Telling Lives

The Seymour Biography Lecture
2005–2023

Telling Lives

The Seymour Biography Lecture 2005–2023

EDITED BY PROFESSOR CHRIS WALLACE

Generously supported by Dr John Seymour and Mrs Heather Seymour AO, the Seymour Biography Lecture provided eminent life writers with an opportunity to explore the business and craft of biography, autobiography or memoir.

Between 2005 and 2009, the Lecture was hosted by the Australian National University's Humanities Research Centre. In 2010, the Lecture moved to the National Library of Australia. The series concluded in 2023.

The lectures reproduced here were delivered in front of live audiences. They have been edited for publication, but we have endeavoured to keep the sense of a spoken text. Some of the original lectures are accessible online at nla.gov.au/stories/talks-and-lectures/flagship-lectures/seymour-biography-lecture.

Contents

Honouring the Biographer's Contract

Professor Chris Wallace
2023

With biographers, you never know what you're getting. Are you getting a toney academic? Are you getting a raffish journalist? My contribution to this series is called 'Honouring the Biographer's Contract'. The alternative title is, 'Biography: Its Part In Our Downfall'. First up, I'm going to invite you to join me in a thought experiment.

It's 2053, 30 years hence. To recap, Rupert Murdoch has been dead for 19 years. He passed away peacefully at 103 years old—the same age as his mother, whom he uncannily resembled—in 2034. I've done the maths: that's a real projection. His estranged wife Jerry Hall, with whom he reunited, was bedside at his death. Elisabeth Murdoch succeeded her father as the head of News Corporation, and immediately realigned the reporting and commentary of its media outlets with reality. News Corp under Elisabeth Murdoch's leadership has fought the good fight to save Earth for human habitation in the face of accelerating global warming, but she's come to the top job too late. Decades of News Corp gaslighting, literal and figurative, has enabled an exponential rise in temperatures on Earth. Extreme weather events are the new normal, habitat destruction and species extinction is generalised, and *Homo sapiens* is next.

Businesswoman Nicola Forrest has liquidated her entire Fortescue Metals Group holding. With the proceeds she's bought X, formerly known as Twitter, and SpaceX from Elon Musk in a fire sale after banks and regulators close in on him over chronic liquidity and governance problems. Forrest renames them XX and SpaceXX. She restores proper labour standards and defeats disinformation on her XX social media platform.

Elisabeth Murdoch and Nicola Forrest have combined forces to evacuate Earth's citizens to Alpha Centauri before we're all wiped out. Murdoch runs the comms on the operation, marshalling support for the exodus and keeping morale up. Forrest runs the evacuation on the SpaceXX fleet. Each country has its own exodus leader linked to the team. In Australia, it's long-serving Prime Minister Tanya Plibersek. In the US, it's President Michelle Obama. Gives you hope, doesn't it? Exodus leadership is not confined to politicians. In Britain, the exodus leader is Tilda Swinton, whom it's generally agreed people will follow anywhere. And in any case, Tilda's mother is Australian, and heaven knows, hybrid vigour is going to be important on Alpha Centauri.

The SpaceXX shuttles begin. Shunning SpaceXX and choosing space transport companies run by their libertarian bros instead, Elon Musk, Lachlan Murdoch and their plutocratic peers struggle to leave Earth in time. These companies' spaceships, put together shoddily by non-union casuals employed through labour hire firms on sub-minimum pay rates, have a high failure rate. Who knew? Musk, Murdoch and friends have to make hard calls about which is riskier: blowing up in one of their libertarian bros' spaceships trying to get to Alpha Centauri, or trying to survive long-term in a subterranean bunker on New Zealand's South Island? Calculations on whether their cellared pinot noir stocks can last out until the 'weather' improves prove pivotal. After all, global warming, it's just a woke delusion, isn't it? And if you've got enough good wine put down, anything's survivable, right?

Writers, artists and musicians are prominent among those shuttled to Alpha Centauri by SpaceXX. You can't transplant and rebuild a shattered species on a new planet without a good starter culture. These particular Earth refugees are vital to *Homo sapiens*' future. But what of the past, the recent disastrous past? On Alpha Centauri, the biographers get together. An uncomfortable question arises, did we contribute to this? Is it something we did? Or is it something we didn't do? Did biographers play a role in the downfall of *Homo sapiens* on Earth?

The Biographer's Contract

Many Seymour Lecturers have canvased the ethics of biography and the ethical obligations of biographers, less so its impact and effectiveness. Ethics and ethical obligations are on biographers' minds all the time. Positively, because of their intrinsic importance, and defensively, to avoid legal action, a real and ever-present threat in the work we do. It's one of the conversations that occur regularly in the Special Collections Room of the National Library of Australia. Am I going to get sued? What am I going to do about it? How can I express something that I know to be true without getting sued? It's a key issue.

With the thought experiment at the back of our minds, I want to turn to three of my predecessors' lectures: those of Frances Spalding, Ray Monk and Richard Holmes. In her 2010 lecture, 'The Biographer's Contract', distinguished art historian Frances Spalding—biographer of, amongst others, Vanessa Bell, Duncan Grant, Roger Fry and Stevie Smith—conducted an expansive exploration of the literal and figurative dimensions of biographers' contracts. She concluded that, 'At the heart of the biographer's contract' lies 'the recording of truth and the attempt to commemorate it'. Spalding then asked:

> Is this still possible in an age of relativism? Not only possible ... but urgently needed, for the truths contained in any unpretentious report, be it a record of a parish outing or a school report, remain the foundation of all literary endeavour.

I agree with Spalding. I want to draw attention to two particular aspects of her lecture—one at this point in it, and a neglected one earlier on in her lecture.

Spalding refers to biography as an aspect of literary endeavour. This is understandable given her distinguished position in the canon of English literary biographers, and the dominance of literary biography—the life-writing tradition—in English letters. But that's not the only tradition. There's also the historical tradition. For much of the twentieth century, biography occupied an ambivalent position in the discipline of history, something which resolved into a secure position only over the last few decades. Much biography is written by historians, and it has properties distinct from that written by biographers working in the literary tradition. Professor Melanie Nolan, Director of the National Centre of Biography here in Canberra, and the current general editor of the *Australian Dictionary of Biography*, argues this point strongly in her book *Biography and Historiography.*

It brings me to the second of Spalding's points to which I want to draw attention. As she said in this room all those years ago:

> there is rarely a moment when a biographer is not faced with some kind of responsibility, to the facts, to ethical issues, to the past, the future, one's audience and to one's craft. The material has to be sifted with intelligent alertness, not just for facts, names, links and connections, but also for the inner life of one's subject. You need an open mind and an open heart to note, with feeling, intellect and intuition, what is being said; to hear also the tone of voice ... being used.

All true. It's a beautiful encapsulation of the biographer's task, especially as conceived of by a literary biographer. (As an art historian writing in a biographical culture dominated by life-writing, Spalding's success may be in no small part due to her ability to combine both literary and historical approaches.)

This segues nicely into Ray Monk's 2014 lecture, 'How Can I Be a Logician before I'm a Human Being? The Role of Biography in the Understanding of Intellectuals'. Monk's lecture focuses on his biography of Cambridge-based Austrian philosopher Ludwig Wittgenstein, *The Duty of Genius*, published in 1990. One of my favourite books. If you haven't read it, do. Follow it up with Benjamin J.B. Lipscomb's, *The Women Are Up to Something: How Elizabeth Anscombe, Philippa Foote, Mary Midgley, and Iris Murdoch, Revolutionised Ethics*, published last year. Monk's Wittgenstein biography is so good it began what for me came to feel like a personal relationship with Wittgenstein—surprising, since his attitude to women was not very good, and I'm a committed feminist. Wittgenstein did rate fellow philosopher Elizabeth Anscombe, at first his student, then his lifelong friend and intellectual interpreter. Wittgenstein and Anscombe are buried diagonally adjacent to each other at Ascension Parish Burial Ground, All Souls Lane, Cambridge. When I'm there, I like to visit and spend a few moments with them. After you read Monk's book, perhaps you will too.

Frances Spalding and Ray Monk are very different people. One an art historian, the other a philosopher. Monk, in fact, specialised in the philosophy of mathematics, which, he observed, you might think is as removed from biography as possible. Yet the spirit and affect of Spalding's and Monk's biographies are similar, embodying the approach described by Spalding I quoted earlier. Monk had a specific purpose in writing *The Duty of Genius*. In the 1980s, he'd worked on Wittgenstein's philosophy of mathematics and concluded that the interpretations of it dominant at that time, by Michael Dummett and Crispin Wright, were flat out wrong. They, Monk said, 'seemed to me misunderstood Wittgenstein's work, but'—and this is crucial:

> misunderstood Wittgenstein's work in a particular kind of way—which was, it struck me, that they'd misunderstood Wittgenstein … it's not a case of misunderstanding, as it were, the words on the page. It's a case of misunderstanding the spirit in which Wittgenstein was writing. It's a question of misunderstanding Wittgenstein.

In writing *A Duty of Genius*, Monk wanted to open up an understanding of Wittgenstein in a way that would allow the Dummetts and Wrights of the world to attain a full rather than fallacious understanding of his philosophy of mathematics. Now, a key part of Wittgenstein's philosophy is that understanding consists in seeing connections. Monk proceeds very much in that spirit in his book. Along the way, readers get a good grounding in Wittgenstein's philosophy.

An example is the famous duck/rabbit picture from Wittgenstein's work, later published in his *Philosophical Investigations*. Said Monk in his lecture, the duck/rabbit is an 'ambiguous illustration'. You see the beak of a duck on the right-hand side of the picture, or you could see it as the ears of a rabbit. At will you can switch between one and the other, Monk said, seeing it 'now as a duck and now as a rabbit'.

> But now ask yourself, well, what changes? What changes when you see it now as a duck, and now as a rabbit?'… In some sense ... you're seeing something different, or rather you're looking at it differently. That, Wittgenstein says, is what the philosopher is trying to achieve. The philosopher is trying to get you to see things differently and that leads him to this notion of the understanding that consists in seeing connections, which was a crucial notion for Wittgenstein.

Monk then canvassed Wittgenstein's concept of family resemblance. Used, of course, figuratively in philosophy, Monk cleverly explained it to the Seymour audience using a literal example: a composite picture, known as a Galtonian photograph, Wittgenstein had made of him and his three sisters superimposed on each other. Monk put this up on the screen to underline that the point Wittgenstein had in mind 'was to see the connections between himself and his sisters. In superimposing one on another, you can in a quite literal sense see the connections. You can see the family resemblances'.

'What does all this have to do with biography?' a relieved audience finally heard Monk ask at this point in his lecture. (I know they were relieved. I was in the audience.) Monk said it struck him that in his quest to convey the kind of person Wittgenstein was, so Wittgenstein's work would be read in the right spirit, what he had to do:

> was not to theorise about Wittgenstein but to describe various things that he wrote and that he said. And the art of the biography is to structure those things, so that the reader now can see the connections, just like somebody looking at that composite photograph can see the connections.

I want you to hold that thought about connections—as Wittgenstein put it, the 'kind of understanding that consists in seeing connections'.

Monk argued this is the kind of understanding that Boswell achieved in his famous *Life of Samuel Johnson*. Said Monk, 'Boswell's method someimes looks haphazard or random. You don't know why he's suddenly talking about Samuel Johnson talking about actresses or whatever, but there's a method to his madness'. By the end of the book, Monk says, you realise you've been given a way of looking at Samuel Johnson, 'a point of view of him':

> Samuel Johnson now makes sense, and that making sense is not just an accumulation of facts, it's an arrangement of those facts. And that, it seems to me, is the art of the biographer. The art of the biographer is to arrange the facts without theorising, without analysing, but arranging them so as to present not just what happened but a way of seeing a point of view of what happened.

This would be a good moment to return to the thought experiment I set up at the outset. Is any of this useful in helping the biographers sitting in Alpha Centauri in 2053, looking back at Earth, wondering if something they did or didn't do had contributed to their necessary exodus from an Earth too hot to sustain human life anymore?

I think it is. I think it is in this way. It begs the question, what is it about biography, the way we practise it, that made us miss the connections that led up to, and necessitated, the exodus in our thought experiment? I'll repeat that. What is it about biography, the way we practise it, that made us miss the connections that led up to, and necessitated, that exodus?

It's not as though related matters have been absent from the genre. Richard Holmes, for example, in his 2008 lecture, 'Biography: The Past Has a Great Future', said,

> The intensity of our concern about the planet, about global and environmental issues, has put the biographical element back into science with a vengeance ... All this has led to an explosion of biographical interest in the creativity of scientists, and the historic context of their work.

That included, of course, Holmes's own *The Age of Wonder*, published to acclaim that same year, 2008. But has it helped us make the connections to stop the catastrophic climate trajectory we're evidently racing along right now, in 2023, evident in extreme weather event after weather event—cunningly rationalised in news reports as 'once in century events' or 'once in 200 year events', insinuating they've always happened, and avoiding mention of their escalating frequency? I would say not.

Let's return to the questions of our biographers on 2053 Alpha Centauri. Did we contribute to this? Is this something we did? Is it something we didn't do? Did biographers play a role in the downfall of *Homo sapiens* on Earth?

Richard Holmes, in his Seymour Lecture, drew attention to what he described as the great tradition of popular biography, both in Australia and Britain, which he argued, 'has proved significant in shaping our different national identities, giving us role models, but also questioning the nature of our societies'. I reserve comment on biography's role in shaping our different national identities and giving us role models, both gigantic topics in themselves. But without delay, I'd like to disagree with Holmes that biography has been effective in questioning the nature of our societies. I would argue that biography—the way it is now written, almost without exception—persistently reinforces the way things are, and that that's a problem, and also that it need not be so.

Ian Donaldson, in his 2006 *Australian Book Review* Latrobe University Annual Lecture titled 'Matters of Life and Death: The Return of Biography', gave a wonderful account of five 'anti-biographers' sceptical of the genre.

I am not an anti-biographer. I'm a biographer who does not want to have to decamp to Alpha Centauri in 30 years time. I've concluded there are things biographers, and historians generally, can and should do to make that avoidable. And I don't mean taking trenchant ideological positions and ramming it down people's throats, something Frances Spalding explicitly cautioned against. There *are* things biographers and historians can and should do to do biography better. This won't be popular with biographers, because who likes being shaken out of familiar models and modes?

The first is to do fewer single-subject biographies and more dual and collective biographies. The overwhelming focus on the individualistic heroic quest story in single-subject biographies needs to be supplemented urgently with collective heroic quest stories if we're to get out of the mess we're in. Contrary to dominant media narratives privileging individual freedom over the broad collective good, we will only get out of this mess by working together. Biography needs to show that this has been done, and can be done again, rather than cling to and reinforce the model of the compelling individual. David McInnis reviewing Margreta de Grazia's *Shakespeare Without a Life*, in the current edition of *Australian Book Review*, paraphrases one of her key points beautifully: 'Prior to Romanticism, one had a genius for something; post-Romanticism, it was possible to instead *be* a genius'. Romanticism did humankind no favours with that shift. As well as reading de Grazia's terrific book, those interested in this topic will be richly rewarded revisiting Isaiah Berlin's *The Roots of Romanticism*, in which his 1965 Mellon lectures are published.

The second thing is to look for and include in biographies the 'negative space' of subjects' life stories. Don't just tell us what they did, tell us what your biographical subject failed to do, the consequences of that failure, its relationship to the success and failure of others, and the implications of that for us all.

The third is to include the future in these stories of subjects past and, if still alive, present. That's necessarily speculative. Include alternative speculations and exercise judgement in weighting them on what those 'negative space' issues have led to or not. Looking back from Alpha Centauri, our doleful biographers reflected on the biographies of political leaders from recent decades, for example. The absence of attempts to see the 'negative space' in their stories, and the failure to make connections between policy failures with a strong 'family resemblance' amongst them, as Wittgenstein would put it, is striking. Had these occlusions been brought to light, there's a greater chance something more could have been done to change path.

Now, is this a biographer's job? To that question I say, if not biographers, who? I would enjoin my fellow biographers to reflect on Frances Spalding's observation that, 'there is rarely a moment when a biographer is not faced with some kind of responsibility, to the facts, to ethical issues, to the past, the future, one's audience, and to one's craft'. Note, 'to the past ... *and* the future'. As we seek to better know the past in order to do the future better, biographers need to find ways to honour more completely the 'biographical contract' and play their role more fully too.

Last Rites

The final section of my remarks is last rites for the lecture series. It has a sweet melancholy about it because all things must end, all lives must end, and, it turns out, all great lecture series must end. The inaugural Seymour Biography Lecture was delivered by Dr Brenda Niall in 2005, titled 'Walking upon Ashes: The Footsteps of a Modern Biographer'. You can tell her subjects are all dead. (Not so mine. Much, much more dangerous.) Dr Brenda Niall, biographer of the Boyds collectively, and Martin Boyd individually, of Georgiana McCrae and Judy Cassab, was an excellent choice as the opening lecturer. Ian Donaldson, then director of ANU's Humanities Research Centre, wrote in the introduction to the published version of the lecture that Niall, 'found that she had more to say about the practise of biography than could comfortably be accommodated in a 15 minute address, and had been spurred into further activity, preparing a monograph for Melbourne University Publishing on this subject'. 'Walking upon Ashes' would eventually grow into Niall's book *Life Class: The Education of a Biographer*, published by Melbourne University Publishing in 2007. Commented *Australian Book Review* editor Peter Rose, reviewing it himself in *ABR*, 'It is good to have Brenda Niall's lucid account of her gradual transformation from academic to biographer'. My own path has been the reverse, from biographer to academic.

There are distant serendipitous links between the first and last Seymour Lecturers that speak to the permeability of Australia's cultural class—in a good way, I think. Mahdi McWilliam (nee McCrae)—my landlord in Sydney in the early 1980s—was the great-granddaughter of one of Niall's subjects, Georgiana

McCrae. Another of Niall's subjects, Judy Cassab, was in a drawing group with my Sydney friend Margaret Fink. Fink was a dear friend of the late Ian Donaldson and his thankfully still alive wife, Dr Grazia Gunn. Ian and Grazia, whom I met through Fink, came to the opening of my then bar, Das Kapital, in the early 2000s. Grazia and I would bump into each other and chat when she was here at the National Library of Australia (NLA), researching one project or another.

Unlike in the 'old country', as earlier generations used to refer to Britain, where class dynamics dominate, these links were democratically and meritocratically forged. While from a book-loving family, when I first arrived in Canberra, aged 16 years and 51 weeks, to enrol at the Australian National University, I had never met the author of a book. I recall finding in the stacks of Chifley Library a book by my Burton Hall non-resident tutor, Cameron Hazlehurst. I remember holding it reverently in my hands, in wonder. It was a hardback on Lloyd George, published by Cape. A little later, my first boyfriend had a hardback book on China's perspective on the world in print with ANU Press. This seemed extraordinary. Books were, and to me remain, magical objects. They engage, they enthral, they can make things happen. If you are not born to the bookmaking world, that is and remains an incredible thing.

I've been an NLA 'reader' now for 46 years. Some things have changed. The old card catalogue's gone for one, and that was a very bad move, NLA. We loved that card catalogue. Of course, we love Trove now too, very much, but can't we have both? Some things have changed. The caf used to be on the fourth floor. It was definitely a caf, not a café. You'll get a sense of it, knowing that doughnuts used to be sold there in cling wrap. Nevertheless, some of the more important conversations of my life happened in that daggy, now long-gone fourth floor NLA caf—not least ANU historian Don Baker, in fatherly tones, dampening my teenage aspiration to be Manning Clark's research assistant one day. It wasn't until reading Mark McKenna's prize-winning biography, *Manning Clark: An Eye for Eternity*, that I understood what Baker was getting at. One of Clark's then research assistants, Lyndall Ryan, was my tutor in first-year Australian history. Ryan's tutes were in her office with an ever-present plate of Iced VoVos, unique in my experience across three universities. What a welcoming gesture it was to young, nervous students. Ryan's career culminated, during her tenure at the University of Newcastle, leading the project to research and interactively map colonial frontier massacres in Australia, 1788 to 1930. It's a depth charge in the reformation of Australia's national identity of which we have barely yet, but will profoundly, feel the impact.

To conclude, I return to the benefactors who have made this long-running biography series possible, John and Heather Seymour. This is how they were described in the publication of that first lecture by Brenda Niall nearly 20 years ago:

> Dr John Seymour was a law lecturer first at the University of Auckland and then at the Australian National University. He also served as a member of the Australian Law Reform Commission. He's the author of numerous books, reports, and articles on juvenile justice, children, and the law and medicolegal topics. His most important book was *Childbirth and the Law*, Oxford University Press, 2000. Heather Seymour practised … as an obstetrician and gynaecologist in Canberra from 1976 until 2001. She was the first woman president of the Royal Australian College of Obstetricians and Gynaecologists, and was made an Officer of the Order of Australia in 1997 for her services to medicine in obstetrics and gynaecology and to the college. After her retirement, she served as the president of the Medical Board of the Australian Capital Territory.

The Seymours' contribution in endowing this series cannot be overestimated. They're professionals, not plutocrats. Yet their active citizenship has brought to our community of thinkers, readers and writers, over the course of 20 years, an extraordinary list of biographers: Brenda Niall, Lawrence Goldman, Jill Roe, Richard Holmes, David Day, Frances Spalding, Robert Dessaix, Jeffrey Meyers, Drusilla Modjeska, Ray Monk, Robert Drewe, David Marr, Raimond Gaita, Richard Fidler, Judith Brett, Jacqueline Kent—and me. And now, concluding not just this Seymour Lecture, but also the long-running series, I'd invite you to join me in saluting the Seymours, and the outstanding writers they supported to come to the national capital over those decades, with a very warm round of applause.

Walking upon Ashes: The Footsteps of a Modern Biographer

Dr Brenda Niall AO
2005

Biographers used to be deferential or envious in the presence of novelists. Deferential because the novel is universally acknowledged to be an art form; or envious because of a novelist's freedom to create. Today it doesn't look so simple. Biographers have become increasingly aware that their work has complex possibilities, complex choices. When I began to write biography, nearly 20 years ago, I used to feel irritated, but also rather defensive when someone paid me the ambiguous compliment of saying, 'Your biography of Martin Boyd was so good—why don't you try a novel?' Routine condolences about 'having to get all those facts' were dispiriting. It's not the facts, of course, but an understanding of the facts that biographers hope to attain.

Today there is less talk about biographical straitjackets, and more recognition of the fact that there are as many ways of writing lives as there are biographers to write them, and that voice and structure are as important as they are in the novel. The fixed points in time remain, but birth and death need not be automatically placed on the first and the last page. The documentary sources must be read and thought about, and put into the context of time and place, but the tyranny of the endnote can be avoided.

For many reasons, biography is not the safe option for the unimaginative writer. It has its risks and adventures. My title, 'Walking upon Ashes', suggests the terrain every biographer crosses in walking into someone else's life. The phrase comes from Samuel Johnson, as he contemplates the risks of writing close to his own time.

> The necessity of complying with times and sparing persons is the great impediment of biography. History may be formed from permanent monuments and records; but Lives can only be written from personal knowledge, which is growing every day less, and in a short time is lost forever. What is known can seldom be immediately told; and when it might be told it is no longer known.

In his own biographer's task of writing *The Lives of the Poets*, Johnson speaks about his uneasiness as he moves towards his contemporaries and their memories:

> I begin to feel myself *walking upon ashes under which the fire is not extinguished*, and coming to the time when it will be proper rather to say *nothing that is false, than all that is true.*[1]

Anyone writing modern biography will share Johnson's unease, though not all will be as sensitive as he was to the feelings of a subject's surviving family and friends. But whether the questions of what can be said appear to the biographer as moral scruples or fear of legal constraints, they are always present. And I think the sense we must all share with Johnson—that there are living fires beneath the ashes—is part of the biographical adventure.

Where is the interest if the feeling of a life has gone? We are all eager to come close to the living fires—although in varying degrees anxious about stepping on hot coals—and if the heat is sometimes alarming, it is also a source of energy. There are always choices to be made, and the biographer's decisions about what can be said will be to some extent determined by temperament and the time of writing. What is unsayable in one period of time may become a matter of course within a space as short as a decade or two, according to the ways in which society judges human behaviour.

My own experience of biography covers a period of time long enough for many changes to have taken place in society—and of course in me too. As a student in the English Department at the University of Melbourne in the early 1950s, I wasn't interested in biography. No-one was. We were New Critics in the making; the close reading of the text was what it was all about. It was one of the certainties of the time that there were three literary forms: Poetry, the Novel and Drama. And as these fitted conveniently into the three terms of the academic year, there was no reason to disturb them. That was still true in my first years of teaching at Monash University, from the early 1960s, and when things began to change in the 1970s, it was literary theory that shook our New Critical certainties and altered our teaching patterns. The author was dead; there was only the text. There was still no interest in biography as a literary form, nor as an area of interest to staff or students in a Department of English. If we had thought it belonged anywhere in a university, we would have consigned it to our colleagues in History.

It was not until the mid-1980s that the chance of writing a full-scale biography presented itself to me. That was a life of Martin Boyd, the novelist member of the Boyd family of artists, on whose fiction I had already written a short introductory study. After Martin Boyd died in Rome in 1972, a trunkful of his papers and diaries was sent back to Melbourne to his nephew Guy Boyd, the sculptor, who was his literary executor. Guy was in some doubt as to what to do with the diaries. He knew that many personal papers had been destroyed—but did the survival of the diaries mean that they were to be spared, or was it his duty to make a bonfire of them? He and his wife, Phyllis, spent long evenings reading them aloud to one another. They both thought them innocuous and dull.

This is where I came in. Guy Boyd allowed me to read the diaries before he gave them, with other Martin Boyd papers, to the National Library of Australia. I wasn't immediately drawn to the diaries; they were mainly a humdrum record of Martin's quietly unhappy last years in Rome. It was the final entries that I found moving. Living alone, very short of money, his novels mostly out of print and often very lonely, Boyd had to face his own death from cancer. He recorded his own frailty, measuring it every day by the number of steps he could take across the room, fewer and fewer each day. 'I grow weaker and weaker and can only hope to die soon,' he wrote. Yet, he could rouse himself to talk to visitors and make jokes about his condition and, as I later discovered, he was at the same time writing letters to friends in England and family in Australia that were funny, spirited and gossipy, with no hint of how desperate, financially as well as physically, his state had become.

I had never thought of Boyd as a battler. He had often presented himself, with due irony, as someone who would always find the softest cushion and sit on it, but when I read the diary entries of these last months, the battler and stoic came to mind. It was from that point—contemplating the way Boyd faced his death—that I felt I wanted to know the beginnings, and as I went back to look at the whole life, including his service in World War I, I knew there was a story to tell.

It was in many ways the ideal distance in time. Boyd was nearly 79 when he died in June 1972. There were many friends who remembered him well, so that I could be sure of getting a varied perspective on his restless, sociable but essentially solitary life. His closest ties were his family: his sister, nephews and nieces. There was no keeper of the flame. Guy Boyd, the nephew who had been chosen as heir and literary executor, did not show any anxiety about what I might write. If there had been lovers, no-one seemed to know them, and to this day none has been plausibly claimed, though there has been plenty of speculation.

Would I be walking on hot ashes? It didn't seem likely, although the cautious and experienced publisher Peter Ryan of Melbourne University Press urged me to get written permission to use any material by Martin Boyd, published or unpublished, in which Guy Boyd as literary executor held copyright. I typed a letter and took it to Guy, who signed it so instantly and trustfully that I felt guilty—what if I did find something? It's one of the hazards of biography that a close relationship with subject or copyright holder can bind the author as tightly as any legal agreement. The Boyd charm and my sense, perhaps mistaken, of Guy Boyd's innocent compliance, would have made me hesitate to use that legal weapon.

As I proceeded to do my interviews, travelling in Martin's expatriate footsteps from Melbourne to London, Sussex, the Lake District and Rome, it all went quite smoothly. His friends remembered him with affection. There were good stories to tell, and a sense of personality began to emerge. So far as I could discern, people talked very freely, rummaged around for old letters and handed them over with no conditions. But I remember one issue of conscience of the kind that Dr Johnson would understand. I was given a bundle of letters written by Boyd to some Cambridge friends. They were good letters: a testimony to his capacity for friendship. They were also performance pieces. Boyd told a good story and he could be malicious.

I had to face this aspect of his personality when, in one of the Cambridge letters, I found a very malicious account of a woman I had already met. She's dead now, but she can remain anonymous, a Mrs X. Now it was perfectly obvious to me from our conversations that Mrs X, a rather sad and lonely divorced woman, had been in love with Boyd. She showed me affectionate letters he had written to her, which, with a slight reluctance that showed how much they meant to her, she let me take back to my hotel to read and return to her the next day. Now what does the responsible biographer do with this situation? I had Guy Boyd's permission to quote anything Martin ever wrote. I did not want to make Martin out to be a saint, and here I had a prime example of his contradictory nature. He was a generous friend to Mrs X, for whom he took real trouble when she was ill and unhappy, and yet he could ridicule her for the sake of a funny story when writing to other friends, who didn't know her and so didn't judge his disloyalty.

Of course, I didn't quote the malicious story of Mrs X. I knew she would read my biography and recognise herself, and she would be devastated. Her love for Martin Boyd, misguided though it was, exemplified Dr Johnson's dilemma. This fire wasn't extinguished. My way out was made easier by the discovery of another letter, not quite as good, but of a similar kind, about another woman, and besides, this woman was dead.

Time and distance, as the 'walking upon ashes' image suggests, have a habit of deciding things for the biographer. I discovered a family secret which would have caused a great deal of trouble if Martin Boyd had been still living. His great-grandfather John Mills, who died in 1841, had been a convict, transported to serve seven years in Van Diemen's Land. That should not have been a problem so many years later, but the family secrecy about his existence did make things complicated for me.

The convict records revealed a quite startling story. John Mills, a Gloucestershire labourer, was convicted of burglary and theft and given the light sentence of seven years because he was only 16 at the time of his conviction. His whole family was active in a group known as the Wickwar Gang, which carried out robberies and thefts for some years before being rounded up in 1827. The Gloucestershire newspapers reported the trial with relish; it was a local sensation. The Mills family was at the centre of the gang, in more than one way. Their kitchen fireplace was the repository for stolen goods, which included silver spoons, a side of bacon and a quantity of rum. At the trial, one brother turned King's Evidence, thereby saving himself, his parents and sisters. Another brother was hanged. The trial was followed by a shooting at the Mills cottage in which Unity Mills, the mother, was wounded. The informer, Thomas Mills, had to leave the neighbourhood for fear of more reprisals.

No matter how much in today's thinking a convict ancestor has risen in acceptability, even to gaining trophy status, I don't think many would relish the wholesale appropriation of other people's goods in the manner of the Mills family. And the hanging of William Mills casts a dark shadow. The story was fully documented, from the judge's address down to the jury recommending the death penalty. Local records included the testimony of the chaplain at Gloucester Gaol, who prayed with William Mills on the morning of his execution. In some circumstances, perhaps, I could simply have told the story of John Mills, but left it in the past as a colourful anecdote, which didn't really impinge on the lives of the twentieth-century descendants. But, as William Faulkner says, 'The past is not dead. It's not even past'.

John Mills was very much present as an influence on his descendants for nearly a century after his death, even though they never knew it. His story had to be told in my life of Martin Boyd because it directly affected the way in which the Boyds grew up. It affected—indeed it created—the family style. Two generations of artists were sustained by the fortune made in early Melbourne by this unpromising young lawbreaker from a Gloucestershire labouring family.

After serving his sentence in Van Diemen's Land, John Mills came to Melbourne, bought land in 1837 in what became the central business district, and established a brewery and several public houses. When he died in 1841, he left only one child, three-year-old Emma Mills, who thus inherited valuable properties, which, after the gold rushes and the consequent growth of Melbourne, made her immensely rich.

The next part of the story sounds like a True Romance, but it is fully documented in public records and private diaries. The convict's daughter, Emma Mills, was given a young lady's education in Melbourne. Aged 17, she met and married the eldest son of the austere figure, Victoria's first Chief Justice, Sir William à Beckett. For this upper-class family, well connected in England, Emma's parentage could hardly have been worse. She would bring the convict stain into the family. Unthinkably, there would be à Beckett children with convict blood. Yet the à Becketts welcomed Emma and, as I read her diaries, I had no doubt of the affection she won from them all; she was an exceptionally charming and lovable woman. Presumably, the affronted gentlefolk of Melbourne eventually stopped gossiping about this intruder's murky antecedents and the story was so successfully camouflaged that Emma's descendants, including her Boyd grandchildren, knew nothing about it. Silence about the origins of the à Beckett money was interpreted to mean no more than the shame of its coming from the profits of the liquor trade. Behind the brewery, the convict stood invisible.

As this story unrolled itself before my fascinated gaze, I was not sure how to deal with it so far as the living Boyds were concerned. Should I tell them first, or just write it and see what happened? There was no question of fencing it off from the main narrative of Emma Mills à Beckett's grandson Martin. As I read his account of his grandmother, I was sure that he had discovered her history and had taken some pains to suppress it. And yet the convict story was crucial as a shaping influence on his own life. There was a long straight line from Gloucester Gaol to penal servitude in Van Diemen's Land, to the Melbourne brewery and its satellite public houses, and to the charming pastoral childhood of the young Boyds, Merric the potter, Penleigh the painter and Martin the novelist, in Sandringham, on Port Phillip Bay, and at their farm at Yarra Glen. Supported by the convict inheritance, which came to them through the bounty of their maternal grandmother, not one of them ever thought of taking a regular paid job. For the next generation—Arthur, Guy and David Boyd—the money had dissolved to nothing, but the certainty of their identity as artists remained. Even their cousin Robin, a professional architect, was slightly embarrassed at being a Boyd who kept office hours.

The basis of the family tradition of unfettered creativity was something Martin Boyd never acknowledged. And his refusal to face it—his denial, in fact, that there was any ungentlemanly matter in his family history—was on record, again and again. He had made himself the family historian; he had drawn family trees and sought out remote ancestors for the Boyds and the à Becketts. But he never mentioned his great-grandfather Mills, nor the Gloucestershire family of labourers with whom, during his long expatriate years, he could have claimed kin.

I could see that Martin Boyd would have been appalled by the story I was about to tell. But would it matter to the next generation—in particular to Guy Boyd? I didn't think it would. But in one of my interviews I was warned that I would strike trouble. The warning came from the writer Geoffrey Dutton who in the early 1970s had embarked on a Boyd family history, which he never finished. 'You won't get them to cooperate,' Dutton told me.

The trouble, he said, would come from Guy Boyd, who after initial friendliness, had suddenly closed the door. This was bad news but I hoped that whatever the problem was, time might have solved it. Yet, now and then, I thought uneasily about the bewildering about-turn described by Dutton, in which Guy—all friendly cooperation and writing pages of his early memories—had suddenly become hostile. Dutton seemed genuinely baffled. His own credentials for writing the biography were impeccable. Well known in the literary and publishing world, with many books to his credit, he was also a close friend of Arthur Boyd and well liked by the other Boyds. A contract from the highly regarded London publisher Secker and Warburg had been signed and everyone was happy. Or so it seemed. But in 1972, when Dutton had spent time and thought on the Boyd biography, and had accumulated a stack of tapes and memoirs, suddenly Guy Boyd put a stop to it all. Talking to Dutton in 1985, I could feel his anger and his puzzlement. I was puzzled too. When I came along, what had changed? What had made Guy Boyd so happily sign away his copyright permissions to me, without even talking about possibly sensitive areas?

I could think of only two matters which might have caused the trouble. The convict story seemed the likely one, but why would Guy Boyd care enough in 1972 to cause a rift with an old friend and by 1985 be relaxed enough to give me a free hand? The other possibility, of course, was that Guy might have been concerned that revelations about his uncle's homosexuality would come out. But that question was not new; people had been speculating for years about it. Guy's abrupt turning against the Dutton book suggested that something happened in 1971 or early 1972, just before Martin's death. And that event, I thought, must have been Arthur Boyd's chance encounter in Canberra in 1971 with the distant cousins from the Mills family who told him the convict story, though in a highly sentimentalised version, with the crimes explained as misunderstandings. Interested and unperturbed, Arthur passed the story on to Dutton who discussed it with other family members. Inevitably, the story reached Martin in Rome, a few months before he died. It did not seem that he was agitated by the news. Indeed, as Dutton told me, Martin gave his blessing for the book: 'the blessing of a dying man', which he found very touching.

While I was still pondering the question, Guy Boyd left Melbourne for Canada and I had no chance to talk to him for the two-year period that followed. As I pressed on with my research, it was Martin Boyd's sexuality that most perplexed me. In interviews with his friends, the question often came to me: what did I think? Had I come across any love affairs? Some said that, of course, he was homosexual and that there must have been lovers, but they couldn't name anyone. Others, like his old friend Max Nicholson, said that Martin never had the courage to commit himself. He would 'gaze at beautiful youths' but that was all. Nicholson, openly gay, rather despised Martin for his timidity. I talked to the former King's College chorister, John Aldiss, whom the middle-aged Martin had invited to tea in the 1940s. He said that Martin was always 'very proper'. That was the note struck in all my interviews with the men, by now themselves middle-aged, who had known Martin in England when they were young. Perhaps there were affairs, they said, but 'not with me'. Is that what they would have said anyway? Perhaps. But I didn't sense any embarrassment or lack of candour. One of them described Martin Boyd's attachment to him as 'sentimental'. No-one spoke of passion.

Then there was the testimony of friends like Quinton Geering and his wife, Jill, who shared Boyd's Cambridge house for more than a year. 'Martin homosexual? Absolutely not. I would have known,' Geering said. Jill Geering thought of him as 'asexual'. Sir Walter Crocker, Australian Ambassador to Italy during Boyd's years in Rome, agreed. 'Too fastidious for casual affairs,' Crocker said, adding that he never heard any gossip about Boyd—and gossip about Australians in Italy usually reached the Embassy. The one strong attachment I had discerned from reading Boyd's Rome diaries and his autobiography, *Day of My Delight*, was with an Italian boy, Luciano Trombini.

With Trombini, aged 16 when they met to Boyd's 57, the relationship was described by Boyd's friends as quasi-paternal, even grandfatherly, or as that of teacher and pupil. Yet Boyd was exceptionally vulnerable to Trombini's moods: his carelessness, his inconsiderate comings and goings, provoked deep sadness as well as anger. And looking back, long after Trombini had married and moved away from Rome, Boyd wrote of this episode as 'the truest friendship of my life ... a happy time, an asset of memory'.

I didn't interview Trombini. It wasn't easy to find him; my time in Rome was limited and my Italian language skills nonexistent. For all these reasons, I turned for help to someone uniquely placed to search out Trombini and ask those awkward questions. Desmond O'Grady, novelist, journalist and friend from our student days in Melbourne, has lived in Rome for many years, speaks perfect Italian and knew Boyd well. After I had returned to Australia, O'Grady managed to trace Trombini, took the train to Milan and talked to him on my behalf. The result was much the same as my own interviews in England. Trombini remembered Boyd as a wonderful teacher, a civilising influence and a generous friend. He was not embarrassed nor defensive in any way. It was evident that he had always thought of Boyd as a very old man. A sexual relationship seemed most unlikely, O'Grady concluded.

Of course, that did not rule out sexual longings on Boyd's part, and as I re-read his novels I could see his own vision of self (or one of them—he was many-sided) in a series of elderly men, pathetic, sometimes absurd in their yearning for a beautiful, indifferent youth. That, I thought, was all I was likely to find, and I was relieved that there was nothing likely to disturb Guy Boyd. There was, however, one last-minute surprise. Sam Wood, an Australian who had known Boyd well in the late 1930s, showed me a letter from one of his cousins in England, recalling her discovery of a long-lasting affair between Boyd and a woman called Margaret Michell. The testimony was the more persuasive because, as she said, she was astonished, having thought Boyd was homosexual.

This letter came too late for me to give it more than a hasty endnote, and because Sam Wood did not think I should publish Margaret Michell's name in her lifetime, it seemed unconvincing to the few readers who noticed it.

In 1988, when *Martin Boyd* was published, there was still a certain hesitation in discussing same-sex relationships. Writers of obituaries used such phrases as 'confirmed bachelor'. David Marr's biography of Patrick White, which changed a great deal in the Australian literary scene, was not yet on the horizon; it would not appear until 1991. Leon Edel, the biographer of Henry James, wrote in some bemusement in 1986, that, having re-read his work for a single-volume abridgement, he had realised that it was 'pre-revolutionary stuff' that took on the genteel tone of former times, and reflected his own 'prairie puritanism'.

If Edel was writing 'pre-revolutionary stuff', so was I. Yet I think my comment in 1988 that Boyd 'repressed and aestheticised his sexuality' was probably right. Except for the surprise disclosure about Margaret Michell, there was no testimony about any physical relationship to which a responsible biographer could refer. If I were to re-write *Martin Boyd*, as Edel rewrote his *Henry James*, I would say more about the complexities of the question, as I did in my later work, the group biography of the family, *The Boyds*, which was published in 2002. But, in 1988, it seemed to me that I had told my readers all I knew, leaving them with as much insight as Boyd's closest friends, with their years of observation and guesswork, had possessed.

My interviews with Boyd's family members and his friends in Australia and England showed me his chameleon quality. The protective colouring he brought to each new setting made him hard to know; so did his habit of keeping his friends in separate compartments. To the intellectuals and bohemians of his 1920s years in Sussex, he seemed one of themselves, not shocked by Jazz Age frivolity, ready for talk of Freud, free love and vegetarianism. A decade later, in rural Cambridgeshire, where he owned a few acres of farmland, with attendant sheep, he wore good tweeds, which did not make the mistake of looking new, and met local squire or rural labourer as if to the manor born. Yet, as he said himself, he 'never quite belonged'. English friends spoke of his 'breezy Australian informality' while there were many in Australia who thought he had become 'very English'. Role-playing came easily to Martin Boyd. No wonder that friends disagreed so sharply about his sex life. They saw such divergent selves.

As I wrote the last pages of the biography, I was almost sure that there was nothing to upset Guy Boyd. And yet, I couldn't quite forget Geoffrey Dutton's warning. With some trepidation I asked Guy if he would like to read my book in manuscript. Ominously, he said he would: 'You know, if there's anything to upset the family, they will blame me'. I suggested that if he didn't read it, he would be in the clear: 'Then they can blame the author'. This ploy failed. Gently, inexorably, Guy said, 'No, I think it's my duty to read it'.

I timed the delivery of the manuscript to reach Guy just as I left for a stay at the Humanities Research Centre, where I was to check quotations from the Boyd and à Beckett papers at the National Library. I didn't give Guy my Canberra phone number, reasoning that if the convict story, or anything else, had upset him, he would have had time to calm down. His friendliness at our last meeting was so obviously unfeigned that I couldn't believe he would torpedo my publication, or even try to censor it. Of course I had his letter, giving copyright permission, but because my liking for him and his wife, Phyllis, had grown so much, I would have been very distressed at any breach.

I had been in Canberra only a day or two when I was called to the phone at the Humanities Research Centre. Somehow, Guy had tracked me down. His first words were reassuring. He had been sitting up half the night to finish the biography and he thought it was wonderful. With a slightly ambiguous compliment he gave the final accolade: 'I never thought that Uncle Martin's life could be made so interesting!'

So all my anxieties were needless. Guy Boyd's attitude to my biography was consistently encouraging and helpful. What then to make of Geoffrey Dutton's experience? Had time resolved a problem? And, if so, was it the convict story or the question of Martin's sexuality? Dutton never knew the reason. His autobiography, published in 2002, records a lasting puzzle and a deep grievance against Guy Boyd. Guy died suddenly just before my own book was published. I hadn't asked him about the Dutton book, and because all the Boyds seemed happy with what I had written—including the convict story—it no longer seemed important.

Just two years ago, I had a hint of an explanation in a casual remark from David Boyd. He recalled a letter from Martin to Guy, saying that Dutton had to be stopped, the convict story must not come out. 'It would ruin me,' were the words David remembered. Martin was dying. Guy was his heir. It was his duty to stop the book and he could not, of course, give Dutton the real reason.

At last there was an explanation that made sense. For all Martin Boyd's frailty in the last weeks of his life, he had strength enough to exert authority over his nephew and heir. It's easy to see why it mattered so much to him. His family research was thorough, even obsessive. He must have known the Mills story, and with its revelation it would be evident to the world that his own gentlemanly pretensions were false. Among his upper class friends in England, Martin had often heard the little convict jokes. 'Boyd is an Australian, but we still have all our spoons,' was one of them. It might not have been so much the convict's existence that would distress Martin Boyd, but his own exposure as having known and concealed this fact. He put a high value on truthfulness—and he certainly had been economical with the truth. So, faced with an urgent plea from a dying man, it seems likely that Guy Boyd would have given his promise, in spite of the awkwardness of offending Geoffrey Dutton. Twelve years later, he didn't see any need to stop me. A version of the story—a sentimentalised tale of mistaken arrest—had been published by David Boyd in 1980. So it seems most likely that Martin Boyd was given the reassurance he wanted before he died, and that particular hot coal in the Boyd story died down to ashes.

Soon after *Martin Boyd* was published, I began to write the life of Georgiana McCrae, the pioneer painter and diarist who came to Melbourne in 1841, and died there, an unwilling exile, in 1890. Here, time was on my side. An earlier generation of Georgiana's descendants would have refused to acknowledge publicly the fact of Georgiana's illegitimate birth, even with the romantic circumstance of her being acknowledged, favoured and taken to live in splendid surroundings by her grandfather, the fourth Duke of Gordon. Some had even fantasised about a missing marriage certificate, which would bring the Australian family into the legitimate ducal line. But in the early 1990s, when I approached the McCrae descendants, the fire beneath the ashes had cooled somewhat. Georgiana's memory was a living thing in her family but they welcomed a biography that would do her justice, and they left me free to do it in my own way.

My task was to work through the accretions of time and legend in a wholly documentary biography; to find Georgiana in her own words, in letters and diaries, and to use public records for the context of her life. Unexpectedly, I found a problem. Georgiana's grandson, the poet Hugh McCrae, had edited her journals for publication in 1934, and since then, they had remained in print as the authentic version of her life. When I compared the published text, *Georgiana's Journals*, with the manuscripts in Georgiana's handwriting—held in the State Library of Victoria and the Fisher Library at the University of Sydney—I could see that McCrae had done a great deal of embellishment and some strategic pruning. Cherished stories, such as an intimate moment with Governor La Trobe, which some had taken to suggest a love affair, were simply not there in Georgiana's text. Examples of her satirical wit were evident, but many more had been added, while her husband, Andrew McCrae, was a much more difficult and grumpy character than he appeared in Georgiana's words. Hugh McCrae had not been editing, in the sense in which we understand it; he had been re-creating his grandparents.

What was I to do about that? First, I had to bypass Hugh McCrae's text and use only the manuscripts; and then to break the news to the descendants. When I told Hugh McCrae's granddaughters, Janet Hay and Anne Humphries, I could see that they were very much taken aback. For their lifetime, they had thought of the published journals as Georgiana's own voice. But, remembering their wayward poet-grandfather, they conceded that livening them up was just the sort of thing he would do. There was never any question of their impeding me by invoking their copyright on the unpublished originals in order to protect the status of the published work. They did not welcome the revelation, but they fully supported me in telling the story. I didn't think they should be too hard on their grandfather, there has been a scholarly revolution in editing since his time, and he had no pretensions to being a scholar.

Georgiana's descendants were not the only ones to take the published version on trust. Several distinguished historians have used it as a primary source, without looking at the originals, so one can hardly blame the McCraes for failing to examine those originals that were available to them. In an attempt to disentangle the texts, I prefaced my biography with an author's note, briefly stating Hugh McCrae's intervention in his grandmother's text, and saying that all my quotations came from Georgiana's manuscript version.

And yet Hugh McCrae's unreliable text, which I thought I could ignore and then supersede, has an enduring life of its own. He was producing his text for Angus & Robertson in 1934, to coincide with the celebration of 100 years of settlement in Victoria. And so he was shaping his Georgiana as a colonial heroine, struggling with physical hardships, burdened by her large family, and the more valiant as a pioneer because her husband, Andrew, gave her no support. The hardships and the strains in the marriage were there in Georgiana's text, but because of Hugh McCrae's almost wholly negative construction of his grandfather,

I was the more alert to signs of affection, which included a love poem written by Andrew and copied into her journal by Georgiana, but discarded by her grandson. I acknowledged the Drover's Wife stoicism of Hugh McCrae's heroine, but in a silent argument with the creator of the phantom Georgiana, I stressed the exile from Scotland and the frustrated portrait painter. I would like to think that my biography wins the argument, but Hugh McCrae's anecdotes are so firmly lodged in public memory that they will probably outlive my less colourful account, from which Governor La Trobe's public appearance, beside Georgiana in a flowered dressing-gown, has been excluded.

My most recent biography is a life of the Sydney-based artist Judy Cassab. There are obvious similarities between Georgiana McCrae and Judy Cassab. Both began their artist's careers as portrait painters. For both, it was hard to balance a commitment to art with the role of wife and mother. Georgiana was an exile from Scotland, to which she never returned. Judy was a refugee, whose Jewish Hungarian extended family was murdered in Auschwitz in World War II. Both kept diaries—an immense asset for a biographer, not only for the information the diaries hold, but for the insight they give into personality.

I used to think that I would never write about a living person. But Judy Cassab's story, as a Holocaust survivor, a refugee and postwar migrant to Australia, and as one of our best-known women artists, was impossible to resist. We first met at the National Library in 1996, speaking at a seminar called 'Constructing Lives'. Her subject was portrait painting and mine was biography. Our friendship began when she unexpectedly asked me, after the seminar, if I would sit for her for a non-commissioned portrait. Very flattered, because I knew her high reputation, I agreed. Six years later, I impulsively telephoned her to ask if she would sit for me for a biography. She hesitated, saying that she had published her diaries: what more was there to say?

I thought that she might well have hesitated because it would be painful to revisit her past, her wartime ordeals. As a young Jewish artist, masquerading as a factory worker under false papers, and hiding in a cellar during the siege of Budapest, she endured physical deprivation and daily terror. Unlike most of her family members, she survived. When I asked her if we could talk about those times, she said firmly that we must, 'because these things have to be remembered'. In this biography, Dr Johnson's metaphor about walking upon ashes takes on a sombre, almost literal meaning. For Judy Cassab, the fires beneath the ashes of Auschwitz must never be allowed to die down.

As to the Cassab diaries, there was a great deal more to say and much, much more than her published volume reveals. All her early diaries were lost, so that there was nothing on record until 1944, when Cassab was 24 years old. Nothing about her childhood, her education and early ambitions, or the first years of her marriage. Nor is there a clear picture of her husband. His Hungarian past and his war experience is missing, and the tensions of their long, loving but difficult marriage are not fully explored. Diaries, moreover, are limited by their day-to-day form. Speaking only to the self, they do not set down what the self already knows.

I suggested to Judy Cassab an analogy between a portrait and a self-portrait. Later, when she gave me all of her diaries to read—only a fraction had been published—I had the uncanny experience of reading the entry in which she recounted and thought about my phone call. By then, I had entered her life as biographer and here was I, on the diary page, where she quoted me as having said, 'It would be MY version of your life'. Did I really stress the personal pronoun so strongly? At any rate that is what she heard and understood.

Intelligent, introspective, capable of sharp self-criticism, Judy Cassab was in many ways the ideal subject for a portrait of a living figure. I often found that she was there before me, anticipating my thoughts. 'But of course,' she would say, as I tentatively put forward an idea. And, to my great relief, she always saw the book as mine, not hers. She made the analogy with her need as a portrait painter to give her own interpretation. She spoke with unqualified disapproval of Lady Churchill's destruction of the Sutherland portrait of Winston Churchill. She was aware, as few people would be, of the artist's need to interpret the sitter's personality.

One of my interviews—a rare chance for a biographer—was with Judy's hairdresser. It happened that I wanted to have my hair cut during one of my Sydney visits; and so, while Louis of Double Bay was busy with the scissors, I asked him about his famous client. He told me the perfect story. When he wanted Judy Cassab to change her style a little, she agreed, saying, 'It's your hair, Louis, I only wear it'. She would not quite have said to me, 'It's your life, Brenda, I only live it'. But she did say, quite sincerely, 'You are the writer; it's your book'.

Astonishingly, this face-to-face encounter between biographer and subject was the easiest of all my books, because our communication was so direct, and because Judy Cassab respected the art of biography and could see my book as something which had a life of its own.

1 Samuel Johnson, 'Addison', in *Lives of the English Poets*, ed. George Birkbeck Hill, 3 vols (Oxford, 1905), 2.116.

Virtual Lives: History and Biography in an Electronic Age

Professor Lawrence Goldman
2006

'Universal dictionaries are no longer possible or desirable. If we would conquer the realm of knowledge we must be content to divide it.' Thus wrote *The Times* on 5 January 1885 in its first article on the *Dictionary of National Biography* (*DNB*), whose initial supplement—the first of an eventual 63 published over the next 15 years—was then about to appear.

Perhaps *The Times* correspondent knew that in 1881, when the Victorian publisher George Smith first conceived of a biographical dictionary and approached his friend Leslie Stephen, the eminent man of letters, to edit it, he had envisaged just such a universal dictionary, including biographies of all the worthies, from all the nations and civilisations. Smith was a worthy himself: the publisher of many of the greatest Victorian writers, including the Brontës, Thackeray, George Eliot, Elizabeth Gaskell, the Brownings, Trollope and Ruskin. He explained in 1894 that his 'first idea was to produce a dictionary of universal biography with many editors and contributions, English and foreign' and from 'that wild attempt he was saved by the knowledge and sound judgment of Leslie Stephen'. Contemporaries approved Stephen's determination to produce a work on eminent and noteworthy Britons only: according to the critic Richard Copley Christie in his review of the first volumes of the *DNB* in 1887, 'The day for the general biographical dictionary is passed. For such an undertaking on the scale of the work before us five hundred volumes would not suffice'.[1]

But perhaps the day for a universal biographical dictionary has returned? With so many national biographical dictionaries now published or in continuous publication; with so many biographical scholars, in so many different countries, now at work; with so much specialised biographical knowledge now available; and, above all, with the technological means to handle vast bodies of information and project them into libraries, offices and homes all over the world, perhaps the time has come to revive Smith's first idea and create that wonder of the Enlightenment, the universal dictionary of everyone; an accompaniment to encyclopedias of everything?

In little more than a decade, the internet has given access to stocks of knowledge beyond the wildest imaginings of Diderot, D'Alembert and their collaborators on the *Encyclopédie*. For those hunting biographical information, it is possible to find details as never before. As things stand, there are online biographical dictionaries for, among others, the British, the Americans and now the Australians, with the Irish to follow in a matter of months. European nations have either launched their own internet biographical dictionaries, or will surely do so soon, turning their many volumes of national biography into web-based resources. We can envisage the linking of these databases and dictionaries into one great biographical corpus of everyone of note who ever lived.

Even if the links are not made, the scholar or casual reader can flick between dictionaries at the click of a mouse. Technology has not only made more information more accessible than ever before; it has also made it possible to compose and compile biographical dictionaries in a fast and efficient manner. The successor to Smith and Stephen's *DNB*, the *Oxford Dictionary of National Biography* (*ODNB*), which was published in 2004, was projected in the early 1990s to be compatible when published with whatever electronic technology might then be in use. That the *ODNB* was produced to time in 12 years owed a great deal to the development of email as a by-product of the internet, making communication with the *Dictionary*'s 10,000 contributors all the swifter, and the transmission and editing of submitted text all the easier.

Contrast this with the labours and the manuscripts of the man who has been credited with compiling the first British dictionary of biography, John Leland, who lived at the time of the English Reformation and was employed by Henry VIII as library keeper and antiquary.[2] Leland compiled a dictionary of British writers which he himself called *De viris illustribus* (when eventually published, in 1709, nearly two centuries after its composition, it was as *Commentarii De Scriptoribus Brittanicis*). Its original title places Leland's work within a genre—the biographical catalogue—that had originated in Renaissance Italy. Ultimately derived from such classical authors as Suetonius and Plutarch, it had been reinvigorated in the fourteenth and fifteenth centuries by writers such as Petrarch and Platina. In gathering material for his magnum opus, Leland spent years travelling through England in the 1530s and 1540s. He visited all the then centres of knowledge, the religious houses and colleges of the two ancient universities, to catalogue their libraries and transcribe their manuscripts. At Leland's death, the then king, Edward VI, assigned his papers to his friend Sir John Cheke, who made them available to two other great compilers of biography of this era, John Bale and John Foxe. But when Cheke left England in 1554, the collection was dispersed among several scholars and patrons. Most of those papers that survived were collected together by William Burton, the Leicestershire antiquarian and elder brother of Robert Burton, author of the *Anatomy of Melancholy* (1621), who in 1632 presented them to the Bodleian Library in Oxford, where they remain to this day.

For a century, therefore, Leland's papers, comprising one of the most important of all sources for historians of England, and an unrivalled corpus of biographical knowledge, which, be it noted, provided crucial information for dozens of biographies in the *ODNB*, were passed around in manuscript from scholar to scholar. In 1576, the author of *The Historicall Description of the Island of Britain*, William Harrison, described the manuscripts as 'utterly mangled, defaced with wet weather, and finally imperfite through want of sundrie volumes … For so motheaten, mouldie, & rotten are those bookes of Leland which I have, and beside that, his annotations are … so confounded, as no man can … picke out anie sense from them by a leafe together'. Let no scholar today ever complain of having difficulty getting access to sources.

Yet this essay is not designed as a mere celebration of new technologies and their capacity to connect and liberate scholars as never before. Rather, this is a cautionary tale which will question our present electronic hubris, and ask whether merely 'having the technology', a phrase of the 1960s, is sufficient? It will ask whether we should do things merely because we can do them? Whether, as scholars and biographers, if we lack a secure rationale for what we do, we are merely producing information for its own sake? Whether the serendipitous nature of the internet may only assist us in piling up irrelevant or unnecessary detail at the risk of losing contact with the major themes? Whether in bringing together hitherto separate bodies of knowledge, each collected and compiled for its own special reason and according to its own conventions, we may do violence to works conceived in isolation of each other? And whether, for these reasons, the internet may be a great leveller, stripping out those elements of style, nature and genre which scholars have prized and respected in the past because they make a work distinctive, unique.

George Smith's universal biographical dictionary is probably within our grasp—but should we want it? Were it to be composed of different sources merely linked together and searchable throughout, I should advise great caution. Scholarly works derive their value from their distinctiveness; to ransack them for information without understanding their rationales—including the way they were composed, by whom, under what circumstances, and for what ends—is to objectify, to vulgarise, to disrespect and to invite error.

To make this perhaps unfashionable case, I want to examine the various notable collections of biography that have been made in Britain since John Leland and consider their reasons for being, the reasons why we recall them today, and, as a corollary, the way in which they should be used by modern scholars. I will begin with those sources of biographical knowledge I know best, the *DNB* and the *ODNB*—published at the end of the nineteenth and the beginning of the twenty-first centuries, respectively—the one growing organically out of the other, including all of its subjects and some of its text, but adding to the range and diversity of the first *Dictionary* through the addition of a further 20,000 lives drawn from a wider range of backgrounds and occupations than before, and including three times as many women.

Immediately, we come up against the contingent nature of all great human enterprises. If we ask why George Smith conceived of a biographical dictionary, one answer is simply that, as editor of the *Cornhill Magazine*, which Smith also published, Stephen was losing his friend a good deal of money. He was putting out a journal that was rather too elevated in style and serious in tone for any likely readership. The circulation was falling, and Stephen had to be moved. Smith, a remarkably wealthy and munificent man, who, it is calculated, lost some £70,000 on the *DNB*, could have sacked Stephen. Instead, he dreamed up a project that would meet the great scholar's interests and talents, though at the publisher's expense.[3]

Similarly, I can say on authority that there would be no *ODNB* today were it not that Colin Matthew, its first editor, who planned the project from which the *Dictionary* emerged, was available in Oxford and willing to shoulder the burdens. In the early 1990s, when OUP considered what was to be done about Smith's *DNB*, which had been passed to them by his family after Smith's death, and which was now outdated and in need of wholesale revision, Matthew was coming to the close of his 14-volume edition of the diaries of William Ewart Gladstone. Matthew had the intellect, the experience and the worldwide respect required to lead a project on this scale; he was also available. Those who invited him to be editor have told me that if he had declined they would not have gone ahead. Scholars are rarely indispensable; but Matthew was rare indeed.[4] He alone made the new biographical dictionary possible.

Beyond personalities, however, we can also explain the origins of the *DNB* and *ODNB* in terms of a wider scholarly rationale. The Victorians had several inferior biographical dictionaries at their disposal, and attempts to compile bigger and better ones had not always succeeded. The first edition of the *Biographia Britannica*, published in eight volumes between 1747 and 1766, was by then out of date. An attempt had been made to produce a second edition, but this had faltered in 1793 after five volumes had been published and they had only got as far as the letter F. This was somewhat better, however, than the record of the Society for the Diffusion of Useful Knowledge—the 'steam intellect society', as it was called—which made a start at a universal dictionary under a committee chaired by the Whig politician Henry Brougham in the 1820s, but gave up after only seven volumes had appeared on names beginning with A alone.

The expansion of historical knowledge in Britain from the 1850s, one of the most notable aspects of Victorian intellectual life, not only made a new dictionary necessary in order to incorporate and make available the new information, but also made it possible as it had not been before. Modern dictionaries of national biography are not only monuments to the nation states of the nineteenth and twentieth centuries, but have depended on the development of historical knowledge, the professionalisation of historical studies and the institutionalisation of history in museums, libraries and archives, for their composition. As the author of the *DNB* article on Elizabeth I, the Rev. Dr Augustus Jessopp, explained in a review of the original *Dictionary*, before the late-nineteenth century,

> the task was then an impossible one. The actual materials for writing the lives of many of our greatest were wanting; the sources of trustworthy information on a thousand questions of fact were packed away in obscure hiding-places; heavy fees had to be paid for the liberty of search in archives public and private; there was nothing answering to the Public Record Office; the great libraries in the country might have been counted on a man's fingers. Societies for printing original documents were unknown; the time for writing English history had not yet come, still less had the time come for investigating the minute facts of personal biography.[5]

By the 1880s, all this had changed. Systematised research has continued ever since, so that, by the mid-twentieth century, much of the late-Victorian *DNB* was showing its age and ceasing to be of much use to scholars. The medievalists among my colleagues tell me that long ago—perhaps in the 1930s or 1940s—medievalists gave up referring to the *DNB* as a source of primary information, and referred to it only as an example of what previous generations of scholars had thought in all their innocence: it had become an historiographical rather than historical source. The enormous expansion of historical scholarship in the twentieth century deserved to be incorporated. Moreover, an ageing *Dictionary* updated by single-volume decennial supplements of those who had died in each decade of the twentieth century was also becoming unwieldy and difficult to use. By the early 1990s, the scholarly and practical rationales for a new edition of the *DNB* were overwhelming.

Beyond these personal and academic factors, those who would really understand these two dictionaries need also to think broadly about the political and social contexts which they embody. I have no doubt that future scholars will look back on the *ODNB* as an exemplar of the liberal values of our age, noting that its breadth and inclusivity reflected the democratic culture which gave birth to it. Matthew set out to include more women in the *ODNB*, and more figures from minorities of all types—religious, ethnic, racial and occupational. He wanted his Dictionary to reflect all sides of life, lowlife as well as eminence—though in this he was merely following Stephen's model, for the latter too had spread the net wider than might be imagined, and was criticised for including too many malefactors alongside the benefactors of society.

Matthew also wanted the *ODNB* to reflect new aspects of our culture, some overlooked as unworthy by the Victorians, such as applied science and engineering, and others simply unknown to them, such as the enormous development of popular entertainment in our own era, which is today the surest and swiftest way to popular fame. Ours is a dictionary which can comfortably include Freddie Mercury, Sid Vicious and George Harrison. The first life in Stephen's *Dictionary* was that of Jacques Abbadie of Pau in France; the very last, that of William Zuylestein of Utrecht. No one, in other words, could accuse Stephen of insularity in his definition of the nation. The *ODNB* builds on this example, and has added many thousands of transnational lives lived by persons who had some attachment to Britain, whether as immigrants to it, emigrants from it, or as figures who never set foot in the British Isles but who influenced its history nonetheless. We have even taken pains to include notable foreign travellers to Britain, whose memoirs of what they saw, offer remarkable insights into British history.

Matthew was also conscious of the timing of his new British biographical dictionary. Intensely interested in the historical development of British political and constitutional institutions, and aware at every turn of the Victorian traditions which underpin so much of British public life, Matthew saw the *Oxford DNB* as marking an epoch in British history. It was compiled and then published during a generation in which centuries of self-government and global reach were giving way to a new identity and constitutional reality within the European Union. Those who knew Matthew appreciated his ambivalence towards these changes, an ambivalence which may be reflected in the breadth and catholicity of the *ODNB*, whose instincts are to include rather than exclude and thus to avoid the difficult business of making a choice about the nation's historic identity.[6] At a point of profound political change whose outcome is not yet clear (for Britain's place in Europe has yet to be determined), the *Dictionary* may be read, in political terms, as indeterminate and undecided, an interim statement which gives due weight to all Britain's international relations and history—imperial, transatlantic and European—without choosing and defining. That is how Matthew wanted it, because it is a fair reflection of Britain's current historical position.

Perhaps counter-intuitively, I would not make a similar argument for the original *DNB*, however: it is not the case, in my view, that the late-Victorian *Dictionary* merely represents what is taken to be a late-Victorian view of the world. But in this matter the problem may lie not with Stephen and his collaborators but with our scholarship and with present-day notions of Victorianism.

Those who have got really close to the *DNB*, Matthew pre-eminently, have not concluded that it is the epitome of supposed and so-called 'Victorian values'. Stephen's letters and speeches from this period repeat his modest ambition that the *Dictionary* prove itself merely in its usefulness to scholars and readers alike. 'He cared not for praise or blame if he had done a good piece of work. He was glad to think that the dictionary had done something to raise the standard of historical and biographical work.'[7] The tone and style of the *Dictionary* was not grandiloquent, rhetorical and imperial, but businesslike, factual and understated, and was praised as such in many quarters.

As one of the contributors, Canon Alfred Ainger, explained, '[t]he motto of the dictionary was of that funereal kind with which they were all familiar, "no flowers by request"'. It is certainly true that many contemporaries wished to see the *DNB* as a national triumph and as the celebration of national achievement. Lord Rosebery, the prime minister, ventured the opinion that it was 'the monumental work of her Majesty's reign', and Stephen's successor as editor in 1890, his former assistant Sidney Lee, born Solomon Lazarus Levi, the son of a London Jewish merchant, was notably more bullish and jingoistic when he came to discuss the *Dictionary* in print.[8] But Stephen's dry, rational, logical and unsparing intellect and his membership of a family famous for their long public agitation against slavery in the British empire, together combined to develop a *Dictionary* in his image.

It is not that Stephen was an unconventional Victorian: it is rather that present conceptions of Victorian culture are stereotypical, narrow and just plain wrong, presenting a pantomime Victorianism of pageantry, propaganda and imperialism. The *DNB* cannot be assimilated into this. Indeed, my own sense is that, like the *ODNB*, the first *Dictionary* is more the product of cultural uncertainty than of imperial self-confidence. Irish Home Rule became the central question of British politics, and the Indian National Congress first met in 1885, the year in which publication of the *DNB* began. Together, they challenged the nature of the United Kingdom and its empire. And, in Stephen, the *Dictionary* had an editor whose own experience of religious doubt, growing since the 1860s and leading him to atheism, was symptomatic of the growing scepticism of the Victorian élite in general—a doubt that was more than merely religious and which, in an existential sense, pervades late-Victorian intellectual life.

In other words, the *DNB* and the *ODNB* have complex and unexpected histories in themselves, which can be understood at various levels, personal, institutional and political. If we pick up a volume, or access one or the other dictionary online—because the DNB is available alongside the *ODNB* in electronic form—it is as well to appreciate these histories. In the search for basic information, this background may be unnecessary, of course; but for more profound work requiring that we understand the provenance of our sources, these contextual and personal factors are crucial. The *ODNB* has been written by 10,000 contributors, 3,000 of whom live outside the United Kingdom, and most of whom work or worked in universities and the equivalent; it was largely funded by a university press with only limited government assistance to the value of less than 15 per cent of the total expenditure of some £25 million;[9] it was typeset by a company based in Pondicherry, India; it was printed by Butler and Tanner, a long-established west country printer with a nonconformist heritage; its website was designed by a company based in Boston, Massachusetts. All these things tell us something and should speak to us as scholars.

And so it has always been. The singularities of *DNB* and *ODNB* may be compared with those of earlier biographical dictionaries, and the comparison will show just how long is the tradition of collecting together biographies, and how complex and varied the reasons for doing so. Today we tend to think primarily of national biographical dictionaries. Recently, Keith Thomas has surveyed the origins and changing forms of national biographical collections, charting their development in Britain in comparison with similar collections undertaken by other nations.[10] But if the specifically national dictionary is the norm in our age of nation states, and at a time when we still organise scholarship into the study of the language, literature and history of discrete national cultures, there have been other ways of collecting and organising biographies in the past.

Some collections, such as that produced in 1620 by Henry Holland the Jacobean printer and bookseller, the *Heroolgia Anglica*, which contained 65 portraits of Tudor worthies, starting with Henry VIII, were simply made for profit alone. Others were compiled for moral and didactic purposes. The Scottish physician George Mackenzie produced his *Lives and Characters of the Most Eminent Writers of the Scots Nation between 1708 and 1722* at a singular moment following the Act of Union with England, in an attempt, no doubt, to celebrate and preserve specifically Scottish achievements and identities. But his purpose was also educative in the broadest sense, and he encouraged his readers to learn from 'the Vertues and Failures of Others'.

We might cast forward also to the Victorian, Samuel Smiles, the misunderstood author of the famous text *Self Help*. Smiles worked in a tradition of exemplary biography and presented the engineers and technologists of Britain's industrial transformation as character models for his audience, examples of commitment, perseverance and the will to make the best of themselves for the good of their fellow men and women. Other compilers had a point to prove and a more personal motive for picking up their pens: it is suggested that Sir Robert Naunton, a minor politician, produced his *Fragmenta Regalia* in 1634 on the personalities of the court of Elizabeth I, and which also offered practical advice on governance to Charles I, to demonstrate to his king that he had not yet lost his faculties and was still up to the job of Master of the Court of Wards. Alas, it did not work: the king dismissed him in the following year, and he died within a matter of days.

For others again, the collection of lives was an extension of the collection of information in general. John Leland planned to write books on the geography and genealogy of England as well as on the nation's authors; bio-bibliography was just part of a vast national project that Leland never completed, but which was taken up again at the end of the sixteenth century by William Camden, whose *Britannia* was first published in 1586, and by the scholars who gathered round him to form the first Society of Antiquaries. The Society's wide-ranging interests fostered developments that culminated in the work of John Aubrey, the remarkable late-seventeenth century antiquarian known for his *Brief Lives of Notable Figures since the Reign of Elizabeth I*. Aubrey was interested in ancient monuments, folklore, topography, place names; why not also the history of people? He worked in an antiquarian tradition which did not differentiate as we do between people, places, natural wonders and man-made landscapes.

Michel Foucault's *The Order of Things* (1966) taught us that the modern disciplinary boundaries we recognise and work with—the way knowledge is organised and divided into separate subjects—is a product of the late-eighteenth century. Before then, biography took its place alongside other and unfamiliar bedfellows, and was an extension of other forms of knowledge. A work like Robert Plot's *The Natural History of Oxfordshire, Being an Essay toward the Natural History of England*, published in 1676, was clearly composed on the assumption that readers would be as interested in the biographies of county worthies as in the geology, flora and fauna of Oxfordshire, and would see no contradiction in reading of all these things in the same book.

The antecedents of our biographical collections, in Britain at least, are largely religious in nature. It is true that secular history was given what may be called a biographical dimension in the writings of a chronicler like William of Malmesbury, whose early twelfth-century *Gesta Regum* is laid out on a reign-by-reign basis, and gives details of the lives of successive kings. However, this process was taken much further in the hands of ecclesiastical writers: hence, for example, the succession of lives of the abbots of St Albans written by the great chroniclers from that abbey, Matthew Paris and Thomas Walsingham, which Paris began in the mid-thirteenth century and which Walsingham continued up to the late-fourteenth century.

Perhaps the most notable figure in the medieval tradition was Henry Kirkestede, once mistakenly known as John Boston of Bury, the fourteenth-century prior of Bury St Edmunds, who compiled for the Bury novices lists of ecclesiastical works, each with a biography of the author, some 674 in total, in his *Catalogus scriptorium ecclesie*. Kirkestede's labours originated a Christian bio-bibliographical tradition in which biography grew out of the attempt to compile lists of manuscripts and books and to tell posterity something about their authors as well, a tradition which continued into the early modern period. Thus, in the late-seventeenth century, William Cave, an Anglican clergyman and patristic scholar, produced a series of works listing all the Christian writers known to him, with basic biographical details appended, from the birth of Christ until Luther. He followed this with a literary history of the writers of the Church, his *Scriptorum ecclesiasticorum historia literaria* in 1688. There was also a separate hagiographical tradition, perhaps starting with the *Sanctilogium* compiled by John Tynemouth, a Northumbrian vicar, in the mid-fourteenth century, which contains the lives of 156 British saints. Later compilations were undertaken by Catholic scholars such as the *Briefe Register or Alphabetical Catalogue* of Nicholas Roscarrock, collected in the early seventeenth century, which contained nearly a thousand lives of the saints of Britain and Ireland.

The urge to collect biographical information seems to have been all the stronger in periods of uncertainty rather than stability. Leland began his quest to catalogue English libraries and manuscripts in 1533 with a commission from Henry VIII in his pocket.

But the dissolution of the monastic orders and the consequent disruption and dispersal of the great learned collections from 1536 gave a new and urgent purpose to his work, and seems to have engendered the idea in him, and also in his friend and co-worker John Bale, later Bishop of Ossory in Ireland, who likewise sought to catalogue and preserve the major manuscript holdings in England at this time, of a biographical dictionary as a necessary companion to a national bibliography. It was not only the manuscripts and books that were in imminent physical danger; knowledge of their authors might perish in the great disruption as well. In his own words, Leland wrote his *Viri illustres* 'so that the reputation of so many learned and elegant writers of our British should not perish'. Leland's major works were unpublished in his lifetime and circulated in manuscript only, as we have seen. Bale, however, published several works of bio-bibliography of which the most famous and important was his *Scriptorum illustrium Maioris Brytannie* (1557–1559), an indispensable source on English medieval literature. Interestingly, at one time Bale possessed a medieval copy of Kirkestede's work, which passed down through the hands of several notable Tudor and Stuart writers and antiquaries.

In a more peaceful era, the collections of the two late seventeenth century antiquarians, Anthony Wood, compiler of *Athenae Oxonienses* (1691–1692), and John Aubrey, who were also long-term collaborators, may be understood as responses to the turbulent passage of Tudor and Stuart History, from the Reformation to the Restoration, which now seemed to have reached a conclusion. Thomas Hobbes had contended that the cause of the Civil War from which he had fled into exile was the uncensored and unchecked religious and political ferment of the universities which, since the Elizabethan era, had become seats of political instability: 'The Universities have been to this nation, as the wooden horse to the Trojans'. Wood's biographical opus on Oxford men and their books since 1500—subtitled *An Exact History of all the Writers and Bishops Who Have Had Their Education in the Most Ancient and Famous University of Oxford*—was thus not as parochial as it might at first seem. Both he and Aubrey reflected the political and scholarly temper of a calmer and more measured age which had deliberately shunned religious and constitutional disputation. But they collected details on the lives of the many notable individuals who had been at the heart of the politics and culture of the 'century of revolution' now ended, conscious, perhaps, of the need to provide a record of its leading personalities. In Wood's case, the politics of biography were not obscure: his sympathies were with the Laudians of the 1630s, his animus to the Puritans.

Other early modern biographical compilations were inspired by a cause: indeed, they became scholarly weapons to be deployed in the religious and political struggles of their age. Bale—bad tempered and 'bilious Bale', as he was called—was strongly anti-Catholic, a bias evident throughout his work. Bale's close friend, with whom he shared information in turn while they lived in England, and also while they were in exile in Switzerland in the 1550s, and whom he influenced profoundly, was the famous John Foxe, compiler of the remarkable *Acts and Monuments*. First published in 1563 and commonly known to contemporaries and posterity as Foxe's 'Book of Martyrs', this was an essentially biographical listing, running to thousands of pages and many changing editions, of those who had witnessed by martyrdom to the truth of the Christian religion from the apostolic age onwards, a process culminating in the Protestant Marian martyrs of the 1550s.

Foxe was not only concerned with his own age but was operating on a scale comparable with the most ambitious of biographical dictionaries of any period or nation. *Acts and Monuments* is in effect cosmic history, recording the establishment of the church, its period of flourishing (roughly between Constantine and Gregory the Great), its deterioration and degradation, and finally the period of 'the reformation and purging of the church of God', which is seen as a fight to the finish between the forces of good—the reformers—and evil—the Antichrist, in the form of the Catholic Church. In the eight-volume edition on the open shelves of the Upper Reading Room of the Bodleian Library, Foxe does not get to the reformers of Henry VIII's reign until towards the end of the fourth volume, and to Mary's reign only in the sixth volume. For a further 300 years, the work inspired anti-Catholicism in Britain.

Like modern biographical dictionaries, *Acts and Monuments* was a collaborative and evolving enterprise, using information collected by Bale and other leading Protestant divines, and the 'fieldwork' of many more humble people using local records. Much of it was written by other hands than Foxe's, though, like a modern editor, he presided. It even incorporated oral testimony from those who had lived through Bloody Mary's reign or could attest to her crimes. Though lesser in length and inevitably unequal in its influence, a reply of sorts to this tradition of Protestant biographising and martyrology was presented in the bio-bibliographical collection of the Roman Catholic priest and English exile, John Pits, whose *De illustribus Angliae scriptoribus* was published in 1619. It contests Bale's bias, and provides valuable information on contemporary Catholic authors.

Later biographical collections were made as part of the struggle between the established church and dissent. The leading Presbyterian minister of the early eighteenth century, Edward Calamy, produced his *Account of Many Others of Those Worthy Ministers Who Were Ejected after the Restauration of King Charles the Second*, which eventually exceeded 2,000 pages, and which listed all the ejected clergyman he had been able to trace who were deprived of their livings after the Act of Uniformity in 1662 for failing to swear their loyalty to the new religious orthodoxy. The work grew out of a chapter of Calamy's biography of Richard Baxter, his *Abridgment of Mr. Baxter's Narrative*, published in 1702. In turn, Calamy was answered by the Anglican John Walker in his *Attempt towards Recovering an Account of the Numbers and Sufferings of the Clergy of the Church of*

England, Heads of Colleges, Fellows, Scholars, &c., Who Were Sequester'd, Harass'd, &c. in the Late Times of the Grand Rebellion (1714), an equivalent book of martyrology, if of less scholarly merit, giving details of those clergy persecuted and ejected by the Puritans between 1640 and 1660.

Like the Reformation, the English Civil War inspired attempts to understand and chronicle it which took a biographical form. *The History of the Rebellion*, by Edward Hyde, first Earl of Clarendon, advisor and lord chancellor to Charles II, and accounted one of the greatest works of English historiography, is punctuated by a superb series of character sketches which have worked their way into popular as well as scholarly memory.

Not all of these studies were partisan, however: one at least, Thomas Fuller's *History of the Worthies of England* (1662), containing short biographies of the most noteworthy figures in each county, was the corollary to his serious historical analysis of the Civil War, and was the culmination of several pioneering works that this Anglican clergyman had researched and published on the Civil War's religious and political origins. These included a study of the leading figures of the Reformation, *Abel redevivus*, published in 1651; *The Church History of Britain* (1655), with its discussion of the Laudian reforms and their effects; and an edition of documents from the famous parliamentary session of 1628–1629, the last before the 11-year period of Charles I's personal rule.

I have provided quite enough examples to make my point clear: that the history of biographical compilation is rich, varied and complex, and has been undertaken for many different reasons, in different circumstances, and often in furtherance of a cause. Specifically national compilations, in recognition and celebration of the nation state, are comparatively recent in origin, and a focus on them may obscure other and older traditions of biographical collection. But this has not been an exercise in antiquarianism in itself, which can be dismissed by the modern scholar as of no relevance to the biographical research that we do today. For these historic biographical collections have an enduring life, their information assimilated over the generations into later, broader and different compilations that nevertheless depend upon the delving and recording of medieval and early modern scholars. In the *ODNB*, some 158 biographies depend upon Leland as a source; Bales's work is crucial to 259 of the included lives; Foxe's martyrology provides information on 224 subjects in the *Dictionary*. Anthony Wood's biographies of the university men of Tudor and Stuart England in his *Athenae Oxonienses* has provided information used for 1,470 separate lives in the *ODNB*; Thomas Fuller's researches are cited 195 times.

Truly, in collecting biographies we stand upon the shoulders of others, those many collectors, compilers, antiquarians and scholars whose manuscripts have gone through many hands and many editions over the centuries; have been discussed and argued over; and have been tested by those who came later. According to Richard Sharpe, 'the way in which Leland, Bale, and [Thomas] Tanner were meshed together, each understanding and building on the work of his predecessors, has given their work a value that has lasted even to the present time'. For these reasons, we can be as sure as may be that the information they left to posterity, though it may reflect a decided point of view, has been scrutinised carefully and those parts of it thought worthy have been transmitted to those who came after—to us, in fact. We cannot be so sure about the vast quantities of information posted indiscriminately on the World Wide Web.

But my argument goes beyond familiar concerns over quality control and the absence of peer review, a term that might have conjured quite other connotations to Sir Robert Naunton in 1634. My concern is also, in the words of Kingsley Amis, that 'more is worse', or in the case of biography, that the very nature of fast searching on the internet will desensitise us to all those many issues—biographical, bibliographical and editorial—bound up in collecting lives and making sense of them, and will lead us to ignore the principles governing the compilations we use and their differences one from another.

My fascinating conversations in the winter of 2006 with the editor of the *Australian Dictionary of Biography* (*ADB*), Di Langmore, and her staff have thrown up just such differences between the *ODNB* and the *ADB*, now happily and most successfully online as well. I admire very much the sharpness and focus of the entries in the *ADB*, even more so now that I appreciate the rigorous checking of each and every fact in a submitted article. For her part, Dr Langmore spoke appreciatively of the style of biographical memoir that has always characterised the *DNB*—the rounded, literary and rather more impressionistic portrait of the life and its context, inevitably longer and more discursive. It is the style bequeathed to us by Leslie Stephen, who had perfected the biographical appreciation rather than the résumé many years before he became editor, and it has come to characterise and distinguish everything we do.

My concern is that in an electronic age that distinction will cease to be appreciated; indeed, may actually deter a researcher in a hurry, looking for information and impatient with the discussion of dress, appearance, character, tastes and style in an *ODNB* article. The internet is for searching and Googling, not for reading and reflecting; we use it in different ways and expect from it different things than we do from *Hours in a Library*, the title of a compilation of Stephen's essays published in the 1870s. Merely in the handling and opening of books, through many different signs and indicators, we can discover something of their purpose and provenance. The internet is much more difficult to decipher and decode.

Hence my message: that to use biographical compilations properly we must use them cautiously, paying due attention to their *raisons d'être*, the circumstances of their composition, their textual history, their use of sources. This applies even to today's biographical dictionaries, written by scholars for scholars, which may seem to have escaped the bias and prejudices of the past. I am saying nothing more than that biographical dictionaries are texts like any other, which must be read with care and used with insight. But if they are texts, then they are something more and other than 'databases' and 'web-based resources', horrid words all.

The internet promotes fast searching among sources of information whose provenance may be unknown and authority difficult to substantiate. We should not use biographical dictionaries, carefully compiled according to the highest editorial standards, as if they are just another of these many sources, some more dubious than others. We should treat them with respect, seeking to understand why and how they have been created, and to what end, for with that knowledge we can use their information with greater accuracy and confidence. National biographical dictionaries of the type that we use all the time have a rationale as records of the historical development and historical consciousness of the nation state: hence the energies devoted to them in so many countries since the age of nationalism in the nineteenth century.

International and transnational collections will also have a rationale in a globalising age when knowing something about figures across boundaries rather than within them may be required. But let there be a rationale: let us do things virtually for a reason, because it will advance knowledge or truly assist scholarship, not just because we can. And let us treat our texts with respect, as complex entities reflecting many different factors in their production.

Andrew Kippis was the editor of the second edition of the *Biographia Britannica* at the close of the eighteenth century. Like other figures we have encountered in the biographical traditions I have sketched, he was accused of bias, by James Boswell among others, though we need to know that Dr Johnson had turned down the position of editor when it was offered to him ahead of Kippis, apparently to his later regret. In the same year, 1777, Johnson signed the contract to produce his own exercise in collective biography, *The Lives of the Poets* (1779–1781). As a Presbyterian minister, a leading dissenter—a colleague, indeed, of Richard Price and the great Joseph Priestley as a tutor at the dissenting academy in Hackney—Kippis was criticised for including too many nonconformist clergymen in his selection of lives, and showing too great a fondness for heterodox doctrines. Alas, his second edition only got as far as the letter F, in five volumes that took more than 15 years to produce, after which the project was killed off. But Kippis penned an interesting preface to his compilation which is worth rehearsing. Biography, he explained,

> may be regarded as presenting us with a variety of events, that, like experiments in Natural Philosophy, may become the materials from which general truths and principles are to be drawn. When Biographical knowledge is employed in enlarging our acquaintance with Human Nature, in exciting an honourable emulation, in correcting our prejudices, in refining our sentiments, and in regulating our conduct, it then attains its true excellence. Besides its being a pleasing amusement, and a just tribute of respect to illustrious characters, it rises to the dignity of SCIENCE; and of such science as must be esteemed of peculiar importance, because it hath MAN for its object.[12]

Kippis's desire to construct a science of man is a classical statement of a central aspect of the eighteenth-century British Enlightenment. His ambition that biography should be the basis of a human science may seem quaint or inappropriate to us now, and perhaps to his contemporaries it was similarly overblown. But the claim that biography should be more than just 'a pleasing amusement' is the final caution in this cautionary tale.

The internet may provide us with information on a scale and at a speed that was unimaginable just a few years ago; but it may also trivialise and denature sources and texts that deserve and require more careful reading and reflection. Kippis intended that biography itself should be elevated 'to the dignity of a science'; my hopes are more modest—merely that in a virtual age we treat biographical information with the dignity that it, and those who have compiled it over the centuries, deserve.

1 R.C. Christie, 'Dictionary of National Biography', *Quarterly Review*, vol.164, April 1887, p.353.

2 James P. Carley, 'The First Dictionary of National Biography', The Lyell Lectures in Bibliography, University of Oxford, Trinity Term 2006, unpublished; Richard Sharpe, 'The English Bibliographical Tradition from Kirkestede to Tanner' in Charles Burnett and Nicholas Mann (eds.), *Britannia Latina. Latin in the Culture of Great Britain from the Middle Ages to the Twentieth Century* (Warburg Institute Colloquia, 8) (London, 2005), pp.86–128.

3 Jenifer Glynn, *Prince of Publishers: A Biography of George Smith* (London, 1986), pp.199–206.

4 Sir Keith Thomas referred to Matthew's indispensability in his address at Colin Matthew's funeral, 4 November 1999, Christ Church Cathedral, Oxford.

5 Rev. Dr Augustus Jessopp, 'The Dictionary of National Biography', *The Nineteenth Century*, 1890, pp.1008–1009.

6 Lawrence Goldman, 'A Monument to the Victorian Age? Continuity and Discontinuity in the Dictionaries of National Biography 1882–2004', *Journal of Victorian Culture*, 11.1, Spring 2006, pp.115–116.

7 *The Times*, 9 July 1897, p.10. Stephen was speaking at a dinner given by George Smith to the editor and contributors of the *DNB* at the Hotel Metropole, London, on 8 July 1897.

8 Sidney Lee, 'Statistical Account', preface to the 63rd and last volume of the *DNB*, 1900.

9 The *Oxford DNB* received £3 million from the British government via the British Academy towards the cost of research. The balance, £22 million, was made up by Oxford University Press, with no prospect of a commercial return on its investment in national scholarship.

10 Keith Thomas, *Changing Conceptions of National Biography. The Oxford DNB in Historical Perspective* (The Leslie Stephen Special Lecture, Cambridge, 2004).

11 Carley, 'The First Dictionary of National Biography', Lecture 1, f.1. Quotation taken from John Leland, 'The Laboryouse Journey & Serche of John Leylande, for Englands Antiquitees, Geuen of Hym as a Newe Yeares Gyfte to Kynge Henry the VIII', in Sharpe, *The English Bibliographical Tradition*, pp.97–98.

12 *Biographia Britannica*, 2nd edn., vol.1 (1778), p.xxi, quoted in Isabel Rivers. 'Biographical Dictionaries and Their Users from Bayle to Chalmers', in I. Rivers (ed.), *Books and Their Readers in Eighteenth Century England: New Essays* (Leicester, 2001), p.157.

Biography and the Struggle for the Soul of Australia

Emeritus Professor Jill Roe AO
2007

My colleagues have been teasing me about being 'on tour'. And in truth the Seymour Lecture is a challenge. It is the same challenge as was put to me long ago in Canberra by Professor Manning Clark who one day, out of the blue, said to me in that formal style which characterised exchanges between staff and students in those days, 'What have you got to say, Miss Roe?' I have recently learned he said it to others too. But the challenge, which I now think was as much to himself as to us, has stayed with me over the years, due these days mostly to Miles Franklin, still a stimulating companion though she died as long ago as 1954. I was 13 at the time and knew nothing of her. It would almost as long again before I heard of *My Brilliant Career*, as it happens from historian Ian Turner. It was longer again before I was invited by the *Australian Dictionary of Biography* (*ADB*) to prepare the entry of Stella Maria Sarah Miles Franklin, which appeared in volume 9 in 1981, and where it all began.

Those of you who know my ways may be relieved to hear that I am not about to deliver another lecture on writing a biography of Stella Miles Franklin. Still, as I have learned from previous work, you can't stick with a subject for a long time without learning a lot from it—there are those who say my mind has been improved considerably by Miles—and often it is inescapable. Besides, continuities matter.

In this lecture, after some essential context and a premise derived from the work of my elders and betters—the historians Manning Clark and Russel Ward—I begin with the literary world to which Miles Franklin returned in Sydney in the 1930s.

I will then enlarge on 'the bushwhackers' she encountered in that world. My star turn will be Michael Sawtell, best known as a Wobbly during World War I, an Emersonian, and strong advocate of Aboriginal citizenship in Sydney from the 1920s to the 1950s, who I researched for the *Australian Dictionary of Biography, Supplement 1580-1980*, published in 2005. A third concern will be with biography and, in a glancing kind of way, its methodological extension, prosopography: that is to say the systematic analysis of occupational and other forms of group biography as a source of insight into social and cultural dynamics. Now that the *ADB* is searchable online, a great storehouse of largely untapped historical knowledge is opening up.

My title is over-the-top, I know. No doubt you wonder what I am going to say about the 'Australian soul', a subject usually left to religious historians. However, it is not such a drab affair these days, as Marion Maddox has shown in her recent book *God Under Howard*, the epilogue of which discusses the Constitutional Conference and shows that in 1998 'God' turned out to be generic word meaning some superior kind of Australian. Maddox thinks it's time to reclaim the soul of Australia. I do too. Here I have recourse to it mainly as a metaphor for the vexatious matter of Australian identity, which I feel it is timely to revisit. I'm sure I am not the only one to feel that a cracked-record assertion of 'mateship' makes little sense in the twenty-first century, for example, or to remember its dark side. More perturbing perhaps has been its gradual militarisation across the twentieth century and its trivialisation by advertising.

Ultimately, I seek to confront some of the simplistic and ahistorical assumptions which have kept, or perhaps I should say returned, 'the struggle for the soul of Australia' to a school yard level. It is my belief that the biographical knowledge accumulated over the past 50 years—it is the 50th birthday of the *ADB* this November and I'm hanging in for the party—is going to make a difference. For a start it will surely show that even such deep-seated phenomena as myths and legends may change over time, and politicians are wasting their breath if they try to impose partial or outdated ones. Melbourne historian John Hirst is quite right to insist that you can't just throw out ideas and values that have shaped people's lives. But we can do better.

In Sydney you learn to watch your back. It is at the least presumptuous of me to set out this. However the problem of identity is of our own times, and it has been long time shaping up. It dates back to the 1950s. In his famous 1954 lecture 'Rewriting Australian history', Manning Clark boldly asserted that the creed of mateship was a poor comforter against the storms of life and threatening skies overhead, but having undertaken the mammoth task of rewriting Australian history, he found it almost impossible to envisage how to proceed. For all the marvellous refreshment of his 1960s approach to the Australian experience, famously recast in terms of the impact of the main European intellectual traditions—Catholic Christendom, Protestantism and the Enlightenment—by the end of his great project he was scarcely able to suppress his disappointment that a new and better civilisation had not emerged in the Great South Land: 'No-one any longer knew the direction of the river of life. No-one had anything to say.' Perhaps the rising generation might be wiser than its predecessors: 'With the end of the domination of the straiteners, the enlargers of life now have their chance.' But he did not say how things had reached this point, and he warned the young would have to choose.

Similarly, in his classic interpretation of *The Australian Legend* published in 1958, Russel Ward touched but lightly on the twentieth century experience, and he too concluded with a warning, that the ethos of the bush workers, carried forward by the labour movement and creative writers, may have become too rigid by the 1950s. 'Today's task,' he wrote, 'might well be to develop those features of the Australian legend which still seem valid in modern conditions.' Ward was well aware of a deep seated problem of racism in the old bush ethos, and he even touched thoughtfully on the significance of the absence of women from 'the nomad tribe'.

So, what has happened among historians in the shaping of national ethos since? A shorthand way to proceed might be to invite you to jot down the two or three authors or titles you have found most significant since Clark and Ward. However, I must call a halt to historiographical background if I am to get to the body of my lecture, by mentioning two very different works of the 1980s. *The Other Side of the Frontier* by a leading historian of the succeeding generation, Henry Reynolds. Our understanding of what happened next has since been greatly augmented, and many more Aboriginal people have entered the national lexicon, but there's a long way to go before Geoffrey Blainey's 1970s vision of an Aboriginal Australian civilisation is fully integrated. The other title I would note is Richard White's *Inventing Australia*, which rethought a sequence of national stereotypes in terms of responses to dominant economic and intellectual forces. The main problem of that was that the stereotypes also derived from the experience of real people in a real world. It is to them I now turn.

On 5 September 1937, British-born journalist and bush writer Will Lawson addressed the Sydney Writers Association on 'Where have the dinkum Australians gone?' Unfortunately, apart from the fact that Lawson's talk was to be followed by a dinner dance in honour of expatriate writer Helen Simpson, who was visiting Sydney to give talks for the ABC and promote her latest novel *Under Capricornia*, nothing more is known of the event. Perhaps Miles Franklin's habit of emphasising that bushmen, not the professors, wrote the ballads has some bearing on what Will Lawson had to say.

Little more is known about the Writers Association. It was the short-lived product of a split in the Fellowship of Australian Writers (FAW). The FAW, which became the main advocate of Australian writers and writing in coming decades, was only seven years old when the first split occurred in 1935, its policies too timid for the live wires. While they were busy ousting the president, college lecturer George Mackaness, for not taking a stronger stand against literary censorship, writers on the left were galvanised by the Egon Kisch affair—a cause celebre at the time due to ham-fisted efforts by the Commonwealth government to prevent Kisch from entering Australia as a guest of the Movement against War and Fascism. It was at Kisch's suggestion that the proletarian Writers League split away from the FAW in 1935. The Writers League was headed by Katharine Susannah Prichard and Jean Devanny and affiliated with the Comintern. That was too much for many of the disaffected, and a year later, in 1936, the Writers League itself split to form the School of Modern Writers, a left sectarian group which lasted well into the 1940s, and the Writers Association, a broader based but short-lived anti-fascist grouping, which rejoined the FAW a year or so later.

In 1937 Will Lawson's most recent works were *When Cobb and Co was King* and *Old Man Murray*. It's a fair bet that by 'dinkum Australians' he meant men from way back, the bushwhackers. What is a 'bushwhacker'? According to the *Shorter Oxford English Dictionary* as revised in the 1930s, the word 'bushwhacker' is of early 19th century American origin, referring to a backwoodsman or a bushranger. *The Australian National Dictionary* first identifies Australian usage in the 1890s. Interestingly, it still had a double meaning then, bushman or fighter, as when members of the Bushman's Contingent for the South African War were referred to in the Melbourne *Tocsin* as 'Bushwhackers'. But it seems that usage did not carry through to the Great War when the colloquial 'digger' came into fashion, and it is now quite historical. When the term's popularity returned in the 1920s it referred only to outback types, often patronised by city dwellers. Today, the *Macquarie Dictionary* tells us it simply means a 'bushy'.

A sign of its reinstatement in the 1920s was a feature film entitled 'The Bushwhackers', launched in Sydney mid-1925. The film was produced by Raymond Longford and Lottie Lyell. There was a governor's preview, and it was released at the Lyceum and the Wintergarden theatres. A romantic tale shot in the wilds of the Burragorang Valley and along the Wollondilly River, south of Sydney, it was widely reviewed. Everyone liked the scenery, but the plot was deemed slight. The main character, who has been lost in the bush and long since given up for dead, returns only to find his wife has married his mate. The self-sacrificing hero returns to a lonely life in the bush leaving the pair to enjoy happiness. The acting was said to be perfunctory.[1]

Some depth was given to the image of the bushwhacker by the young P.R. Stephensen in the 1920s. Amazing as it now seems, this 'wild man of letters' wrote *The Bushwhackers: Sketches of Life in the Australian Outback* in London in the late 1920s and published it there under the imprint of his modernist Mandrake Press. It seems Stephensen was challenged by the images of the Australian bush in D.H. Lawrence's *Kangaroo* (1923). Though slight, his sketches are forceful and heartfelt and his country is diversely peopled. The title tale protests against instant European exploiters of the land—my notes say laconically, 'then the bush whacked them'—and there are portrayals of Willy Ah Foo, the tormented market gardener, and of 'Black Alf', who died on his horse, as well as portrayals of legendary events, such as the alien ceremony of the cremation of Napro Singh and the tragic outcome of the man who accepted a wager to lift a one ton weight. Stephensen's view of the bush at the time was too harsh and challenging for what was then the common currency. Lawrence simply thought 'Inky' should have taken more time over his sketches. Nettie Palmer accorded them more serious attention, acknowledging a passion for the land and a rich idiom in what are said to be recollections of his boyhood at Biggenden in central Queensland.[2]

The person who liked them most was probably Miles Franklin, then also living in London, who had previously been uplifted by expatriate poet Mary Fullerton's *Bark House Days*, a memoir of Mary's youth in the wilds of Gippsland.[3] Mary and Miles had several important things in common. Both were female, and therefore not likely to be seen as 'bushwackers'. Both felt themselves to be handicapped as writers by their limited rural education. But both wrote what they knew out of their rural experience.

How Miles came to draft the roaring tale of Danny Delacy in the prize-winning *All that Swagger* (1936) is too elaborate to tell here. Danny Delacy was based on her paternal grandfather, a young Irish immigrant who arrived at Yass where he began as a labourer and within a decade was drawn to the mountain country in the south. In some ways, Danny is a more confident extension of 'Brent of Bin Bin', the persona Miles chose for her three-volume pastoral saga published in England 1929-1931. Miles had been experimenting with the pseudonym since at least 1925, and as dedicated readers of *My Brilliant Career* will know, Bin Bin East and Bin Bin West were holdings to the east of Brindabella.

A question I wish to put before you this evening is that maybe the bushwhackers were now mostly to be found in books? Or, at least, that is where they still counted. What significance should be attached to the surge in bushwhacker writing in the interwar years? As Will Lawson's titles may indicate, the writing of popular regional stories by 'townies' was in full swing by the 1930s, and bushwhacker folklore was being collected—for example, in *Packhorse and Waterhole: With the First Overlanders to the Kimberleys*, Gordon Buchanan's record of his father Nat Buchanan's droving feats across northern Australia, material subsequently utilised by Ernestine Hill and Mary Durack.[4] Ernestine Hill (1899–1972), Rockhampton-born, spent most of her life after the death of her husband in 1933 travelling and writing about inland Australia, firstly *The Great Australian Loneliness* (1937).

The outstanding example of popular outback writing has to be Ion Idriess. Beverley Eley's informative biography of 'Jack' Idriess shows how the gold-mad young prospector from Broken Hill and Far North Queensland became a disciplined writer of Australiana down south when his luck ran out—'the Boswell of the Bush' and one of Australia's most successful authors. Looked down on by the middle classes, his books taught countless ordinary Australians from the 1920s to the 1950s their history and geography, my father among them, and to a certain extent even me.

Idriess was astonishingly prolific. In the 1930s, when he got into his stride, he published nine books. In chronological order: *Lasseter's Last Ride* (1931), *Flynn of the Inland* (1932), *The Desert Column* (1932), *Men of the Jungle* (1933), *Gold, Dust and Ashes: The Romantic Story of the New Guinea Goldfields* (1933), *The Cattle King* (1936), *Man Tracks: With the Mounted Police in Central Australia* (1935); *Forty Fathoms Deep: Pearl Divers and the Sea Rovers of Australia* (1937); *Over the Range: Sunshine and Shadow in the Kimberleys* (1939). Most of these books were written upstairs at the old Angus & Robertson headquarters in Castlereagh Street, with the help of a few whiskies in the morning. Some, for example, *Lasseter's Last Ride*, are still in print. No wonder more self-conscious or ambitious writers found him too much or simply left the country!

D.H. Lawrence may have been the most significant visiting writer of the 1920s with something to say to Australian readers about the bush. When Miles caught up with *Kangaroo* almost a decade later, she recognised its importance, remarking to a new friend—American publicist Hartley Grattan—that reading it was like walking over a freshly ploughed paddock. But other recently arrived writers of the time contributed more to the popularity of bush writing: for example, Arthur Upfield, Thomas Wood and William Hatfield.

These days Arthur Upfield is probably the best known of this trio, and I will have a little more something to say about him shortly. Thomas Wood, a musician as well as a writer, came to Australia in 1930 to conduct music exams, and after two years traveling the country, wrote *Cobbers*, a classic work published in London in 1934, which though affectionate does not eschew critical comment. (The *ADB* entry on Wood was written by Russel Ward.)

William Hatfield was a draper's son born in Hampshire in 1890 who always dreamed of going to Australia, and in 1912, aged 19, decided to migrate. He worked his passage and jumped ship at Port Adelaide, setting off immediately for the interior. After a hard day's walking he found himself at Glenelg. Soon after, he was recruited by Elder Smith and on his way north to begin almost 20 years at every conceivable outback job. A skilled bushman, Hatfield always wanted to write about his experiences, but his efforts in the 1920s were unsuccessful. The extent of those efforts is not fully clear from his engaging memoir, *I Find Australia,* published in England in 1937, but we can get some idea of his preoccupations from his first successes *Sheepmates* (1931), a station tale of central Australia, and *Desert Saga* (1933), about an Aboriginal boy. Hatfield did return to England briefly in the 1930s, but it is no surprise to find him back lecturing on conservation in the 1940s.

English immigrant and Gallipoli survivor Arthur Upfield's detective novels, featuring part Aboriginal Detective Inspector Napoleon Bonaparte—presently attracting renewed, if contested, attention—also date from the 1930s. *Winds of Evil,* set in outback NSW, was published by Angus and Robertson in 1937 and is still an interesting book to read. Upfield, it has been rightly said, gives a worm's eye view of awesome natural grandeur, a sense of human inadequacy in a dominating continent.[5]

Stephensen was not so much a writer as a man on a cultural mission. His most important contribution to debate came with *The Foundations of Culture in Australia: An Essay Towards National Self Respect,* published by his new patron W.J. Miles in 1936, a vigorous assault on 'the garrison'—that is, excessive overseas influences—which asserted that all cultures are created locally. Stephen's descent into authoritarian nationalism in the late 1930s is well known. Less well known, or at least less easily absorbed, is Stephensen's influence on some younger men. It was Stephensen's essay that encouraged the Orroroo-born teacher and poet, Rex Ingamells, to write *Conditional Culture* published in 1938, which was an important, if flawed, attempt to harmonise white and black cultures. At the level of oral history, Laurence Gooley, then a young Sydney clerk, heard people talking about Stephensen on the train, and this awoke him to a lifelong sense of the importance of Australian literature.

Conditional Culture is especially significant here. Firstly, because of its historical perspective; and secondly, because of its subsequent influence. Ingamells was able to capture the cultural moment.

> Thoughtful introspection must lead us to serious consideration concerning the aboriginal question ... The stage has been reached, when after a vigorous era of

> colonization, Australians should take stock of the past and present and so give effective thought to the future.[6]

Furthermore, Ingamells' initiative led to the formation of the Jindyworobak Movement, the main cultural conduit of bushwhacker values in the 1940s. By then, Miles Franklin had marshalled some of her own memories of bush life and had a better grip on cultural currents. Stephensen had tried to expand his sketches too, but this came to nothing. His real contribution was to publish Xavier Herbert's epochal portrayal of northern Australia, *Capricornia*, in 1938 and in the same year to shadow-edit and publish *The Abo Call*, journal of the Aborigines Progressive Association.

Thinking about the failure of both Miles Franklin and P.R. Stephensen, who both returned to Australia from England in late 1932, to get far with their exalted ideas of a national literary culture based on a unique bush experience prompts some questions about the fiercely contested character of literary life in 1930s Sydney. Recent research on the coming of modernism to Australia in the interwar years has led me to the following broad conclusion (since it is my conclusion, I hope you won't mind me quoting myself):

> In the interwar years, the forces of modernism made more headway in Sydney's 'sea coast of Bohemia' than elsewhere in Australia. Yet with all roads from the depressed hinterlands leading to Sydney, there were plenty of keen (though less well documented) advocates of an indigenous (as then defined) bush culture too. The result was 'a conflict of opposites', with ideological and class tensions tending to cancel one another out and little space left for the idea of a national literary culture ... (it was evident that) the lines were simplistically drawn between those committed to the 'gum tree' school and those who felt themselves above and beyond it, though, as she [Miles] rightly observed, unlike the English oak, the alphabet of the eucalypt was hardly known.[7]

We usually think of the battlers making for the bush in the Depression, but they also came in from the bush. In 1938, drover 'Billy Miller' turned up at the FAW with Gordon Buchanan. A true example of the bushwhacker genre, Miller—whose real name was Linklater—had run away from a harsh Presbyterian childhood in Adelaide in the 1880s, and for over 50 years lived the bush life in Northern Australia. He was in town mainly because of eye trouble but also in hope of help with his memoirs. Besides his smattering of classical education, he also knew several Aboriginal languages. It was too late for anyone to help him as a writer, though with his daughter he did publish *The Magic Snake* on Aboriginal legends in 1940, and he died soon after. The life of Billy

Miller is documented in the *Northern Territory Dictionary of Biography* edited by David Carment and colleagues.

Adelaide seems to have been a breeding ground for the later bushwhackers. When Billy Miller visited Sydney he called on Michael Sawtell, whom he had known up north before World War I. 'Mick' Sawtell now ran a health food shop in Victoria Arcade, which served also as the headquarters of the Emerson Society. (Sawtell was the president and possibly the only member.) By the 1930s he was also a leading figure in the emergent campaign for Aboriginal citizenship.

He was often heard speaking in the Domain, and regularly at one or other of the two theosophical halls in the city. Sometimes he turned up at the FAW, though usually as a speaker. In fact, he would speak anywhere provided people paid his expenses. His favourite subjects were great thinkers, especially Plato, Aboriginal life and beliefs, theosophy and the occult and, of course, Emerson. In later life, he became an enthusiast for turning the coastal rivers inland, a theme expounded not only by engineer J.J.C. Bradfield who gave us the Sydney Harbour Bridge, but also popularly for a wide audience by Idriess in *The Great Boomerang* (1941). In literary terms, Sawtell was constantly searching for the great Australian essayist to stand alongside his American hero Emerson.

Sawtell was a marvellous subject to research. For the best biographical experience you need someone who has lived life to the full, preferably in interesting places, and has a mind of their own. And it helps if there is some secret or quirkiness. I am no Manning Clark, but I, too, prefer the ones who are a bit on the wild side. Sawtell was born in Adelaide in 1883, son of an optician and his Swedish-born wife. He attended the elite St Peters College where he did well, but soon after went to work on a Kidman cattle station east of Lake Eyre where he made friends with young Aboriginal workers. He worked the Birdsville Track, eventually moving northwards to Borroloola on the Gulf of Carpentaria where he spent six months reading in the extraordinary, and later Carnegie-funded, Borroloola Library—in itself the epitome of the old bush self-education through the tradition of 'swapping books', so admired by Joseph Furphy and skilfully exploited by J.F. Archibald in the Bulletin. Nicholas Jose's *Black Sheep: Journey to Borroloola* (2002) is an interesting modern commentary of the now legendary library.

Sawtell then went west to Yampi Sound, chanting socialist verse while droving his cattle. It was wild country beyond Derby and he was soon driven out by local Aboriginal people. It was there that a passing missionary gave him theosophical literature. What he found in it was the theosophical teaching that all human beings were equal regardless of race and equally capable of evolving to a higher plane of existence. Perhaps in keeping with developments in contemporary anthropology, theosophy was then especially interested in Aboriginal spirituality.

From Yampi, Sawtell trekked to Perth, where he joined the Perth theosophists and became a Wobbly during World War I. By 1917 he was in Parramatta Jail for industrial disruption at Broken Hill. Back in Adelaide in the early 1920s he married a schoolteacher, but the marriage was short lived. Somehow he made his way back east picking up work wherever he could. By the later 1920s, he was working in a factory in Sydney. In October 1937, a month after Will Lawson posed that question about the dinkum Ozzies at the FAW, Sawtell was at the Savoy Theater a few blocks away holding forth on theosophy and the Aboriginal culture—and if the amount of press attention his talks and actions subsequently attracted is any guide—well on the way to becoming one of Sydney's great characters.

There are several press photos of him standing on his head meditating in his book-lined sitting room in Darlinghurst. Close up, however, his enthusiasm was probably too much for ordinary humans to bear. After hearing Sawtell at the Fellowship on one occasion, Miles Franklin sighed that oratory was obviously a male disease.

It is perhaps self-indulgent of me to spend so much time on Sawtell. However, Sawtell has not previously been researched and he is a good example of the quality of new knowledge in the pages of the *ADB*. Clearly Sawtell was not an average bushie, or even typical of the bushwhackers. Nonetheless I suggest he is a pivotal character who came to rest between the formally educated professionals and the self-educated, pragmatic, 'school of hard knocks' types, and his living illuminated richer possibilities than the trite values allegedly derived from the old bush culture usually proposed for our allegiance.

It has been argued that the urban intelligentsia of the 1890s created the Australian legend. Perhaps they did. But many of them came from the bush in the first place, like Lawson and latterly Sawtell, and also Ingamells. They were all bush intellectuals by origin just as was Miles Franklin, and though I can no more than mention him, the lyric poet John Shaw Neilson. Such speculation leads me into the third area to be considered in this lecture. What more might be found in the volumes of the *ADB* about bushwhackers and the old bush culture? What did they have to say? How much of the retrievable knowledge is relevant now?

From researching one relevant life, that is the life of Miles Franklin, I at least have a fair idea of what the most useful categories of inquiry would be. After family, the people she learned most from as a girl were bush teachers, local newspaper men, and sundry bearers of cultural information such as musicians and librarians, though not, it must be said, bush clergy. A chronological listing with names would go as follows: Charles Auchinvole Blythe, her Scottish-born tutor at Brindabella, who had been a journalist in England as a young man and sometimes contributed leaders to the *Tumut Times*; Mary Ann Gillespie, an Irish-born farmer's daughter from Grabben Gullen, about 30 kilometers north-west of Goulburn, the teacher at Thornford Public School who tried to improve her mind on weekends in Goulburn; Thomas Hebblewhite, the London-born editor of the *Goulburn Evening Penny Post* in the 1890s, who might have chosen to work on the *Bulletin* but preferred to set up in 'Australia's first inland city'; and maybe some musicians at the two Goulburn cathedrals. Later at Penrith, proximity to Sydney overshadowed all other cultural influences but local political influences were significant. As in Goulburn, there was a sizable population of railway workers supporting the new Labor Party, votes for women in New South Wales was a big issue, and her father, who would have passed any bushwhacker test, was able to briefly make a mark as a town councillor. Even at his lowest after entering in bankruptcy in 1896, John Franklin could assert, in the only extended—and, I must warn you, largely unpunctuated—communication with his daughter to survive, his god-given right to think for himself.

> I know I have a law full right to think simply because no one else knows what my thoughts are thank god for that although I may have to consult some of my reverend seniors & those educated in the school where nature is only a fool I suppose that you will be glad to hear I thank god for something, well I do but not the god of gold selfishness envy hatred malice pride pomp & worldly show & hundreds of other names, but the one I thank is the god of reason science art love and beauty ... now as you maybe endowed with the power to think for yourself, you can think out what sort of a god I thank.[8]

During her years away, Miles's contacts with the Australian bush were maintained through people like former squatter Philip Sydney Watson. In America and again in England she encountered Watson, who had worked at 'Gregory Downs', the Watson family's station near Burketown on the Gulf of Carpentaria, in the 1880s, and retired to Melbourne. Watson's father had been a spiritualist and in 1905 'P.S.', as he was usually known, became an accredited Christian Science practitioner. As 'Kangaroo', he once sent Miles a postcard from New York addressing her as 'Dear Wombat', and his 1920s letters to her combine droving details and Christian Science admonition.

On her return to Sydney in the l 930s Miles was able to renew links with her old teacher Miss Gillespie who had retired to Hurstville, and through her met Will Carter who had also taught in bush schools all his life, was recently retired and also living nearby. With the help of the Hurstville paper, *The Propeller*, Carter established the Propeller Young Writers' League of which Miles became patron. Carter was a prolific contributor of 'Australianities' to the rural press, and he did his bit to keep her name before the reading public upcountry.

All of the 'bushwhackers' in Miles's early experience were really professional people with some formal education, the 'hard core' of the rural intelligentsia. In those days the rural working population was even greater than it was in the 1930s, but ordinary bush workers seldom appear in Miles's recollections. Let's take a look at them now. If you type in under occupation the sometimes more settled category of 'farm and station worker' of *ADB Online*, no less that 157 matches will come up, which is quite a surprise since an entry in the *ADB* signifies more than occupation. Bush workers are also quite numerous. Maybe that's partly because of quite a few shearers. Not surprisingly, itinerants and unskilled workers are fewer. Still, some among them stand out as bush intellectuals.

A classic case must surely be 'Scotty' Mowbray', another Scottish-born and educated figure roaming the wilds of Australia. 'Scotty' served in the British Army all over the Empire before settling for Australia, where he became a swagman and occasional contributor of 'Aboriginalities' to Archibald's *Bulletin*. In 1901 he wrote to the Governor-General, Lord Hopetoun, to point out that the bush proletariat had not been invited to the G-G's investiture. 'He did not wear his learning lightly', author Gerry Walsh writes. But Mowbray died too soon, at Narrandera in 1903. Victorian-born Donald McGillivary, horse-breaker, the self-styled 'Professor McGillivray', lasted until 1921. Better still is central Australian bushman Bob Buck, another Adelaide lad, largely self-educated, a fount of bush lore who became famous as the man who found Lasseter's remains (probably). Miles met him when traveling with Frank Clune in 1937 and he died in Alice Springs in 1960, aged 79. Although it's a category slide, most impressive of all may well be Aboriginal tracker, stockman and clever man Mick McLean ('Irinyili'), who was born near Pirlakaya well in the Simpson desert and retired to Port Augusta in 1971, devoting himself to preserving the cultural knowledge of the northern Lake Eyre basin. It probably goes too far to include champion NSW rabbiter Joe Copeley, who with his brother once trapped 288 rabbits in a day. Joe's life story is touching but there's not much 'soul' in it.

Among the professionals or the more formally educated bush workers, teachers were the largest group. There are lots of them in the *ADB*. In the first 12 volumes covering lives to 1939, there are 124 people listed as teachers, and that's not counting art teachers, dance teachers, music teachers, school principals, technical educators and university teachers, who are listed separately. By now the educational world, or should I say industry, is so complex there are no such simple index entry as 'teachers'. However teacher is probably the easiest of all occupational groupings for us to imagine as cultural agents, and I have already cited two bush teachers, though neither are at *ADB* level. Instead I would like to recall a research trip to upper Eyre Peninsula in South Australia last January, where I found many deserted and now quite isolated one teacher school sites, still fenced, with plaques giving dates of operation, which in the case of Eyre Peninsula was usually in the early 20th century when the rail and closer settlement opened up much marginal land there. Instead tucked away on a standalone site beyond Poochera there's a large and impressive looking area school, evidence of renewal & resilience.

A more manageable and possibly almost as wellunderstood category is newspaper editor. Once every country town had a newspaper. Some were quite small and parochial. Even so, it is remarkable how much those editors packed into their pages once the telegraphic cable transformed communication with the wider world in the 1870s. Hebblewhite is probably exemplary. He also had a large personal library which he generously made available to aspiring writers, as recently recalled by Canberra writer Mena Calthorpe. More widely influential than Hebblewhite was Christopher Crisp, editor and proprietor of the *Bacchus Marsh Express*. From the 1880s until his death in 1915. The *ADB* entry on Crisp prepared by Jim Rundle—once a student of Don Baker—shows him to have been so insightful and generally respected for his knowledge and his views as to be consulted by important federal politicians.

Then there was Mary Garland, of whom I learned from Patricia Clarke's study of early women journalists and editors in *Pen Portraits*. Mocked by the *Bulletin* as 'Carcoar Mary', she was, like all the early women country newspapers editors of note, a widow. After the death of her first husband Edward Boyle in 1880, she took over the *Carcoar Chronicle* and ran it and the *Mt McDonald Miner* both apparently, until her own death in 1929. A woman of strong principles, 'she could not be turned aside from her convictions'. She sounds just like Miles Franklin's Grandma Lampe, who died in Tumut in 1912.

A particular rigidity of the bush culture and the intellectual life which helped to sustain it into the twentieth century is the comparative absence of women's voices. Ward did touch on this as an aspect of the political economy from which the legend grew. However, there was probably more room for self-expression than we imagine. It's just that in those days of journalistic anonymity, it's hard to trace. Miles Franklin's first identifiable publication was a report on the Thornford School Picnic in the *Goulburn Penny Post* of 26 March 1896 'By a Correspondent', written when she was aged 16, and it seems there may have been even earlier contributions. We only know about her 1896 contribution because she included the information in a letter to Charles Blyth.

A great deal of new information about the lives of influential Australian women has been researched and published in recent volumes of the *ADB* and especially in the 'catch-up' supplement. One stand-out regional life from the period is of librarian Grace Perrier, who was born in Rockhampton in 1875, daughter of a railway porter and his Irish born wife. After a convent education, she joined the Rockhampton School of Arts as a junior library assistant in 1889, rose to head the library when it was taken over by the council in the late 1940s, and after 63 years' service, retired reluctantly in 1952. She was trained on the job by scholar librarian N.M.M. Davidson, and she died in 1975 aged 103, after numerous local honours were bestowed upon her. The *ADB*'s NSW working party is now also on the track of Sybil Kauffman of Canowindra, who is said to have collected thousands of first edition books and stored them at home, and when forced to move to a nursing home, was driven by her niece to tend them. She never married, and died as recently as circa 1988.

In the *Oxford Companion to Australian History*, Graeme Davison has noted the amazing resilience of the Australian Legend. I have been trying to suggest something of the intellectual richness lying behind it, created out of experience of working in the outback and by the effort to live with and understand the land itself. I do this not because the riches of civilisation at first posited by Clark should be set aside. That would be absurd. Nor is it because I want to see the code of the nomad tribe postulated by Russel Ward reinstated. Rather it is because fifty years on it seems clear the old variables of heredity and environment, which underpinned the differing visions of both Clark and Ward, now seem so inadequate. For the pivotal volume 4 of his *History of Australia*, Clark chose the biblical subtitle 'The Earth Abideth Forever'. But what if the civilisations we have enjoyed mean it cannot? It is here that the lives and thoughts of our predecessors have an important bearing. Russel Ward feared the legend would be too rigid. Paradoxically, it has become too flaccid. Likewise, Manning Clark expressed, elliptically it is true, a warning to latter-day deconstructors. Seeking to defeat the black dog of despair and nihilism in 1979, he wrote to the Monaro David Campbell, 'one can live without many things, but not without a love for the people at large'.

There has been a tendency to patronise the bush intellectuals of the early twentieth century. It is in part due to what historian E.P. Thompson famously called the enormous condescension of posterity. It is also due to lack of biographical and other historical knowledge. I trust I have shown that the bush intellectuals stood not for a simplistic notion of mateship, but for a more profound engagement with the realities of this country. Arguably its key features were the egalitarianism of self-expression, the authority of lived experience, and an appreciation of the power to the land, integral to which was a rough-hewn respect for the qualities and knowledge of its original inhabitants. The struggle for the soul of Australia these days is to a large extent a cooked-up affair of publishers and the media, plus the pollsters and the spin doctors, and the Bushwhacker tradition is exploited rather than studied or understood. However, it remains part of our cultural inheritance and at the least, serves to remind us to take care, lest, as in the old adage, we wake up one morning and find ourselves in a valley of dry bones.

1 *Australian Dictionary of Biography*, Volume 9, Melbourne: Melbourne University Press, 1970; Andrew Pike and Ross Cooper, *Australian Film 1910–1977*, Melbourne: Oxford University Press, 1970, pp.666–67

2 Nettie Palmer, 'The Bushwhackers', *The Bulletin*, 16 October 1929, p.5, nla.obj-606262949; Munroe, *Wild Man of Letters*, Queensland: University Press Queensland, 1992, pp.79–81

3 *Bark House Days* was published in Melbourne in 1922.

4 Miles Franklin, 'A Book of Lore', *Australian Mercury*, August 1935, vol. 1, no.2, (review of Gordon Buchanan, *Packhorse and Waterhole: with the first Overlanders to the Kimberleys*, page proof).

5 Stephen Knight, 'Upfield, Arthur William (1890–1964)', Australian Dictionary of Biography, National Centre of Biography, Australian National University, adb.anu.edu.au/biography/upfield-arthur-william-8900/text15635, published first in hardcopy 1990

6 Rex Ingamells, *Conditional Culture*, Adelaide: F.W. Preece, 1938, p.17

7 Peter Kirkpatrick, *The Sea Coast of Bohemia: Literary Life in Sydney's Roaring Twenties*, Queensland: Lucia, 1992; Geoffrey Dutton, *The Innovators: The Sydney Alternatives in the Rise of Modem Art, Literature and Ideas*, Melbourne: Macmillan, 1986; Eileen Channin and Steven Miller, *Degenerates and Perverts: The 1939 Herald Exhibition of French and British Contemporary Art*, Melbourn: Miegunyah Press, 2005, p.45

8 John Maurice Franklin to Stella Miles Franklin, 7 December 1896, Franklin Papers, vol. 48, Mitchell Library, State Library of New South Wales

Biography: The Past Has a Great Future

Richard Holmes
2008

Just before I flew to Australia to deliver this year's Seymour Lecture, I heard an ABC broadcast on the BBC World Service. The Australian commentator was talking about the centenary of the birth of Donald Bradman, the 'great Don' with his famous Test batting average of 99.94 runs. He said that Bradman was a peculiarly Australian role model because he was a *sporting* hero, and because he knocked the hell out of the British bowling. Slightly carried away by the moment, he added: 'We still need those founding fathers—we've had no George Washington, no Abraham Lincoln ... Don Bradman fills a biographical gap.'

I am interested by this idea of filling the biographical gap. I want to address the importance of the great tradition of popular biography, both in Australia and in Britain. It has proved significant in shaping our different national identities, giving us role models, but also questioning the nature of our societies.

To do this, I want to start by paying a personal debt. My first biographical essay, a study of the suicidal Romantic poet Thomas Chatterton, was published nearly 40 years ago, in John Murray's *Cornhill Magazine*. It was printed alongside the first part of Alan Moorehead's stirring autobiography, *A Late Education: Episodes in a Life* (1970). This led to my discovery of one of the greatest Australian popular biographers and historians of the previous generation. Three of Moorehead's short but powerful books from the 1950s and 1960s—*Gallipoli* (1956), *Cooper's Creek: The Real Story of Burke and Wills* (1963) and *The Fatal Impact: An Account of the Invasion of the South Pacific 1767–1840* (1966)—were decisive in changing public attitudes. Although previously considered a war correspondent and popular historian, Moorehead (1910–1983) achieved a significant type of collective biography, and all three books have remained in print for half a century. Warfare and friendship, exploration and personal endurance, colonial exploitation and ethnic responsibility: these have become major Australian themes. Moorehead's works alerted me—and the world—to a different Australian cultural viewpoint and helped to establish a new postwar Australian identity.

I know there is a current reassessment of the significance of Moorehead, with Ann Moyal's fine biographical monograph, published by the National Library of Australia (2005) and drawing on its extensive collection of his papers. Significantly, Moorehead decided against leaving his papers to an American university, despite being offered a considerable amount of money to do so.

The inspiration behind Moyal's work was anticipated in an important introduction by Manning Clark to a new edition of *The Fatal Impact* in 1987:

> Moorehead always had the gift to anticipate the groundswells in public opinion. In *Cooper's Creek* he was out in front in that huge swell of interest starting in the history of Australia ... not as a branch of British colonial history ... but making it Australia-centred .... helping to show it was interesting to explore the minds of the heroes and heroines of Australia.

Seen from the outside, biography will always be a study of national identity, not just because of its choice of subjects but also because of its manner of treatment. It is the *relationship* between the biographer and the subject that creates the distinctive identity.

I have been struck by other notable works by Australian biographers in which there is a clear sense of new identities being forged, of new social questions being raised. Let me mention just three published in the past two decades.

The first is David Marr's fine biography of the novelist *Patrick White* (1991), which examined the old cultural tensions between Australia and England, the question of homosexuality, and the notion of art as revelation or revenge.

Brenda Niall's wonderful multi-biography, *The Boyds: A Family Biography* (2002), crossed five Australian generations, starting with a true but almost folkloric Australian archetype: the former convict's beauteous daughter who marries the handsome son of a High Court judge and founds a dynasty. Niall's biography, ingeniously constructed, moves between the various Boyd houses in a series of subtle, sliding narrative panels. What a significant moment it was for Australian biography when Niall abandoned the idea of writing a biography of Edith Wharton and turned to the Boyds.

Peter Rose's *Rose Boys* (2001) was a new kind of family memoir, transforming what starts as an Australian sporting biography into an extraordinarily acute, intimate and disturbing account of his brother's car accident and subsequent quadriplegia. In its brave emotional risk-taking, *Rose Boys* bears comparison with John Bayley's controversial memoir of Iris Murdoch (1998).

These are major works that are helping to shape a distinctive Australian inheritance—'filling the biographical gap'—and launching what I believe will prove to be a golden age of Australian biography. Australian biography is becoming more and more distinct from the British form, both in style and subject matter. I sense a certain new pride taken in Australian biography. This is rather different from the mildly apologetic attitude affected by many British biographers, including me. Nonetheless, there are still clear parallels, which I would like to explore.

It has always been characteristic of the British tradition to approach the genre of biography with a certain good-humoured scepticism. As long ago as the eighteenth century, Samuel Johnson's learned friend Dr Arbuthnot observed, 'Biography has added a New Terror to death'. One could compile an anthology of such gentle witticisms, which, in the English manner, often disguise serious reflections. 'Every great man has his disciples,' observed Oscar Wilde, 'and it is usually Judas who writes the biography.'

What is certainly true is that in Britain today we are immersed, not to say drowning, in a sea of biography, autobiography and memoir. According to figures recently produced by British Book Watch, no fewer than 4,000 new biographical titles are published per annum. The earnest student of the form would need to read ten biographies a day to keep abreast of developments.

Mind you, this figure includes the personal memoir, which has become immensely fashionable in recent years. Distinguished British authors who have followed this trend, moving significantly from biography to autobiography, include Michael Holroyd (*Basil Street Blues*, 1999); Lorna Sage (*Bad Blood*, 2000); and even my old teacher George Steiner, in *My Unwritten Books* (2008).

Memoirs of the more populist kind lay great emphasis on unhappy or dysfunctional childhood experiences. Some versions have been derided as 'misery memoirs'. In Australia they tend to be called 'triumph over tribulation' tales. Huge sales figures have also been achieved by disguised or ghosted 'misery memoirs'. One example is Andrew Morton's *Diana: Her True Story in Her Own Words*, secretly compiled from taped interviews with the princess and originally published in 1992. Sales of Morton's book now run to more than two million copies.

British television now has a dedicated biography channel. Biographical series such as *Secret Lives*, *Reputations* and *Who Do You Think You Are?* have proven popular here and in Britain. The National Portrait Gallery in London runs frequent exhibitions featuring contemporary celebrities and publishes series of books on biographical subjects.

The British Library recently launched a kit known as *The Family History Box*, which offers biographical entertainment. It is just like the old chemistry sets we used to have as children.

Meanwhile, the internet hosts numerous sites for genealogy, family history, surnames and clans. The internet's famously free, and famously unreliable, Wikipedia is essentially a kind of 'do it yourself' biography. And we all now know what it means to 'google' someone.

Biographical films are all the rage, having cleverly usurped the British love of costume drama, especially when a heroine is at the centre. Recent examples include biopics of Elizabeth I and the current monarch, Beatrix Potter, Jane Austen, and the glamorous eighteenth-century Duchess of Devonshire, based on Amanda Foreman's outstandingly successful life of *Georgiana*, an avatar of Diana, Princess of Wales.

Perhaps the most significant recent biographical development in Britain was the publication of *The New Oxford Dictionary of National Biography* (2004). I realise that this was the subject of the 2006 Seymour Lecture: Lawrence Goldman's 'Virtual Lives: History and Biography in an Electronic Age', but I would like to make a couple of points here.

The new *ODNB* expands the original number of individual lives from 38,000 to 50,000. It is no longer written by a small team of scholars. Rather, it has become a communal project, gathering contributions from no fewer than 12,000 biographers. Although all of the old entries have been retained—if briskly rewritten—*ODNB*'s principles of selection have radically changed. In essence, the notion of 'achievement' has been greatly widened and democratised. There are fewer clergymen, aristocrats and bureaucrats; more women, workmen and rogues. Or as one critic remarked, 'less bishops and more actresses'.

This democratising zeal is not exclusive to Britain. I note that the National Library of Australia is developing its *People Australia* database. Australia's National Portrait Gallery, whose new home by Lake Burley Griffin will be opened in early December 2008, will pioneer new methods of biographical presentation and juxtaposition.

Biography in the University

The movement that has developed most decisively during my lifetime has been the teaching of biography. Tertiary courses now flourish in Britain, Australia and the United States, and to some degree in France and Germany. The study of biography has revived Literature as one of the traditional 'humanities', rescuing it from the deserts of Literary Theory and reviving the ideals of Creative Writing courses.

In Britain, this new pedagogical phenomenon began at the private University of Buckingham in 1998, in a course run by Jane Ridley. It was followed in 2000 by the University of East Anglia (UEA)—already famous for its Creative Writing course—which set up an MA in Life Writing under Lorna Sage, largely inspired by the novelist and critic Malcolm Bradbury. It was a bitter irony that both Sage and Bradbury were dying of chronic illnesses. Neither of them lived to see the MA course properly take root. I recently met Lorna Sage's first and only pupil, a young woman who is now a radio broadcaster. She told me that Lorna never spoke of her own illness but sometimes, during their one-to-one seminars 'wept over the unhappiness of other lives'.

In 2001, UEA appointed its first professor of biography: a working writer, not an academic. This happened to be me. This was my first and only academic post in 40 years as a working biographer. To inaugurate the MA, I gave a lecture to the Oxford Faculty of English entitled 'The Biographer Who Came in from the Cold', named after John le Carré's famous spy novel (1963). I taught at UEA for six years. Now I am 'The Biographer Who Got Out of the Kitchen'.

After some initial doubts, I do not believe that teaching biography will paralyse it with theory. On the contrary, it should develop the creative future of the form and produce new generations of young writers who will 'go forth and multiply', biographically speaking!

My own students had wonderfully varied backgrounds: doctor, barrister, financial journalist, housewife, television researcher, ex-headmistress, social worker, company director, taxi driver, primary school teacher, Pakistani air force pilot, Japanese retail manager, Nigerian poet.

Pleasingly, several poets defected from Creative Writing to Life Writing. Poets make excellent biographers. One of them now runs a new writers' project at the British Library Oral History Department. Five of my students have already published their own books: notably Druin Burch's fine study of the eighteenth-century surgeon Astley Cooper, memorably entitled *Digging Up the Dead* (2007), a reference both to surgical and biographical practices. My Pakistani air force pilot was Mohammed Hanif, whose first novel, *A Case of Exploding Mangoes* (2008), started life as an essay about Plutarch, the dreams and forebodings of tyrants, and General Zia-ul-Haq. It was longlisted for the 2008 Booker Prize.

One of the major lessons we learned was this: no biography, however good, is definitive. It is important to understand how a series of biographies on the same subject shape and change a reputation through time. To learn about biography, you must view it comparatively. For instance, there are at least eight good lives of the eighteenth-century feminist Mary Wollstonecraft, and all repay study, from William Godwin's original memoir of 1798 to Lyndall Gordon's biography of 2005.

Apart from the UEA, other MA courses have sprung up: in Oxford, under Hermione Lee; and at London University, under Andrew Motion and Blake Morrison. Lisa Jardine, the distinguished scholar of seventeenth-century science, has founded the Centre for Editing Life and Letters at Queen Mary, University of London. Last year, the new University of Kingston founded 'The Centre for Life Narratives' and posted an important mission statement on its website.

A Biographers' Club has been founded in London and runs a notable website. Even the Royal Society, austerely dedicated to scientific papers and traditionally opposed to scientific lives, is launching a new series, *Memories in Science*, to mark its 250th anniversary in 2010.

Such developments have not been restricted to Britain. Perhaps the first university course in biography offered anywhere in the world was founded here in Australia, at Griffith University, in the 1970s. The National Library of Australia's oral history project began at the same time. Biography has been taught at Monash University and La Trobe University since 1996. The Biography Institute, in Canberra, was founded in 2005; its conferences and workshops are attended by writers, academics and postgraduate students from around the world.

Because of the good offices of Dr Geoffrey Cains, the National Biography Award was founded in 1996; the National Biography Award Lecture, also administered by the State Library of New South Wales, followed in 2003.

Reflecting on the kind of biographical issues that are being debated in universities and at conferences around the world, I have come up with the following:

- the significance of the cult of celebrity, and the generation of pseudo-biographical forms, notably on the internet (e.g. Facebook)
- the creative impact of biography on other media: film, television, photography, portraiture and even ballet (e.g. the recent 'biographical ballet' about George Gershwin, produced in Paris in 2008)
- the revival of biography within narrative history
- the use of biography as a bridge to fields of specialist knowledge, such as philosophy or the physical sciences
- the development of biographical exhibitions, using physical objects (so-called 'object biography'), photographs, video loops and sound archives
- ethical questions such as the biographer's invasion of privacy
- the big philosophical or epistemological questions about the nature of human understanding, empathy and subjectivity (e.g. how far can we ever know another human being?).

One of the most suggestive indications is the sudden and rapid expansion not merely of biographies but of books *about* biography, studying the genre as a literary form. The Subject Index at the British Library currently lists 363 English language titles under this heading. It is no coincidence that 80 per cent of these titles were published after 1990. Here are just nine of the most influential recent ones: Ian Donaldson, James Walter and Peter Read (eds): *Shaping Lives: Reflections on Biography* (1992); Paula R. Backscheider's *Reflections on Biography* (1999); Michael Shortland and Richard Yeo (eds): *Telling Lives in Science: Essays on Scientific Biography* (1996); Michael Holroyd's *Works on Paper: The Craft of Biography and Autobiography* (2002); Peter France and William St Clair (eds): *Mapping Lives: The Uses of Biography* (2004); Hermione Lee's *Body Parts: Essays on Life-writing* (2005); Thomas Söderqvist (ed.): *The History and Poetics of Scientific Biography (Science, Technology and Culture, 1700–1945* (2007); Brenda Niall's *Life Class: The Education of a Biographer* (2007); and Nigel Hamilton's *How to Do Biography: A Primer* (2008).

In my view, the study of biography at university can become a complete, new humanist discipline. It can also keep an eye—or watching brief—on the new 'para-biographic' forms now multiplying, such as internet blogs (of which there are now more than 110 million); CD sleeves; author statements, profiles and interviews; the self-correcting Wikipedia entries on the Internet; and—if anyone can bear to look at them—celebrity and reality television shows, which continue to burgeon like exotic hot-house jungle plants.

Nonetheless, the primary aim of teaching biography remains the written form: to recover a great tradition, establish the study of comparative biography, and lure students from theory and back to the actual practise of research and writing. It highlights the central importance of the biographer–subject relationship to the study and understanding of biography as a form. Above all, though, it aims to teach the art and craft of biographical narrative—storytelling.

Biography and Storytelling

People often suggest that the future of biography lies in a radical change of form, in the development of fractured or postmodern narrative modes. Brian Matthews's experimental and award-winning biography *Louisa* (1987), a Po-Mo biography of Henry Lawson's heroic mother, is one example. It used multiple biographic voices and dramatised self-questionings. It will be fascinating to see what Matthews does in his biography of Manning Clark. Peter Ackroyd's *Dickens* (1990), with its flamboyant insertions of fictional interludes, is another example of this technique. Julian Barnes's *Flaubert's Parrot* (1984) used a fictional biographer—Geoffrey Braithwaite—to explore factual, or counter-factual, questions about Flaubert (e.g. what colour were Emma Bovary's eyes?).

My own book *Footsteps: Adventures of a Romantic Biographer* (1985), in which the biographer continually steps in and out of four different Romantic 'frame' narratives (the lives of Stevenson, Wollstonecraft, Shelley and Nerval), might claim to be a fourth. It is interesting that all these experimental works appeared in the mid-1980s, a period when we all wanted to 'shake the cage' of conventional biographical form and see what happened.

The traditional art of storytelling will always be central to biography and its power. What we may need more is a change of subjects or a development in our ideas of the kind of material that biography can deal with. It is new biographical subjects which will redefine the narrative form, not vice versa.

Even if it is not presented chronologically, biography always takes the form of a human story, a narrative action, an *agon*. This has been so since the earliest *Parallel Lives* of Plutarch (c.120 CE). Plutarch launched the great narrative melodramas of biography: Alexander's self-destruction, Julius Caesar's assassination, Antony and Cleopatra's love affair. In his prologue to his *Life of Alexander*, Plutarch summarised his approach: he would tell 'not history, but lives'. He would look for the inside story, the intimate gesture, 'an expression or a jest', that revealed true character. He would narrate 'the souls of men'. (As his Elizabethan translator Sir Thomas North wryly observed, Plutarch was interested 'not only in how many battles Alexander won, but how often he was drunk'.)

When I suggest that biography is non-fiction storytelling, I mean the following. It has a protagonist, a time sequence, a plot, and a dramatic pattern of human cause and effect. Its essential discipline is secular; it resists supernatural explanations. Even Plutarch is sceptical about the gods, though he is fascinated by dreams. The rhythm of biographical narrative is that of suspense/mystery followed by resolution/explanation. The basic unit is the anecdote, strung along the narrative like beads on a string.

But there are numerous epistemological problems in storytelling. How reliable or selective are our sources? What are the vagaries of human memory? In what sense can one write he or she 'thought' or 'felt' something? How far can we 'know the other', philosophically speaking?

There is a powerful school of French sceptics—Sartre, Barthes, Derrida—that questions the fundamental authenticity of the narrative form. But there is also a counter Anglo-Saxon body of informal theory which explores the idea of 'identity as narrative', expressed in the philosophy of Alasdair MacIntyre (*After Virtue*, 1981), the histories of Simon Schama and the shrewd critical accounts by the American critic Paul John Eakin (*How Our Lives Become Stories: Making Selves*, 1999).

These were addressed at a theoretical level by Professor Ian Donaldson in his brilliant 2006 *ABR*/La Trobe University Annual Lecture 'Matters of Life and Death: The Return of Biography', which responded to a number of anti-biographers, notably the British Marxist critic Terry Eagleton, who accused it of 'bourgeois linearity'; Roland Barthes, who announced the death of the author; and Stefan Collini who argued that it was sociologically unrepresentative.

On a more practical, writerly level, I would suggest that nearly all biographical problems can be answered by finding appropriate forms of narrative. A good example of this is one of the earliest breakthroughs in popular biography, Daniel Defoe's *Life of Jack Sheppard* (1724). Here, a master storyteller brought traditional forms of narrative to bear on a new and subversive subject, and, in the process, completely transformed the genre. Defoe's treatment of Jack Sheppard (1702–1724) was revolutionary. In an age accustomed to biographical eulogies of the good and great, how could Defoe create a significant biography of a petty thief?

Defoe was writing in an early and much neglected biographical tradition, known to scholars as the Newgate Calendar or Prison Confessions. From the period 1720–1760, 1,200 male and 58 female 'confessions' have survived. These were usually brief, homiletic biographies written by the Newgate Ordinary (the prison chaplain) and sold as cheap pamphlets. Mostly, they were lives of the failed, the lost, the forgotten, the condemned.

With brilliant originality, Defoe—himself a former inmate at Newgate—stood the genre on its head. He reversed the reader's expectation. Before his execution, Jack Sheppard had escaped not once but three times from his death cell. Defoe presented Sheppard not as a miserable petty thief but as a heroic and resourceful escape artist. Defoe set out to show his pluck, his humour, his incorrigible determination—and his terrible cockney jokes. He has Sheppard remarking of the visiting clergymen, 'In Newgate, a File is a more valued gift than a Bible'. After his penultimate escape, Sheppard proclaimed with cheerful blasphemy: 'Yes, Sir, I am the *Shepherd*, and all the Jailers in the Town are my *Flock*; and I cannot stir into the Country but they are all at my Heels *baaaa-ing* after me'.

Defoe's publisher, Applebee, inserted a single engraving of Jack's third escape route, showing the amazingly ingenious and resourceful way he evaded the locks and chains of the notorious 'Castle' death-cell. The engraving was like a strip-cartoon in nine panels, a visual narrative, which closely followed Defoe's breathless account from room to room in the prison. Using Jack's own words, Defoe described how Jack unpicked his shackles, climbed up a disused chimney, broke through six locked doors in the dark, crept through the prison chapel, clambered over the spiked roof and lay there listening to St Sepulchre's church chime the midnight hour. Faced with a final 20-foot drop onto a flat roof, Jack had the self-command to return to his cell and fetch a blanket to use as a rope. Finally, exhausted, he slept for two hours before descending into the street. Defoe makes this escape saga both a gripping piece of storytelling and a vivid demonstration of Jack's indomitable character. Indeed, it is a kind of *Pilgrim's Progress*:

> Being got to the Chapel, I climbed over the iron Spikes, and with ease broke one of them off for my further [lock-picking], and opened the Door on the inside … Here I came to another massive Door, which being fastened by a very strong lock, my spirits began to fail me … But cheering up, I wrought with great diligence, and in less than half an hour, with the help of the Nail from the Red Room and the Spike from the Chapel, wrenched the Box off—and so made the Door my Humble Servant!

While still at liberty, Sheppard began to hear stories and ballads about himself. This quickened his own sense of identity: 'That night I came to a cellar at Charing Cross, and refreshed myself very comfortably with Roast Veal etc, and heard about a dozen people all discoursing about Sheppard, and nothing else was talked about while I stayed amongst them'.

After Jack's last escape, he stole a set of gentleman's clothes, rings, and sword, picked up two pretty girls, and had the audacity to hire a coach and ride back under the very gateway of the Newgate Prison arch. This, as told by Defoe, was a stroke of theatrical genius and a brilliant assertion of a transformed self, a new and glorious identity:

> I now made an extraordinary Appearance, and from a Carpenter and a Butcher was now transformed into a Perfect Gentleman; and in company with my Sweetheart aforesaid, and another young Woman her acquaintance, went into the City, and were very merry together in a Public House not far from the Prison … and drank three quarters of a Pint of best Brandy …

Defoe's short biography ran to eight editions in six weeks. In a touching gesture, he handed a copy to Sheppard on the gallows. In death, Jack had been given another life. It turned him into a legend, and one could see how easily his story could transfer into other media. It did so: John Gay's hugely popular eighteenth-century *Beggar's Opera* (1728), numerous Victorian music halls, a thriller by William Harrison Ainsworth (1839), Bertolt Brecht's *The Threepenny Opera* (1928), a Hollywood film and, most recently, a television dramatisation.

It also reaffirmed the value of the Lost Life—and launched a tradition which can be traced back to Samuel Johnson's *Life of Mr Richard Savage* (1744), and which includes Alexander Masters's highly original *Stuart: A Life Backwards* (2005) and Ben Macintyre's comic-thriller biography, *Agent Zigzag: A True Story of Nazi Espionage, Love and Betrayal* (2007).

Biography and the Future

Finally, let me turn to the broadest panorama: the future of biography; or rather, its *futures*, for biography has always been destined to have separate roles in different cultures. The tasks to be carried out look subtly different between a post-imperial England and, if I may say, a pre-republican Australia. They are certainly very different in France and the United States.

As far as Britain is concerned, many biographers now sense what Jonathan Bate—a leading Shakespeare scholar who has now turned Romantic biographer of 'John Clare'—has recently called 'the approach of a paradigm shift'.

It is true that the traditional form of major Life and Times biographies, often in two volumes, are still being written, often magnificently: Claire Tomalin on Samuel Pepys (2002); Hilary Spurling on Henri Matisse (1998, 2005); Hermione Lee on *Edith Wharton* (2007); and, most recently, Michael Holroyd returning to mighty form with his massive study: *A Strange Eventful History: The Dramatic Lives of Ellen Terry, Henry Irving and Their Remarkable Families* (2008).

Yet, clearly, something is happening at the cutting edge. There is a widespread questioning of the traditional forms and chronology, and a fascination with briefer and more experimental work. There is renewed interest in marginal and subversive subject matter. The monolithic single Life is giving way to biographies of groups, of friendships, of love affairs, of 'spots of time' (microbiographies), or of collective movements in art, literature or science.

Many concern what Virginia Woolf called 'neglected lives', or collective lives, those held together for an historic moment by a common endeavour, place or ideal, and therefore not dependent on the 'single life' or traditional womb-to-tomb story. In consequence, because of the unusual nature of their subjects, they tend to develop unusual narrative forms.

Let me suggest nine popular and highly influential biographies that indicate this new pattern. Some of these titles are frequently proposed as harbingers of a 'paradigm' change in biographical forms, but they really mark a rediscovery of different kinds of subject matter. They are Holroyd's *Basil Street Blues*; Bella Bathurst's *The Lighthouse Stevensons* (1999); Lucasta Miller's *The Brontë Myth* (2001); Jenny Uglow's *The Lunar Men: The Friends Who Made the Future, 1730–1810* (2002); Masters's *Stuart: A Life Backwards*; William St Clair's *The Grand Slave Emporium: Cape Coast Castle and the British Slave Trade* (2006); Anne Wroe's *Being Shelley: The Poet's Search for Himself* (2007); Linda Colley's *The Ordeal of Elizabeth Marsh: A Woman in World History* (2007); and Frances Wilson's *The Ballad of Dorothy Wordsworth* (2008).

The narrative form of each of these books is highly unusual: for instance, the meta-biographical layerings of Miller's Brontë book exploring the phenomenon of the 'Brontë industry', and the tragic, reversed chronology of Masters's life of his down-and-out subject.

But lives may be 'experimental' in a different sense: not because they concern obscure or marginal or ethnically undervalued subjects, but simply because they appear difficult, specialised or remote from common concerns or culture. Johnson is famously reported by Boswell as saying that 'he could write the Life of Broomstick'. But could he write the life of a particle physicist or a pure mathematician or indeed a Newton?

The writing of scientific lives represents perhaps the most significant new field in British biography, and it has already challenged many assumptions. For years, biographies of individual scientists have been traditionally regarded as a form of children's literature. Their narratives have taken the form of simplified 'eureka stories': Isaac Newton and the fall of the apple and the instant discovery of universal gravity.

It has also been the convention of science biography to ignore or at least be nervous of the mistakes and dead ends of scientific research. The messy process of actual research and experiment is ironed out as the Whig history of endless progress. Men and women of science are assumed not to have inner or emotional lives at all, but to be icy blocks of cheery rationalism, 'men in white coats'. For nearly the whole of the twentieth century, it was assumed there were Two Cultures, and that arts-educated people could never speak to, let alone understand, the scientist, and vice versa.

The intensity of our concern about the planet, about global and environmental issues, has put the biographical element back into science with a vengeance. We realise that science does not—cannot—exist in a human vacuum. We want to know what drives individual scientists to make their discoveries, and especially their mistakes; and how they feel about non-scientific things—love, religion and politics, for example. Renewed interest in the ethical dilemmas posed by scientific discovery requires a humanist response which the enquiring spirit of biography is ideally placed to provide. All this has led to an explosion of biographical interest in the creativity of scientists, and the historic context of their work. Here are some of the striking new works this has produced: Dava Sobel's *Longitude* (1996); Michael Shortland and Richard Yeo's *Telling Lives in Science: Essays on Scientific Biography*; Lisa Jardine's *Ingenious Pursuits: Building the 17th Century Scientific Revolution* (1999); Janet Browne's *Charles Darwin: Voyaging* (1995) and *The Power of Place* (2002); Patricia Fara's *Newton: The Making of Genius* (2002); Anne Thwaite's *Glimpses of the Wonderful: The Life of Philip Henry Gosse, 1810–1888*

(2002); Jenny Uglow's *The Lunar Men*; and Walter Isaacson's *Einstein: His Life and Universe* (2007).

Science biography confronts a central question of our age: how far can we *trust* scientists as guides to survival on our planet; whether science is a source of hope or dread.

My new book, *The Age of Wonder*, is an attempt to grapple with these challenges in the form of a collective biography, or what I have called, rather sportingly, 'a relay race of scientific stories'. The book covers the fields of astronomy, chemistry, geographical exploration, ballooning and experimental surgery at the turn of the nineteenth century. It re-examines such classic scientific tales as how Davy invented the Miner's Lamp, how William Herschel discovered the new planet Uranus, how Joseph Banks went in search of Paradise in Tahiti, and how Mary Shelley invented the most famous scientist of all time—Dr Frankenstein.

The Age of Wonder is set at exactly the time when the great Romantic writers and poets were championing emotion and subjectivity, and supposedly turning against rationalism, objectivity and science. Yet writers such as Coleridge, Keats, Shelley, Byron, Goethe and Mary Shelley were absolutely fascinated by science. The real subject is what I have called 'scientific passion': the inner lives and drives of scientists, and their impact on writers and the way we all imagine the world around us.

My book is subtitled 'How the Romantic Generation Discovered the Beauty and Terror of Science' because, right from the beginning, science has held out both promise and menace, both progress and destruction, precisely the dilemmas we face right now. I argue that it was the Romantics who first faced them two centuries ago, and that biography is the way of finding how we got here. The past has a great future, indeed.

Finally, and even more broadly, one may wonder what might be the future task of biography in emerging countries such as China, India, Russia, Iran and South America? It should not be forgotten that each of these has a fabulously rich tradition in fiction and poetry, and even film: yet biographically they are largely an unknown quantity, except for ideologically motivated Lives of the Great Leaders: Mao, Stalin, Ghandi, Genghis Khan, the Moguls—many in fact written by western biographers.

Here again we can see the old historic tension emerging between the traditional 'Great Men' school of biography, and the modern impulse to recover 'Neglected Lives'. From that point of view, one might say that the finest Russian biography of recent years, though cast as a fiction, has been Alexander Solzhenitsyn's *One Day in the Life of Ivan Denisovich* (1962).

In these countries, notions of not only human rights but of genealogy, privacy and individual identity itself may still be radically different from ours.

It is a fascinating question how far biography as a form may in fact depend on the existence of liberal democratic institutions and the freedoms that go with them: relative freedom of expression, largely uncensored publishing, generally unrestricted libraries and open archives, and a secular culture of self-expression and self-development.

Can biography flourish in radical Muslim states? Can true biography flourish in any kind of one-party, authoritarian state? The answers are not simple: after all, it could flourish under the Roman emperors and the enlightened despots of eighteenth-century Europe.

One might hazard the guess that biography will do better in modern India than in China because of the prosperous professional and middle classes in India, its multicultural diversity and its strong popular grassroots tradition of folksong, stories, poetry and now film. It is true that oral history has growing significance for China, exemplified by Xinran Xue's *China Witness: Voices from a Silent Generation* (2008), an attempt to tell the true story of Mao's Cultural Revolution through scores of personal interviews. Yet even this book was written in London, and is not being published in Beijing.

These are large questions, and they will reverberate in coming years. But as one who has believed passionately in the wonderful form of biography, its unique combination of the critical and imaginative spirit, and who continues to struggle with it after nearly 40 years in the field, I offer them to you here in Australia and leave them confidently in your keeping.

And on that suitably apocalyptic note, I shall bid farewell with my 'Ten Commandments for Biographers':

1. Thou shalt honour Biography in all its Living forms and Experiments.
2. Thou shalt not covet thy neighbour's Novel.
3. Thou shalt recognise that Biography is a celebration of Human nature in all its glorious Contradictions.
4. Thou shalt demand that it be greater than Gossip, because it is concerned with Justice.
5. Thou shalt require that though it chronicles an outward career (the Facts) it reveals an inward life (a Comprehensive Truth).
6. Thou shalt see that this Truth can be told again and again, unto each generation.
7. Thou shalt greet it as a Life-giving form, as it is concerned with Human struggle and the Creative spirit, which we all share.
8. Thou shalt relish it as a Holiday for the human Imagination—for it takes us away to another Place, another Time, and another Identity—from which we can come back refreshed.

9. Thou shalt be immodestly Proud of it, as it is something that the English have given to the world, like cricket, and parliament, and the Full Cooked Breakfast … and the Australians have re-invented like the Sydney Opera House and the open-air Barbecue.
10. And lastly, thou shalt be Humble about it, for it demonstrates that none of us can ever know, or write, the last Word about the human Heart.

Writing Political Lives

Dr David Day
2009

Biographies are all the go. When I recently presented a publisher with a proposal for a history of Antarctica, she suggested instead that it be titled, *Antarctica: A Biography*. And why not? As she pointed out, Peter Ackroyd's *London: The Biography* had been a popular and critical success in a way that *London: The History* may not have been.

As the renowned biographer of Dickens and others, Ackroyd made some attempt to justify calling his history of London a biography, pointing to historic allusions to London as a human body. 'We must regard it as a human shape with its own laws of life and growth', argued Ackroyd. And thus able to have a biography. It seemed a new idea at the time, and the book had a big impact.

In fact, it wasn't as novel as it seemed. Ackroyd was following in the footsteps of Christopher Hibbert who, 31 years previously, had written *London: The Biography of a City*. Hibbert had also written 'biographies' of Rome, Florence and Venice. There have been similarly titled books on Berlin and Paris. More recently, we have had Michael Pye's *Maximum City: The Biography of New York* and John Birmingham's history of Sydney, which he rather cannily called an 'unauthorised biography'.

Even countries have had biographies. In 2000, Philip Knightley published *Australia: A Biography of a Nation*, while last year Nigel Watt published *Burundi: The Biography of a Small African Country.* On a larger scale, there has been a biography of the earth and even a biography of the universe, written by a self-styled spiritualist.

Mark Kurtansky went in a different direction with his sensitive portrayal of a fish, called *Cod: A Biography of the Fish That Changed the World*. If the humble cod has a biography, it is not surprising that so too has God. There have also been so-called 'biographies' of the American dollar and of the English language.

Has this attempt by marketers to force such disparate books within the genre of biography leached all meaning from the term? Or has it simply broadened the definition and enriched the genre? Certainly, the *Oxford Dictionary*'s definition of biography as being 'the history of the lives of individual men' has long been redundant. Yet there is still considerable scope for biographies as they were originally understood, which is to chart the course of a life and set it within a wider context.

It seems to be traditional for historians who do biographies to begin lectures of this kind by implicitly apologising for their work or launching into long justifications, as if the writing of biographies somehow lacked intellectual credibility. Forgive me if I don't do this. Rather I want to take its credibility as given and reflect instead on the challenges and possibilities of writing political biographies, and specifically my experiences in writing biographies of three Australian prime ministers.

I began my academic life more than 20 years ago with a book on the wartime conflict between Robert Menzies and Winston Churchill, which was something of a biographical snapshot of those two men. As I argued in the book, it was a time when Menzies believed that his political days in Australia were numbered and he glimpsed the chance of a political career in London, even to the extent of him being the person to replace Churchill as (Britain's) prime minister.

It was a political long shot by a politician who was fast running out of options in Australia. But it was not a total fantasy at a time when Australians regarded themselves as British and when it was not uncommon for Australian politicians to have a second political life in Westminster. Former Australian prime minister George Reid did it, Billy Hughes was urged to do it, Andrew Fisher tried to do it and Stanley Melbourne Bruce was soon to do it.

Menzies was encouraged in his ambitions by leading political and military figures in Britain, who were concerned by a string of military defeats and by Churchill's almost dictatorial direction of the war. Menzies also had support from some leading newspapers in Britain and the United States, some of which rated Menzies as the person most likely to succeed Churchill. Although we now see the elderly Churchill as a great monolith casting his shadow over the entire Second World War, that was not the case in mid-1941, when his hold on power was relatively tenuous. But it was still sufficient for Churchill, once he was made aware of Menzies's ambition, to do what was necessary to thwart it, by simply preventing Menzies from returning to London.

Amidst the great crash and din of armies battling around the Mediterranean in 1941, and with the war in the balance, the political struggle in London was little more than shadow boxing. It never came to a definitive climax, although it did lead to Menzies's resignation, forced upon him by colleagues who thought that the first duty of an Australian prime minister should be to Australia.

Had Menzies been successful in transferring his talents to Westminster, and then toppling Churchill or even just curbing his power, the direction of the war and the history of the world would have been changed.

While my book certainly did not attempt to offer a complete portrait, the story of their lives during those dramatic days in 1941 provided insights into their lives and careers as a whole. It revealed both the political desperation and astuteness of Churchill in mid-1941, and showed the divided loyalty of Menzies, who tried to establish a political career in London and was forced by his failure to carve out instead a political future in Australia.

After that brief foray into biographical writing, I shied away from it for the next ten years or so, perhaps picking up on a feeling among colleagues that it was not what serious historians did. It was too nineteenth century, too much of the 'great man' at a time when historians were focusing on 'everyman' and 'everywoman'. Indeed, there was a dearth of Australian political biographies in the 1980s.

It was not until the late 1990s that I decided again to focus on an individual life. A biography of John Curtin was an obvious book to do. My work on the Second World War gave me a good grasp of his time as an inspirational war leader, while earlier work that I had done on the labour movement during the First World War had shown Curtin in a radically different light, as an anti-war activist and international socialist. Here was an interesting contradiction at the centre of a life that was lived to the full and set against the backdrop of the twentieth century's most dramatic events.

That was the public side of Curtin's life. But the private side was just as intriguing, and became even more so the more I delved into it. Not only was he troubled throughout his life by alcoholism and a chronic skin complaint, but he was laid low several times by the effects of bipolar disorder, or, as it used to be called, manic depression. In these two things, Curtin and Churchill had something in common. For both, the alcohol was a way of keeping their feelings of despair at bay.

From the beginning, I wanted to deal seriously with Curtin's whole life, rather than write a political biography that treated everything prior to him becoming prime minister as a prelude to those final four years of his life. I wanted to blend the personal and the political and compose, in so far as it is possible to do so, a portrait of the whole man. So the book was titled *John Curtin: A Life*.

I particularly wanted to treat his childhood seriously, believing that it would enrich the understanding of his later life. Moreover, childhood is interesting for its own sake. It has always puzzled me how biographers can sometimes rush through the early years of their subjects, as if there was little to be discovered there. Yet we are all shaped by our childhood experiences and take the memories and formative effects of those years into our adult lives.

Politicians perhaps even more so. For they are not only driven to exercise power and achieve political ends, but also driven to live out their lives in the public gaze and crave public approval, knowing all the time that it must ultimately end in the ashes of rejection and defeat for most of them. Certainly, political leaders freely acknowledge the role of their early years and of families in shaping their public lives.

The late US Senator, Ted Kennedy, the youngest of four boys, recalled just prior to his death how his father encouraged the brothers to compete against each other, causing him to feel inadequate compared with his older, high-achieving siblings. 'As I think back to my three brothers', mused Kennedy, 'it sometimes has occurred to me that my entire life has been a constant state of catching up'.[1]

Yet sibling relationships are often neglected by biographers. Despite the many biographies written about Churchill, most readers would think he was an only child. John Charmley's book on Churchill makes just one glancing reference to his brother, Jack. Others omit him altogether. Churchill himself made only four slight references to Jack in his own memoir, *My Early Life*. It was not until 2007 that Celia and John Lee's book, *Winston and Jack*, went some way to redressing the neglect of the brother who played an important role throughout Churchill's life as rival for his parents' approval and affection and later as financial adviser and sometime political sounding board.

It is unlikely that Ben Chifley's two brothers left him with feelings of inadequacy. But he did have the pain and trauma of being separated from his parents and two siblings at the age of five, when he was sent from Bathurst to live with his widowed grandfather and his aunt on a small farm outside of Bathurst. He would have been there into his adulthood, had his grandfather not died when Chifley was 14. The farm was set just too far away for Chifley to have frequent contact with his immediate family, although Chifley's blacksmith father would occasionally ride out on horseback to visit his son and father.

It would be unusual if this did not leave Chifley with feelings of rejection and a heightened need for affection, which he got partly through his political life. The experience also helped to shape his political style. After being sent from Bathurst by his parents, he spent his adult life striving to intimately involve himself with the life of the town and many of its public institutions. He never tired of telling his colleagues to stay in close touch with their electorates. For Chifley, it would have answered a political and psychological need. He was never so happy, he said, as when driving down the hill towards the lights of Bathurst. It may also have been a factor in him deciding to emulate Curtin and not live in isolation in The Lodge, but continue, as prime minister to stay with other Labor MPs at the Kurrajong Hotel.

The effect of siblings does not end with childhood. The long illness and eventual death of Chifley's younger brother from a heart attack in May 1948 would have reminded Chifley of his own mortality. It would have been a factor in pushing him harder in the late 1940s to implement Labor policies, such as bank nationalisation, regardless of the public reaction. Likewise, three of Andrew Fisher's brothers predeceased him by decades, two from accidents and one from illness. Along with Fisher's time working down the mines, and the slow death from black lung of his miner-father, it would have impressed upon him the fickleness of life and made him perhaps overly protective of his own health.

It could explain why Fisher grasped at opportunities to take long breaks from the burdens of office, whether it was during prolonged visits to Britain, an extended visit to South Africa or several weeks spent travelling in New Zealand over Christmas 1914, as Australian troops prepared to leave for the war. They were curious diversions at a time when Labor had been handed power in both houses of parliament and had an opportunity to implement its program. And the concern about his health played a role in Fisher's unfortunate decision to resign and hand office to Billy Hughes, who would go on to tear the nation apart.

It is not easy to reconstruct childhoods when the subjects themselves have not left any illuminating memoir of their early years. That was certainly true of Fisher, Curtin and Chifley, who only made occasional references to their childhoods. Moreover, some of these references were contradictory or misleading, or were silent on important episodes in their life.

There are several references over the years by Fisher as to when he first went to work as a child in the coal mines, each time giving different ages, ranging from nine to 13. The latter age was the most likely, as it was illegal for a child under 12 to work in the mines. Yet Fisher may have been content for the younger age to be part of his political narrative. Similarly, Curtin claimed that his father had been a police sergeant, when the official record shows that he had never been more than a constable. And Chifley offered no explanation as to why he had been sent by his parents to live with his grandfather for nine years.

Despite the difficulty of knowing that some questions will never have definitive answers, biographers should not be deterred. Looking further afield can sometimes produce surprising results. The official correspondence by inspectors visiting Chifley's primary school provided insights into his education at the hands of an alcoholic, part-time teacher. It also included a revealing letter from his grandfather.

In the case of John Curtin, a reading of the police file of his father's service revealed a shameful incident in Port Melbourne, when his father got into trouble after fondling a shop assistant while doing his nightly rounds. Curtin avoided being sacked but was transferred to Creswick. It showed there was a shadow over what had been depicted as an idyllic country childhood. And there was more. Those same files also detailed his father's later retirement from the force due to ill-health, supposedly brought on by rheumatic arthritis, although his death certificate would show that he had died from syphilis. Again, it was something that John Curtin probably had in common with Churchill.

Aside from the official files, there were newspaper accounts of Constable Curtin's rough treatment of skylarking children who made fun of his physical infirmity, and there were scattered references to his later life as a struggling publican. There were also newspaper reports suggesting that Curtin's parents had, at different times, employed two Creswick women as carers for their son. It is not clear why this would have been necessary.

Further glimpses into the early lives of these political leaders came from walking the ground and getting a feel for the lives they lived, whether it was by fossicking for relics in the remains of the earthen-floored farmhouse that had been Chifley's childhood home, or walking the narrow streets of inner-suburban Brunswick to discover the several humble houses that Curtin's impoverished parents had rented and to imagine the life they must have led. They always stayed within the tight confines of Brunswick's so-called 'Irishtown' and within easy furniture-carrying distance of their previous abode.

Glimpses into Fisher's childhood could also be gained from walking the village streets of Crosshouse, or the neighbouring Ayrshire market town of Kilmarnock, where he would spend evenings in the reading room of the Cooperative Library, intent on self-improvement. Or it might come from standing, as Fisher later did with his son, before the imposing statue of the Scottish rebel William Wallace outside the Royal Theatre in Aberdeen. Fisher would have told his son of Wallace's exploits, just as his own father had told him tales of Wallace as they rambled across the undulating countryside around Crosshouse, where Wallace was reputed to have fought some of his fights against the English occupiers.

Wallace wasn't just an Ayrshire hero. The family tradition of the Fishers maintained that Wallace was their ancestor. Whether true or not, Fisher believed it and used a small notebook to transcribe the inscription at the base of Wallace's Aberdeen statue about refusing to live 'under any slavish bonds'. Wallace's example became part of Fisher's childhood sense of self. It was something powerful he could draw upon in later life, whether it was fighting against unfair conditions in the workplace or supporting the Allied cause against Germany.

Without this association with Wallace, Fisher's election commitment in 1914 to support Britain to 'our last man and our last shilling' seems a curious declaration by a Labor leader who had opposed the Boer War and spent his political life trying to engender a national spirit among Australians. Of course, the commitment was an attempt to ensure his election victory after Fisher had been denied his expected re-election the year before. But it was more than that.

The statement was also an echo of Wallace's defiance of the English, with the language and the sentiments harking back to Fisher's childhood in Ayrshire. As Fisher would later tell an audience in London, it was 'far better our sons should die honourably fighting than live to become enslaved'. And at least some young Australians went off to war and died as a result of Fisher's unqualified commitment to Britain. He had made their enlistment a matter of honour. Fisher may have moderated his language somewhat if he had known that 60,000 young Australians would die in the battles to come.

While Fisher led Australia into the war, young John Curtin was among a minority of Labor Party members who opposed it from the beginning and was jailed when he later opposed the attempts by Billy Hughes to introduce conscription. Yet Curtin would go on to be hailed as a war leader himself and to introduce conscription in 1943, albeit just for the Australian region.

Perhaps the most memorable image of Curtin is of him pacing late at night in the garden of The Lodge, unable to sleep while a convoy of Australian troops was returning, on his instructions, to defend Australia. His historic decision had been taken in defiance of appeals and threats from Churchill and Roosevelt. Not only was he defying two world leaders whose support was essential for Australia's defence, Curtin feared that the troops might come to grief crossing the Japanese-controlled waters of the north-eastern Indian Ocean. Hence his late night pacing in the garden.

As Curtin privately confessed to a close friend, he was not made to be a war leader. Amidst all the worries of the war, he was concerned that his longtime friends from his days of opposition during the last war would be critical of the decisions he was being forced to make during this war. That was not his only concern.

Curtin had long wrestled with personal demons and sought to keep them at bay with alcohol. Exploring these questions has been difficult for biographers. Lloyd Ross was prevented by Curtin's widow from publishing his biography in the 1950s, with its mention of Curtin's alcoholism, until after she had died. Even then, Ross left out evidence that Curtin had continued to drink after becoming Labor leader in 1935, when he had promised his colleagues he would stop. The drinking was both a disease and a symptom of a deeper angst.

Although some still argue that a politician's private life should be shielded from the scrutiny of biographers, it is difficult to write a meaningful biography if significant parts of the life are kept off limits, as Curtin's widow tried to do. Elsie Curtin would have been sensitive about more than just the alcoholism. There were also Curtin's bouts of depression, which affected him so badly in January 1942, as the Japanese fleet steamed towards Darwin, that he was unable to cope and was forced by his colleagues to recuperate for two weeks in Perth. Other times during the war, he locked himself away for days at a time in his office.

Some parts of a person's life are kept so private that they can not be detailed with certainty. When Curtin's Presbyterian wife refused to admit a Catholic priest to The Lodge in July 1945, as Curtin lay dying upstairs, it is likely that Elsie was doing more than respecting his attitude to religion or preventing his deathbed return to the church of his birth. Curtin's visceral response to the Catholic church went much deeper than a philosophical rejection of its teachings.

Indeed, Curtin became disillusioned with the Catholic church at an early age. Although we may never know for sure, it was perhaps prompted by a traumatic experience as an altar boy in a Catholic church in Charlton in country Victoria. Whatever the cause, he sought his salvation elsewhere, turning briefly to the Salvation Army in his teenage years and then to the Sunday evangelism of the Victorian Socialist Party. He steadfastly refused throughout his adult life to step inside a Catholic church, not even for the weddings of close friends.

When Curtin was prevailed upon as prime minister to attend the rededication of a Presbyterian church in Canberra, the minister called on him to speak to the congregation and was disconcerted to see Curtin 'shivering in the presence of church people'. Curtin said it was 'the hardest speech he ever had to make in his life'. Although biographers and their readers might want certainty, we can only wonder what lay behind those words. Was carving his name in the timber of the Charlton church a way of retaliating against the forceful priest with a commanding presence, who had once threatened to take a horse whip to a newspaper editor?

With perhaps a priest and his father—who was known around Brunswick as 'Bumble'—having let him down, Curtin turned to other male authority figures. Tom Mann of the Socialist Party, described by Curtin as the 'man of men' who had 'made their socialist faith possible'; Frank Anstey of the Labor Party, who had told Curtin that his socialist faith could move mountains; and General Douglas MacArthur of the American army, who relieved Curtin of some of the onerous decisions he might otherwise have had to make.

Curtin had described Mann and Anstey as the 'white lights' that had safeguarded him from the 'rocks of dismay'. Each of these figures would disappoint Curtin in their turn, Mann by leaving Melbourne in 1909 and returning to Britain, Anstey by retiring from parliament in 1934 and extinguishing his socialist flame, and MacArthur by pushing on to the Philippines and leaving Australian forces behind.

Ben Chifley too had a troubled relationship with the Catholic Church, which could not countenance his marriage to a Presbyterian and refused him the sacraments thereafter. Although some have denied it, as if it somehow diminishes Chifley, he seems to have fallen out of love with his wife Elizabeth soon after and found love elsewhere. But the couple continued to keep up appearances, and their former house in Bathurst continues to do so, with its double bed in the front bedroom and no sign of the curtained-off alcove in the adjoining study in which Chifley slept when he was at home.

Although some of Chifley's extended family have attempted to wall off parts of his life from view, and have denied that there was anything amiss in the marriage, sufficient evidence remains to suggest otherwise. The most obvious evidence was Chifley dying from a heart attack in his Kurrajong Hotel room in the company of his long-time secretary Phyllis Donnelly. Refusing to call a doctor, he was eventually rushed to hospital where a priest deemed he had been alive long enough to have the last rites and so warrant a Catholic burial.

The manner of Chifley's death inevitably gave rise to rumours about his relationship with Donnelly, although the focus of Chifley's affections seems to have been elsewhere. According to his one-time campaign director, it was Phyllis's sister, Nell, with whom he had bought a house, who was the real love of Chifley's life.

As Chifley's death showed, not even political leaders can avoid the fact that every life has a conclusion. And it may not end as they might like. But the place and manner of a political leader's demise can be illuminating for a biographer. It's not just the medical facts that can be gleaned from a death certificate, or the financial facts, and sometimes feelings, which can be discovered in a will.

Chifley's death offered insights into the man. As other politicians enjoyed a ball in nearby Parliament House to celebrate the jubilee of the Parliament, the 'man of the people' spurned the high-faluting festivities for an evening apparently listening to the wireless in the company of Donnelly. Yet even this image was somewhat misleading, for Chifley was also fond of powerful American cars and had his shirts specially made in Melbourne.

After his death, Elizabeth Chifley declined the opportunity to go to Canberra and waited in Bathurst for the funeral. While Prime Minister Menzies and the rest of the mourners continued to the graveside in the Catholic section of the cemetery, where Menzies wept openly, the car carrying Elizabeth Chifley left the long procession and returned home.

Curtin had also died in office, apparently unable or unwilling to acknowledge that the progressive heart disease from which he was suffering would end in his demise. Too ill to fulfill his duties as prime minister, he nevertheless stayed on in The Lodge, cared for by Elsie, who had been mostly absent from Canberra during the previous four years. There was no sign of Belle Southwell, the manageress of the Kurrajong Hotel, who had been Curtin's companion in Canberra, and who had done so much to keep him off the grog.

While Curtin and Chifley held onto power far longer than they should have, Andrew Fisher left office of his own choosing, albeit under considerable political and financial pressure. And he resigned to become high commissioner in London, which was a position of some power, considerable prestige and a much higher salary. He would die in London 13 years later, imprisoned by his dementia in an upstairs bedroom of his Hampstead house.

Fisher's long decline into a twilight world caused particular difficulties for a biography that purported to deal with his whole life. There was little material about the last six or seven years, when he was increasingly cut off from the world. I tried to get around this by beginning each chapter with an imagined episode during his long decline, based upon two visits that I made to the house in Hampstead, a sparse account by his daughter and my own recent experience with my father-in-law.

Those opening paragraphs were also a way of asserting the role of imagination in biographical writing, although the publisher undermined the effect somewhat by putting them in italics, as if to say that the author's imagination was not at work in any other parts of the book. Which of course is nonsense.

Lastly, I would like to return to the question of ownership. Not that the question of ownership is restricted to biographical writing. Some might argue that an historian who had not fought in the Second World War shouldn't have the temerity to write about it. Or that a white Australian shouldn't write about Aboriginal history. That such writers are effectively stealing stories 'owned' by others.

Similarly, some have argued that biographers have no right to trespass on the private lives of public figures. Relatives of both Curtin and Chifley certainly thought so and restricted my access to some material about their private lives or declined to answer when questions were posed about aspects of their private lives that could shed light on their public persona and their performance as leaders.

It is not only families who have a sense of ownership and with whom a political biographer has to contend. There is also the relevant political party, which might claim to have a stake in the biographical outcome, particularly if it has commissioned the book. There are also the party supporters to be considered, the prospective readers of the book and, of course, the subject of the biography themselves.

Where a political biography purports to encompass the whole life, there is no way for the biographer to avoid intruding into the private life of their subject. After all, a political life is not just concerned with smoke-filled caucus and cabinet rooms. It is also about friends and family, loves and rivalries, hopes and fears. It is about exploring the human condition in all its richness and complexity. A biographer intent on bringing a subject to life, and allowing readers to see a larger meaning in that life, has to draw on all the available material and the power of their own imagination to do so.

1 *The New York Times*, 3 September 2009.

The Biographer's Contract

Professor Frances Spalding CBE
2010

The business of authoring another person's life is problematic and potentially dangerous.

You need to be brave to write biography. It's not just the labour involved, nor the obsessive research which often involves more travel and hours of work than can be deemed cost-effective, but it is also the fact that it requires a self-exposing judiciousness. At every stage in the procedure, decisions are made, not with the backing of any committee or support of a line manager, but usually by the biographer alone. The rightness or wrongness of these decisions affects not only the selection and handling of the material used, but almost every aspect of the project, from the initial negotiations with descendants of your subject, the literary executor or interested parties, to the publicity that surrounds the book's publication. Few of us get by without erring at some point.

Biographies, as you will know, can be distorted by flattery or idealisation, or dulled by a superfluity of small facts. At one point, while writing my biography of the painter Vanessa Bell, I was so enthused by the closeness of the relationship between Bell and her sister Virginia Woolf that, in detailing their lives, I quoted a letter that mentioned a sponge bag, a forgotten sponge bag. As one reviewer rightly pointed out, it was one detail too many. And, for a while afterwards, critics, whenever they came across another over-stuffed example of this genre, referred to the author as belonging to the 'sponge bag' school of biographers. I felt deeply chagrined to be the source of this infamous label and still today have such a horror of sponge bags I can scarcely bear to bring one with me when I travel.

But there is rarely a moment when a biographer is not faced with some kind of responsibility, to the facts, to ethical issues, to the past, the future, one's audience and to one's craft.

The material has to be sifted with intelligent alertness, not just for facts, names, links and connections, but also for the inner life of one's subject. You need an open mind and an open heart to note, with feeling, intellect and intuition, what is being said; to hear also the tone of voice or the irony or hyperbole that is being used. I find it important at relevant moments to let the voice of my subject come through by means of quotations from their letters. It is in this way that the reader can catch, very precisely, a wry observation, a momentary hesitation or a characteristic way of looking at things. It is important, too, to catch the register of a person's vocabulary. For instance, if Vanessa Bell, who was a stoic, admitted 'agitation'—a fairly mild word, you might think—I knew that something was seriously wrong. But there are times where a biographer, feeling his or her way into another's mind, finds scant help. Samuel Beckett, for instance, refused point blank to engage in any discussion about the meaning of his work. I experienced a similar silence when I went, as a biographer, to the British Council in London, in search of Stevie Smith.

As a poet, Stevie Smith is best known for the three tragi-comical short verses that form 'Not Waving but Drowning'. It's a poem that has universal appeal. Most of us, after all, do at some point know what it is like to feel disorientated, out of step, emotionally exiled, finding ourselves, as the character in Stevie Smith's poem says, 'much further out than you thought/ And not waving but drowning'. In the late 1960s, the British Council had brought out LP recordings of poets reading their own verse, and in connection with this, they had asked every poet concerned to send in biographical details. I was well advanced with my biography of Stevie Smith by this stage, but I went to hear the British Council in order to see if what I had written chimed with what she herself thought was significant. A fat, bulging file was put in front of me, and leafing through its contents, I learned what busy lives poets lead, what a lot of prizes they win, residences they fulfil, wives they have and how extensively they travel. Finally, I arrived at Stevie Smith's biographical details, which amounted to two type-written sentences: 'Born in Hull. But moved to London at the age of three and has lived in the same house ever since'.

Why struggle with this genre, you may ask, in the face of such a flight into anonymity. Aware of the difficulties that biography presents, I am still sometimes astonished when young academics tell me they are making it the vehicle of choice for their first major publication. Such a move would have been unwise for several decades. From the 1940s onwards, while the textual analysis of New Criticism held sway, and on through the sixties and seventies, while Parisian theory created one orthodoxy after another, this allegiance to biography might have damaged your chances of gaining tenure. Poststructuralist and deconstructive theorists questioned the notion of the individual as an originating point of consciousness and sought to disconnect the life from the work. It is a delicious irony that the fame of Roland Barthes's 1968 essay, 'The Death of the Author', has become a major reason why his name lives on. Nevertheless, for many years biography was shunned by academia. It was thought to be conservative, regressive, blindly humanist in its assumptions and not alive to the crises, conflicts and discoveries that have exploded the kind of classic narrative on which biographies have traditionally depended.

And yet, in the twenty-first century, like the mysterious smile on the Mona Lisa, biography continues to fascinate with its suggestion of the known and the unknown. Today, it is not only popular but it also carries intellectual authority. It is interesting to see how intelligently and acutely it is used today to access politicians, and not least here in Australia, in the wake of Kevin Rudd's rise and fall and continuing political activity. Biography is also now firmly embedded within academia. This lecture coincides with the intensive week-long residential course 'Using Lives', which brings to Canberra students from all over Australia who are working on theses in some way shaped by biographical subjects and methods. And here and in England, certain universities are actively promoting the writing and study of biography, and employing leading scholars in order to do so.

Some of the questions that are being asked of biography today include the following: How does a biographer combine factual accuracy with innovation? Must a strong narrative drive be at the expense of contingencies? What kinds of selfhood are on display in the presentation of identity? How do we reconcile the private individual with the performative nature of public life? And should biographers imitate Boswell and promise 'veracity' about themselves as well as their subjects? What is our responsibility to a past, which in some ways remains open, not completed, while we write about it in the present and for the future? Is there a place in biography for postmodernist indeterminacy? Such questions can make biographers nervously aware of the multiple questions and commitments they must keep in mind.

If there is a twenty-first-century development in all this, it is, I think, the sudden rise in popularity of 'life-writing'. This variant term, a literal translation of the medieval Greek from which the word 'biography' derives, has been used to suggest that the graphic representation of life can take many forms and find more outlets than the traditional cradle-to-grave biography. One noticeable aspect of the work emerging from 'life-writing' courses is the greater degree to which personal narrative, reflection and theorising mesh together.

Sometimes a biographical essay is accompanied by a psychosocial analysis of its content or an enquiry into the play of gender roles within it. Whether or not this agrees with one's needs as a reader, it must be admitted that this explosion of interest in biographical writing, among people from all walks of life, would have pleased Dr Johnson. 'No species of writing seems more worthy of cultivation than biography', he wrote in 1750 in the *Rambler*, 'since none can be more delightful or more useful I have often thought that there has rarely passed a Life of which a judicious and faithful narrative would not be useful'.

I worry, however, that if a biographer is primarily motivated by a desire to prove a specific ideological point or a political theory, his or her subject is likely to suffer. However, it would be foolish to try to establish a set of rules for biography, as it is a hybrid and fluid genre, always spilling out of neat packages and persistently reshaping its enquiry as the questions that interest each generation change. This is one reason why there can be no such thing as a definitive biography. But an absence of fixed rules or goals does not mean there are no *external* constraints and *internal* restraints affecting the biographical project. For the biographer deals not with fictional characters but real people, and with that comes responsibility. The more the biographer is aware of those responsibilities, the more she or he will feel themselves to be under contract. Hence the title of my lecture: 'The Biographer's Contract'.

A biography cannot sail free on the author's imagination. It is instead tied to facts and often watched over by interested parties, be it a widow, a literary executor or a keeper of the flame. Of course, there are many kinds of biography, from the scholarly edifice to the breezy framing of celebrities, and therefore there will be many kinds of contract. If a biographer is aiming at shock, voyeurism and titillation, his or her contract may be similar to that of an assassin. At the other extreme, biography may harbour the kind of dutifulness that curtails enquiry and upholds the status quo. But even the most daring or inventive biographer comes to recognise that biography is necessarily a *constrained* art form. This may be true of all creative acts. Paul Valèry, in his 'Introduction to the Method of Leonardo da Vinci', published in English in 1929, states the following:

> An author preparing a discourse, and meditating on it beforehand, finds himself at once *source, engineer* and *constraining influence*. One part of him is the impulse; another foresees, arranges, suppresses; another, remembering and deductive, keeps an eye on the material, preserves the harmonies, makes sure of the permanence of the *calculated* design.

It is an interesting description of the creative process, and in particular of the verbal architecture that the biographer must construct. The word 'judicious', as you've perhaps noticed, has already come up twice, once in Johnson's desire for a 'judicious and faithful narrative'. As mentioned, a biography is not like a sailing ship steering out to sea with the wind of imagination in its sails. It is more like a tent fixed to the earth, and if one of its pegs is only loosely in place, the endeavour can come crashing down, as with Ian Hamilton's abortive attempt to write a biography of J.D. Salinger.

So, anyone embarking on a biography needs to think carefully about the ways in which she or he is contracted to the project. The standard dictionary definition of a contract is 'an agreement on fixed terms'. The *Oxford English Dictionary* defines it further: 'Proceeding from or showing sound judgement; marked by discretion, wisdom, or good sense'. And as a verb it can mean 'to effect by agreement'. Now, there is obviously room for manoeuvre here. Certainly, there may be times when the biographer needs to reject discretion. And there will be more contracts than the written agreement between publisher and author. In its standard version, this insists that the book's material must be original, in no way a violation of any existing copyright; that it must contain nothing obscene, libellous or defamatory; and that all statements purporting to be facts must be to the best of the author's knowledge and belief true.

Biographers like myself, who work on subjects within living memory, whose written words are still in copyright, know how unwise it is to embark on a major project of this kind without first seeking an agreement with the literary executor regarding access to papers and permission to quote. And there are often various other conditions on which spoken or written agreement is sought at this stage. Some biographers, for instance, ask if an embargo can be placed on relevant archives or documents not yet in the public domain, so that, while they are at work on their subject, no-one else can access this material. This kind of agreement firms up the grounds on which one can proceed. But a biography can be written without copyright approval or authorisation. Peter Ackroyd boldly produced a ground-breaking, useful biography of T.S. Eliot, despite being denied access to the letters or the right to quote more than a few lines of any poem.

At the outset, biographers need to be aware of interested parties, those to whom they will be in some way indebted, contracted or committed. Again, it is wise to establish agreements of some sort at the start, lest a vital dependency is suddenly withdrawn.

It struck me, recently, that this diplomacy and preparatory work is rarely discussed by practitioners of biography in the prefaces or acknowledgements of their books. Sometimes we glimpse these constrictions in passing. Earlier this year, David Marr revisited his biography of the writer Patrick White in order to deliver the Menzies Lecture at King's College, London. Titled 'White's London', he unfolded White's long-standing and ambivalent relationship with this city. Marr wove into his talk a riveting portrait of White, touching on his ambition, sexuality, wit, greatness, tetchiness, censoriousness, among other things, and he ended with an explanation of why news of White's death, rather surprisingly, reached most Australians via London, the city that shaped White and had formed his other home. Interestingly, in an aside, we learnt that White had read through the manuscript of Marr's biography—and here I quote Marr—'in front of me, slowly, over nine agonising days'. We can readily guess at what made those days so agonising. Was Marr perhaps anxious about the extent to which he had fulfilled or contravened expectations? Had there been spoken or unspoken agreements between him and White? And was he, at that moment, acutely aware of awkward tensions between his various commitments—to his material, to his subject, to his own self, to history and posterity, to his craft, and to his readers?

Property, permission and copyright are legal issues. The law, by means of copyright, protects our written words. But there is no copyright on the facts of our lives. Hence the relative freedom surrounding the making of biopics. The subject of a recent television biopic in Britain was Lord Longford, the Labour peer who befriended the child murderer Myra Hindley after she was imprisoned for life. One of Longford's daughters, Rachel Billington, was asked what she thought of the film. She was careful to praise Jim Broadbent, the actor who had played her father, but then admitted it had been painful to see on screen her father being sacked from government by the actor who played Prime Minister Harold Wilson, when in fact he had resigned. And to see her mother played as a dithery old lady, when she had been an elegant, specially alert woman of considerable intellect, and an outstanding biographer. Worryingly, the power of film enables these distortions to lodge deep in public consciousness. Despite the uncovering of many inaccuracies and false statements in T.E. Lawrence's *Seven Pillars of Wisdom*, his name is still treated with a certain hagiography owing, I think, to the lasting power of David Lean's film, 'Lawrence of Arabia'.

Hence, too, the frustrating experience of Iris Murdoch's biographer, Peter Conradi. After speaking at a literary festival on Iris Murdoch, a woman came up to him and, with reference to some detail, announced: 'You got it wrong in your book'. Why do you say that, he asked? Her reply: 'It wasn't like that in the film'.

The need to achieve good audience ratings no doubt shifts film and TV biopics towards dramatic solutions that ignore brute facts. A biography is differently analysed, its truths scrutinised over time and checked by many interested parties. Many of the problems confronted by biographers who write about those within living memory arise from imperfect contracts between the biographer and the literary executor or the spokesperson for the family or the deceased person's estate. If these are written contracts, the precise terms have been inadequately stated; or they are tacit agreements, with nothing on paper; or they are imagined contracts, imagined because they exist in the mind of one party only and have not been properly communicated to the other, therefore no agreement has been reached. Often these contracts concern sensitive information.

My only encounter with situations of this kind have been fairly trivial. One arose while I was writing the life of Charles Darwin's granddaughter Gwen Raverat. As her name suggests, she had married a Frenchman, Jacques Raverat, who began to suffer from ill health. It remained undiagnosed until he tried to enlist in the French Army at the start of the First World War, when it was discovered that he had multiple sclerosis, or disseminated sclerosis as it was then called. By the end of the war, when they tried to start a family, he had already more or less lost the use of his legs and, because of this partial paralysis, they had to seek help with conception. They were ahead of their times in this, for the simple process involved was, in those days, officially only used agriculturally. I was surprised to be rung up, not by the two daughters of the Raverats, but by a more distant member of the Darwin family who simply said: '*We* do not think it should be mentioned'. I noted the use of the royal 'we' in connection with the Darwin family, and was astonished that a Darwin was asking me to suppress information that reflected advanced thinking. I responded diplomatically, pointing out that the topic was passed over in a paragraph or less and saying that I would discuss it further with the two daughters. In fact, they had no problem at all with the relevant paragraph and the information was not censored.

There had been an earlier moment with that book when I had thought I was up against a more difficult issue. The two daughters had noticed some anti-semitic remarks in their father's early letters and asked if they could be ignored. I was able to point out that one or two passages from these letters had already been published in a biography of Jacques's friend, Rupert Brooke, and that it would therefore be foolish to try to cover up this aspect of his nature. It could, with reference to his French upbringing, the long-running Dreyfus affair and the anti-semitism in France and in certain French newspapers, be place within a wider context and thus to some extent be, not excused, but explained.

In both instances, I felt that the constraints initially proposed would have compromised my independence and integrity. Anti-semitism and multiple sclerosis are public concerns and a biographer's audience can be far-reaching. It seemed important to me, from the point of view of other sufferers of multiple sclerosis, to mention the difficulties the Raverats had faced. In addition, the constraints suggested by the family, however well-intentioned, did not fit with today's society, whose ethics entail a belief in openness. Readers today generally believe that there should be no censorship or idealisation, a belief that goes hand in hand with the growing resistance, in many spheres, to authority. But for the nearest and dearest of a famous person, the situation may not be so cut and dried.

Nigel Nicolson, the son of the diarist and diplomat Harold Nicolson and of Vita Sackville-West, aristocrat, poet, novelist and gardener, had no qualms about publishing *Portrait of a Marriage,* his mother's account of how she and Violet Trefusius left their husbands and fled to Continental Europe in order to have a passionate affair. But it is clear from Nigel Nicolson's own memoirs, and from my slight personal acquaintance with him, that he was by nature a rather private man. And when he gave Victoria Glendinning permission to proceed with her biography of Vita, he made one condition: that when listing all the women with whom his mother had affairs—and there were a great many—she was not to mention the affair Vita had with her sister-in-law, Harold's sister. Glendinning respected this request. In the book, she simply says that the two women were very close. She felt certain that anyone who had read that far would be able to recognise what was implied.

Censorship in this instance was merely an English nicety, Vita's affair with her sister-in-law being a step too far in Nigel Nicolson's mind. The two women were not blood relations and it was not a case of what Canon Law calls 'prohibitive consanguinity'. But this was precisely the issue in the case of Fiona MacCarthy's biography of Eric Gill. MacCarthy, a razor sharp journalist and a leading authority on the history of design, refused to do as others had done and turn a blind eye to passages in Gill's diaries which referred to incest with his sisters and daughters and sexual relations with dogs. Two previous writers had noted this material and kept silent. But this was dynamite information, for Eric Gill was widely regarded as the greatest English artist-craftsman in the early twentieth century. He was also a devout Catholic and a central figure on the founding of three Catholic art and craft communities laid down on semi-monastic lines.

To this day, MacCarthy remains perturbed by the outcry that greeted this book. Its publication coincided, in England, with the Cleveland child abuse scandal, a notorious case, involving incest, which ran for many weeks in the British press and media, and heightened public revulsion at this crime. But what specifically hurt MacCarthy was the sudden turning away of Gill's literary executor, Walter Shewring. The latter had worked with Gill, had gone on to be a schoolmaster at Ampleforth, a famous Catholic boarding school in Yorkshire, and though not a monk, as are other teachers at this school, he had lived a celibate life. In an essay looking back on her relationship with Shewring, MacCarthy has recounted how it developed, from the first formal meeting in a barren waiting room in the school, where a cup of tea and shortbread biscuits were the only nod to conviviality, to what became regular festive outings to Marmaduke's Haunted Bistro in York, where Shewring would order two bottles of Corvo wine and the conversation flowed. After one of these meetings, MacCarthy gave Shewring a finished typescript of the manuscript. He promised to check the source notes, but rather surprisingly said, with regard to the text, 'I leave that to you'. MacCarthy was certain he knew that it revealed incest as this had privately created issues before among Gill's closest associates. Afterwards, a letter arrived from him acknowledging that she had illumined a great deal, and with it came a schoolmasterly list of corrections on points of detail. Then suddenly came another message from him, scrawled urgently on a half-sheet of lined paper, telling her that 'our acquaintance and correspondence must now cease'. MacCarthy shook with sobs as she read it. She concluded that the family had informed him of their hostility to the book and he had been obliged to side with them in what became a bitter vendetta against her. It needs also to be said that, when the book came out, MacCarthy published an article on Gill in a Sunday newspaper which went a step further than the book and also named, in connection with incest, one of Gill's daughters who was still alive. Story has it that this daughter did not mind but that her children took enormous offence.

MacCarthy, who went on to publish a prize-winning biography of William Morris, writes:

> The book *Eric Gill* had been my first full-length biography. I began it in a state of naivety, imagining my only loyalty lay with Gill himself and the truth relating to the bizarre contradictions of this single human life. What I had not been prepared for was the fact that in searching out the truth, especially the truth of a near contemporary, you impinge on other interconnected lives as well, stirring emotions, resurrecting memories. In the dangerous complexities of writing a biography, the book on Eric Gill was my baptism by fire.

What comes through here is her humility in acknowledging her naivety. But this confession also raises another important issue. Should a biographer respect the right to privacy of those still alive? As mentioned previously, there is no copyright on the facts of our lives and, in Gill's case, it would have been impossible to expose incest without naming the members of the family involved. But there are many cases where a biographer is wise to exercise discretion when touching on lives that are still being lived, and may feel silently contracted in this respect.

Given the disturbing paradoxes that Eric Gill's life presents, it is a relief to find the critic Elizabeth Hardwick, when writing about Thomas Mann, talking about 'the inexplicable balancings in one soul of heredity, historical moment, character and choice'. Virginia Woolf would have agreed with her use of the word 'inexplicable'.

'We do not know our own souls,' Woolf wrote in her essay 'On Being Ill', 'let alone the souls of others'. But what is the biographer to do with such observations? Hold back judgement and resist from comment? Critics and reviewers often get very irritable if a biographer withholds comment or refuses to offer a view. Yet, there is integrity in this position and sometimes it should be adopted. Nevertheless, a biography with no views would make very dull reading.

Interestingly, Elizabeth Hardwick was herself the victim of biographical abuse when her former husband, the poet Robert Lowell, used her personal letters in some of his poems, changing them in places to suit the needs of his verse. Lowell had been a poetic touchstone to another poet, Elizabeth Bishop. He was also Bishop's friend, mentor, patron, ally and almost-lover. But Bishop was shocked by Lowell's use of Hardwick's letters and saw it as a desecration of poetry and personal dignity. She condemned him unequivocally. '[Aren't] you violating a trust?' she wrote. 'Art isn't worth that much. It's not being gentle to use personal anguished, tragic letters that way—it's cruel.' Somehow their friendship survived, though, as William Boyd mentions in a recent article on Bishop, its equilibrium was never fully recovered. But I am grateful to Boyd for also drawing attention to another quotation from Bishop's letters, which speaks directly to us biographers. 'My passion for accuracy', she writes, 'may strike you as old-maidish—but since we do float on an unknown sea, I think we should examine the other floating things that come our way very carefully; who knows what might depend upon it'.

And so we come to what is perhaps at the heart of the biographer's contract—the recording of truth and the attempt to commemorate it. Is this still possible in an age of relativism? Not only possible, I would suggest, but urgently needed, for the truths contained in any unpretentious report, be it a record of a parish outing or a school report, remain the foundation of all literary endeavour. Here is that great anatomist of melancholy, W.G. Sebald, looking back over what distinguishes the best scholars on the work of Kafka.

> Today if you pick up one of the many Kafka studies to have appeared since the 1950s, it is almost incredible to observe how much dust and mould have already gathered on these secondary works, inspired as they are by the theories of existentialism, theology, psychoanalysis, structuralism, poststructuralism, reception aesthetics or system criticism, and how unrewarding is the redundant verbiage on every page.
>
> Now and then, of course, you do find something different, for the conscientious and patient work of editors and factual commentators is in marked contrast to the chaff ground out in the mills of academia … it seems increasingly that … all [who] have concentrated mainly on reconstructing a portrait of the author in his own

time, have made a greater contribution to elucidating texts than those exegists who dig around in them unscrupulously and often shamelessly.

The poet Geoffrey Hill, when asked why his poetry was so difficult, replied 'because people are difficult'. And because people are difficult, writing biography remains a complex task, full of often unresolved tensions. It requires awareness of tradition as well as innovation, boldness as well as diplomacy and sensitivity. You can simplify a life to make for easy reading, but do not forget that similar reductions, omissions and silences have been used by totalitarian regimes not to commemorate human life but to support its denial. A biography that communicates effectively encourages us to empathise with an age or a people or a race or class different to our own. It brings the past closer to us and thereby thickens, enriches and challenges the present. Moreover by looking at history through the life of an individual, we come closer to the particularities of the period and they can become freshly vivid.

Recently, a friend told me of the lively response on the part of one intellectual to the news that a certain writer had died. 'Oh good,' he replied, 'now I know that I have got all of him on my shelves!' Let's hope his collection also contains a copy of this writer's life.

Pushing against the Dark: Writing about the Hidden Self

Robert Dessaix
2011

If you're a theatregoer, then somewhere along the line you're bound to have seen *The Government Inspector*—Nikolai Gogol's comedy about a rapacious nobody being mistaken for a government official by the citizens of a nameless provincial backwater. (Needless to say, they too are nobodies, greedy to be somebodies.)

And at one point, you might remember—since it's a line that will have evoked both your contempt and your compassion—the fussy fool Pyotr Ivanovych Bobchinsky, a local landowner who fails to exist to the point of being almost indistinguishable from his companion Pyotr Ivanovych Dobchinsky, says to the government inspector, who actually isn't one:

> I beg you most humbly, sir, when you're in St Petersburg, say to all the different bigwigs there—the senators and admirals: You know, in such-and-such a town, your Excellency, or your Eminence, lives Pyotr Ivanovych Bobchinsky. Just say that: lives Pyotr Ivanovych Bobchinsky ... And if you're speaking to the sovereign, then say to the sovereign as well: in such-and-such a town, your Imperial Highness, lives Pyotr Ivanovych Bobchinsky.

And the government inspector, who isn't one, pockets his 65-rouble bribe and, being a windbag, declares that he will be pleased to be of assistance.

Even when I first read these lines at the age of 18 at university here in our own St Petersburg, I felt knocked sideways by them. I didn't quite understand why, but I knew they cut straight to the quick of something deep inside me—some tight little knot of anxiety, or even anguish, that I'd tried for years to ignore.

'In such-and-such a town, your Excellency, or your Eminence, lives Pyotr Ivanovych Bobchinsky. Just say that …'

Even then, certain though I was of so many things (as most of us are at 18—you've got to start *somewhere*), even then, bound up in a tiny ball inside me, was the suspicion that I, too, was after all at root just another Bobchinsky. In fact, more than that: I suspected that most of us, in the final analysis, were just a crowd of Bobchinskys and Dobchinskys, stumbling around in semi-darkness, sending messages to different bigwigs living in the light—excellencies and eminences of various kinds—saying: 'I exist'. Not much more to begin with, whatever form our first messages might have taken (essays, poems, papers, a short story or two)—just 'I exist'.

Gogol's point was almost certainly religious: without God, even these senators, admirals and, for that matter, the sovereign himself would also fail to exist in any meaningful way. 'Corks' is Gogol's word: they would all be just common and garden 'corks', 'the sort you seal bottles with', and nothing more, if there were no God to give their being a particular meaning—an identity, as we might say.

I doubt that Sid Vicious, though, or Edith Sitwell, say, or many of the other notables whose names appear on the spines in the Biography section at your local bookstore would have agreed with Gogol about their ultimate insignificance in a godless universe, and I'm in two minds about it myself, but Gogol's viewpoint still gives me pause. When, as sometimes happens, I see my own first book, *A Mother's Disgrace*, an autobiography, or perhaps a memoir, on a bookshop shelf beside biographies of Diaghilev and Dickens, or at least sandwiched somewhere between Roald Dahl and Dawn French (if I'm lucky—it's often stuck in Fiction), I always avert my eyes. In this parade on the bookshop shelves of the celebrated and the wounded, I feel too blatantly exposed as a cork. I can almost hear Gogol aping Bobchinsky's unctious patter as he whispers in my ear: 'In such-and-such a town, your Excellency, or your Eminence, lives Robert Dessaix'. After all these years—not all of them spent in total obscurity—I'm Bobchinsky again.

At this point, I usually take rapid refuge in Crime or Travel, but today I'm going to be braver. Enough averting of the eyes: today I'm going to unpick that little 'knot of anxiety', as I called it, first felt a lifetime ago on reading those lines in *The Government Inspector*. Today I'm going to stand my ground, and ask what sort of storytelling I should be doing to take my place unblushingly beside the bigger D's. In other words, I'd like to talk today about recounting penumbral lives, lives that lack the historical significance or celebrity status of lives lived in the limelight. I want today to talk about pushing back the dark.

I'm not the only Bobchinsky on the shelves, of course. In recent times, there's been an explosion of what has been called 'life writing'—not a term I warm to, I must admit, but it's popular at the moment, I know, and does several jobs at once.

During his Seymour Lecture three years ago at the National Library, Richard Holmes noted that you'd need to read about ten biographies a day to keep up with what was being published in English alone. As a matter of fact, I've just finished reading the biography of an American snail, a particular snail, not just any snail, who until recently lived in Maine—this is life writing taken to the extreme. I'll never step on a snail again. And beyond the bookshops, blogs, I understand, are numbered in the tens—perhaps by now the hundreds—of millions, publicising the minutiae of private lives, or at least of alter egos. And then there's Facebook and Twitter and all the other social networking sites allowing both non-entities and celebrities to chronicle the course of their daily existences, to map the vagaries of their minds. Lives are ceaselessly dramatised in the cinema and on television as well—and not just Xerxes's and Henry VIII's, either. Indeed, every last Dobchinsky and Bobchinsky in the universe, it would seem, turns up sooner or later on *Australian Story* or *Who Do You Think You Are?* Who indeed.

I am less interested in the burgeoning array of forms these narratives take, by the way—memoirs, diaries, whole-life chronicles, costume dramas, photographic retrospectives, Facebook pages—than in *why* this is happening. What do we think we're doing? What Plutarch or Lytton Strachey or Richard Holmes thought they were doing is more or less clear: they were giving historical figures substance, even a nobility, and therefore our own present lives a past, a grounding in something bigger than we are. But what do those of us who are not Solon or Queen Victoria or Paul Keating think we're doing when we turn our lives into art? And, more interestingly, when does what we do seize our readers' imaginations most strongly, transfiguring them in a burst of lambent moments? That's the point, after all, isn't it.

Well, I know what I thought *I* was doing when I wrote my first book, *A Mother's Disgrace*. I was bringing things that had been hidden out into the light. I was lighting a flare. *Something* must always be uncovered in life-writing: if not new information, then new perceptions, new ways of seeing, relationships we had not anticipated—with the author, sometimes—at the very least a new way of styling the self.

At the time I wrote *A Mother's Disgrace,* I was not quite Bobchinsky—Bobchinsky's whole life is sunk in obscurity, lived out unnoticed in a penumbra of chattering meaninglessness in a town with no name. I was at least on the radio—in any event, I impersonated myself on the radio every week; I'm not sure that *I* was on the radio. As Borges put it so deftly in his one-page piece called 'Borges and I',

> I live, let myself go on living, so that Borges may contrive his literature, and this literature justifies me … I am destined to perish, definitively, and only some

> instant of myself can survive in him. Little by little, I am giving over everything to him, though I am quite aware of his perverse custom of falsifying and magnifying things … I do not know which of us has written this page.

I did not always know which of us was talking on the radio. For that matter, which of us is talking now?

If I was indeed on the radio, I was on a station that only a few of the intellectually curious listened to (the chattering classes, I think they're called, or the latte-sipping elite—you know the kind of listener I mean, how could you not?). Yet for all the talking I did—ten years of it—something remained hidden. I hardly knew what it was until I began writing, but something was. Something always is. Illuminate any private life, for instance, and you'll reveal papered-over cracks in public myths—about adoption in particular, in my case, about mothers and sons, about families. 'The greatest drama of humanity,' David Grossman, the Israeli writer, said, 'is the drama of the family'. Really? Well, I don't have one. Not the sort Grossman has in mind. And never will have. As a narrator, where does this leave me?

In addition, like everyone here today, I lead a double—or even triple or quadruple—life, not all of it in the light. Or at least I try to and hope you do, too. Fernand Pessoa, the Portuguese writer, said that he had a whole orchestra of selves playing away inside him. At the very least, in addition to the viola you heard on Radio National, I had an oboe, a flute and possibly a triangle tuning up in another room.

What's hidden need not be shameful—it needn't be a matter of confessing to bigamy or watching Channel 10. It just has to be a hidden self, or two. A time comes when, to ripen as a human being, you're ready to reconfigure the self you present to the world, to cock a snook at pious stereotypes, to bring out of hiding the darker sides, the raw or quirky sides, the facets you know some will mock, the unhealed wounds. You want at last to fill out and take your place in the world. Just like Bobchinsky, in other words—or Dobchinsky, who begged the government inspector (who wasn't one) to make his illegitimate son legitimate: *that* was quite close to home—but with more flair.

So when out of the blue the chance came to send a message to St Petersburg, I did. In *A Mother's Disgrace,* I gave myself a life. I gave the voice on the radio roots in the suburbs—and beyond, of course, in Russia—as well as in a certain unfashionable religious cast of mind, in intimate relations, in failed relationships, and in origins once considered shameful. The story spiralled like coils of smoke around an emptiness—or at least wisps of story (about dozens of things), the one curling into the other, twisting upwards and inwards, tightening.

As a consequence, the emptiness seemed to have a shape—the void was given a shape by the spiralling story—but it was still a void, a shaft of emptiness. Perhaps I wrote like that, spinning a looping skein of stories around a silence, to avoid plunging into it. Perhaps the reader kept reading to avoid the same fate. With hindsight I wonder if that's what I always do in my books (being a Bobchinsky): give nothingness—or at least incoherence—a shape by unreeling a thread of stories *in* it, as a staircase gives shape to the void in a stairwell.

Some biographies have had a void at their centre as well, not because the lives in question were obscure, as mine certainly was when I began writing, and still is, compared to Ricky Ponting's, but because little is known about their subjects: biographies of Socrates, for instance, or Cleopatra or even Elizabeth I. Here, too, the writer has had to give a hole a shape by describing the doughnut, as it were, rather than the hole. Virginia Woolf, in her essay 'The Art of Biography', got very cross with Lytton Strachey for concocting too much doughnut in Elizabeth's case, thereby turning biography into art, she said, when it should remain craft. I'm not quite sure what Woolf thought the difference was between art and craft: as far as I'm concerned, if a beautiful handmade chair can be sat on, it's craft. If it falls apart when you sit on it, it was art. An exquisite teapot that pours well is craft. If the tea splashes all over the place, it's art. (I have both kinds.)

Be that as it may, at least Socrates's, Cleopatra's and Elizabeth's lives were worth imagining. Nebulous as these figures might now appear, a bit short on detail, we do know that they lived abundantly. They were not mere Bobchinskys, flailing for attention.

When I first started to read biographies—about the time I first read *The Government Inspector* as a student in the early 1960s—the notion of writing a life to give shape to nothingness would not have entered my head. In those days, before bleating narcissistically into the ether became fashionable, one knew one's place. The life narratives I came across—Tolstoy's, for example, or Lenin's or Richard Burton's or some other worthy's—were researched retellings of lives that mattered, the lives of the bigwigs in St Petersburg themselves (the senators, admirals and sovereigns), not just lives that should be brought to their attention. No Bobchinskys *there*. These were crowded lives, densely woven lives that added up to something, recounted from cradle to grave. This was the heyday of the definitive biography. Take Arthur Rimbaud's life, for instance. By the age of 26, Rimbaud—well, let me quote from his biographer Graham Robb (also the biographer of Balzac, Baudelaire, Hugo, and more recently of Paris itself—biographies of cities being quite the fashion). By the age of 26m Rimbaud had 'worked as a pedlar, an editorial assistant, barman, farm labourer, language teacher, private tutor, factory worker, docker, mercenary, sailor, tout, cashier and interpreter … he'd been arrested in three countries and repatriated from three others'. He had been, I might add, on intimate terms with some of the most remarkable writers and political thinkers of the age, not to mention with Verlaine; committed at least a dozen imprisonable offences with impunity; survived war, revolution, illness, a gunshot wound, his own appalling family and rounding the Cape of Good Hope. And he had, without meaning to, also altered the course of literary history, changing ideas across the world of what poetry could be. *By the age of 26*. He still had a whole new life gun-running in East Africa to go. Not a likeable sort of fellow, not a saint, not a pillar of church or state, not a worthy —unlike the subjects of the earliest biographies—but not just Miles Franklin or Elizabeth Taylor, either. Definitely busy. And definitely wounded. A 'one-man, alternative *comédie humaine*', Robb calls him.

Robb, by the way, calls biography an 'optimistic genre'. It's an interesting word. I suppose he means that it engenders hope—hope of significance, of coherence, of narrative thrust, of validation, at least in somebody's sight(the gods', originally, I assume, or God's, or the nation's, or history's—*somebody's*). Nowadays I think that most of us writing up others' lives—or our own—are more modestly optimistic. We know before we start that redemption is a long shot. We're more likely to aim, as the best portrait-painters do, at a compelling likeness with plenty of sweep.

But why did I resort with such alacrity to autobiography in the first place all those years ago, if that's what *A Mother's Disgrace* was? It has all the earmarks of a memoir, actually, rather than an autobiography: it's fragmented, a curling necklace of arresting moments, far from all-encompassing, opinionated, intimate and at least dotted, if not peppered, with scandalous disclosures—illegitimacy, bathhouse adventures and so on—the sort of thing that Frenchwomen of slender virtue disclosed in the earliest memoirs, although as a rule about bishops and other pillars of society they had crossed paths with. But why leap into memoir or autobiography and not have a stab at a novel?

One reason is that, like Lytton Strachey—at least according to Virginia Woolf— and, I'm sure, many other writers, I doubted my purely creative powers. And so, like Strachey, I turned to writing a life narrative: my own, interwoven with my mother's. In fact, I didn't so much *doubt* my ability to invent as not even contemplate it.

In later books, I did invent, up to a point. I certainly telescoped and told stories back to front, although in my second book, *Night Letters*, which I called a novel although it sprang from my life as surely as *A Mother's Disgrace* had, I felt so self-conscious about writing 'pure fiction' that I actually wrote the completely fictional story of the amulet (some of you might remember that flight of fancy) in italics, as if to say: these pages were written by someone else, I've inserted them into my story, but I'm not responsible for what he's written.

On the day I arrived in Paris a few years ago to launch the French edition of *Twilight of Love* (a memoir, if I must name a genre, about my love affair with Turgenev and his with Pauline Viardot), my publisher and translator took me off to lunch straight from the station so we could get to know each other in person after a year of emailing. At around two o'clock, she said to me: 'Well, I should let you go, I suppose—you'll be wanting to go and meet Daniel'. (Daniel pops up at several points in the book as a Parisian friend of mine—a kind of *raisonneur* figure, asking awkward questions, bringing me back to earth.) 'Actually,' I said, 'Daniel doesn't exist. I invented him'. My publisher was not just nonplussed, but flabbergasted. 'But he's so *real*,' she said, slowly lowering her expensive spoonful of *crème brûlée* back to her plate, 'so completely French, so believable. Perhaps you should be writing fiction'. I do, of course, write fiction, all the time, as I've said, but rarely call it that. I generally call it memoir or autobiography. I gossip—that's really what I do. To call what I write 'fiction' would raise expectations I can't fulfil.

The books about Turgenev and Gide (*Twilight of Love* and *Arabesques*)—by the way, my most recent books—seem to fit most happily into the very modern sub-genre of memoirs of readers' relationships with writers, such as Geoff Dyer's best-selling diary of his failure to write a biography of D.H. Lawrence, *Out of Sheer Rage*. We learn nothing about Lawrence, but a lot about Dyer apropos of Lawrence. Many of you will have read Janet Malcolm's account of her involvement with Chekhov, *Reading Chekhov*, and then there's Nicolson Baker's *U and I* about his imaginary friendship with John Updike—all of them ludic (playing on the boundary between fact and fiction), all of them unscholarly (or at least unacademic) and all of them as much about the writer's own thoughts and experience as about the subject's.

There was more to my choice of autobiography when I started writing than a simple doubt about my ability to write fiction. When I began writing, like many other Westerners at the end of the twentieth century, I think I was losing faith in the purely fictional narrative. (That's a phrase I've borrowed from David Lodge, by the way, who has ruminated on this loss of faith at length.) I don't know how widespread this sense that pure fiction is in an exhausted, decadent phase is, but I suspect that many of my contemporaries, both readers and writers, share my ebbing faith.

There's always talk of the death of *something*, I know—the book, newspapers, conversation, even God—but Mark Davis, for instance, of the University of Melbourne, predicts that 'reading, studying, writing and publishing literary fiction will increasingly become the preserve of "true believers"'. A small niche market, in other words. Certainly the *Times Literary Supplement* these days devotes no more than a few pages to recent fiction: philosophy, religion, classical studies, history, science, biography, medicine, memoir, travel, criticism, even poetry—almost everything but fiction, it seems—is reviewed in its pages. Yet it was as recently as 1963 that Marguerite Yourcenar said, 'In our time the novel devours all other forms; one is almost forced to use it as a medium of expression'. Not any more, one isn't.

Why this lack of faith in fiction at the moment? It's tempting to blame post-modernism: after all, the post-modernist sensibility distrusts the very idea that a reality can be captured or created by language while also disdaining the traditional boundaries between genres (between fiction and non-fiction, say, or the autobiographical rant of a stand-up comic and the family memoir of a writer like Edmund de Waal—*The Hare with Amber Eyes*—indeed, the very boundary between truth and lies, some might say). Consequently, when we feel compelled to write, perhaps many of us these days naturally tend to shy away from pure artifice and seek out hybrid forms. There may even be something decadent about the arts in general at the present time, something stunted and sickly about the modern fascination with form, and we instinctively sense that hybridity could replenish the stock. Certainly, as I wrote *A Mother's Disgrace*, I found myself to some extent fictionalising my own autobiography, and then later I found myself infusing my fiction with autobiography and biography: in *Night Letters,* for instance, or *Corfu*, or my books about Turgenev and Gide, autobiography, biography and fiction are interlaced.

What other source might there be for this worldwide craving to record 'my life'? Drowning in a sea of facts on the one hand and beautiful lies on the other, do many readers, for instance, simply hanker after a *relationship* with someone when they read? With Alan Bennett, Karl Marx, Michael Kirby, Wordsworth or even Alexander McCall Smith's fictional Mma Ramotswe—it doesn't matter with whom, so long as it's felt to be a real, developing relationship.

Are we also less interested in the twenty-first century in national identity than once we were? At least in the West. Not so long ago, it was taken for granted that a good biography would tell us not only all we needed to know about Caravaggio or Shelley or Marcel Proust, but also what it meant to be Italian or British or French at a particular point in history. A good biography was almost like a pilgrimage—a tour of sites of cultural significance. Nowadays, I doubt that many think the question of national identity worth asking—*at least with regard to themselves*. Indeed, from my point of view, the current fashion for nationalist clap-trap in the media actually signals a crisis of confidence in national identities, a growing suspicion that being 'Australian', for instance, means less to many Australians than barracking for the Pies, say, or being an architect or a Christian.

'Placelessness' is the word describing contemporary sensibilities that struck a chord with me most recently. Large numbers of us nowadays float placelessly above the world's nation-states, cocooned in our own private memories, allegiances and dreams. Malouf puts it more gently: our idea of our Australianness, he says, is becoming less pressing—but also more subtle and more complex. I certainly believe that there's a growing disaffection from public life. What, exactly, in Australian public life are thinking Australians meant to identify with at this historical moment? 'What *is* Australia, anyway?' Dante asks in Malouf's *Johnno*—one of the first works of Australian fiction I ever read, as it happens, 35 years ago. Even 15 years ago, when I began writing, it would not have occurred to me to try to capture anything except my own suburban story. I, too, would have been hard pressed—and still am—to articulate what the word 'Australia' signified beyond its obvious geographical meaning. And so we retreat into private lives, which were not, broadly speaking, the subject of biographies in the English-speaking world until about 200 years ago.

If pure fiction is losing its mass appeal, though, or at least its pre-eminence, pure fact may not be faring much better. For a start, we're awash with facts these days, swamped by wave after wave of them from the moment we wake up in the morning. Sometimes, while the kettle's boiling, I make up a word—just random syllables that come into my mind—and then google it to see what happens. Without exception a fact pops up: my little spurt of gibberish turns out to be a town in Albania or a politician from Uttar Pradesh, a boy band in Nova Scotia or the Chinese word for octopus. My fantasy turns out to be a fact. And when it comes to the past, I suspect that the facts now belong on the internet. If what you want is the facts about some worthy's life, or even some nonentity's, then google him or her, go to Wikipedia.

What we now want from a biography, I think, or autobiography, is the very thing that Virginia Woolf, writing 72 years ago, said that we have no right to want: art. Not only art, obviously, but art nevertheless. Which is why Christopher Hitchens's rather savage attack on *The King's Speech* and the film's light-fingered approach to history missed its mark, surely: we don't go to the cinema for a history lesson, we go to be transported. By art. We're adults, we know legerdemain when we see it. What we object to is shoddy legerdemain, not sleight of hand in itself. And we love the illumination of dark corners of the soul, having quite a few of our own, if we're honest with ourselves. Throw in a king or two, a war and Wallis Simpson and you've got it made, really, haven't you.

When I began writing, there was no internet, no Wikipedia—there were libraries and archives—but I think I knew enough about myself after a decade or two impersonating a scholar at various academic institutions, writing the usual sort of scholarly article for journals that virtually nobody read and even a book or two (so little read that I actually burned a pile of them in the backyard to free up a bit of storage space in the cupboards in my house). I think I knew enough about myself when I began writing real books to know that the mere arrangement of facts was not my forte. In any case, as a Bobchinsky (more or less—certainly not a Tony Blair or David Bowie), the facts about my life—birth, adoption, school, university, marriage, divorce, realignment—were hardly worth chronicling for their own sake. The public would have to be seduced into reading about my life by something else. The question was: by what?

Most obviously, by the telling. The main themes of nineteenth-century novels, as Ian McEwan has pithily observed, are present in the life of any tribe of bonobos: 'alliances made and broken, individuals rising while others fall, plots hatched, revenge, gratitude, injured pride, successful and unsuccessful courtship, bereavement and mourning'. So it's all in the telling, isn't it. Artful retelling is the non-bonobo bit of what I do. That's what I meant when I said that I'd like to talk, not just about what we think we're doing when we write about our own lives or others', but about what will seize the readers' imaginations and transfigure them. It's not such a problem for the biographers of Agatha Christie or Colette, but, for all the Bobchinskys and Dobchinskys now sending messages to the capital, it is.

From a storytelling point of view, there must also be an event that changes us, I think, a kind of nub to loop around, something to kick-start the spiralling. It could be anything—any small epiphany, really, anything (as I say in *Arabesques*) 'that fits like a key into the clamp on our soul, unlocks it and throws it wide open, letting who we are come spilling out at last'. Even when I'm writing a memoir through the prism of someone who is far from being a nonentity—Ivan Turgenev, for instance, or André Gide—I like to circle around an epiphany: falling in love for life at the opera, agreeing to have coffee with Oscar Wilde in the casbah in Algiers.

In the case of my first book, it was the first meeting with my biological mother in my mid-forties. What, you might ask, is seductive about that particular twist in my tale? Who, apart from my mother and me, would care whether I met her or not? Almost nobody (and I know this) is interested in what *I* have encountered on my journey through life, but almost everybody is interested in mothers, questions of blood and in how selves are fashioned, particularly their own. Almost everyone is interested in unspooling their *own* lives from time to time and rummaging amongst the loops and curls. My life is there (as Balzac's, say, or Chatwin's, probably isn't) to give my readers the words to reconfigure their own.

Perhaps that sounds a little abstract, a touch bland. It's not just a matter of getting readers to retell their own lives as they read. A good book, according to the English author Michael Morpurgo, 'finds cracks' in the reader. It 'seeks out' these cracks and, I assume, worries at them, lays them bare. This chimes with my own experience as a writer. Virtually every letter I have received from readers of my books begins, 'Thank you for this book' and then switches to retelling the reader's life—sometimes at great length—taking pleasure in the dovetailing of our lives, as well as in the differences between them, in the fresh perspectives on mothers or adoption or Russia or religion or some other element in my story, in the restyling of the self that a good book offers, rather than in information. And then the letter homes in on one of the faultlines that my book has shone a light on—a breach or faultline in the *reader's* sense of self, not mine. Naming it at last in the light of what I've written seems to give pleasure. Michael Morpurgo might be right; it might be desirable in any book to keep us under its spell—but in the autobiography of a Bobchinsky it may well be essential.

But there's more to it than simply coming up with a dramatic twist to fan out from or seducing the reader into complicity with your story, tricks no traditional subject of a biography or autobiography—no Thucydides, Thackeray or Thatcher—would need to stoop to. 'Seizes the readers' imagination and transfigures it' is art. Virginia Woolf, as I've mentioned, in her essay on 'The Art of Biography' was insistent in that rather bossy way of hers that biography was craft, not art, 'a rest from the intense world of the imagination', and that while Strachey's biography of Queen Victoria was a 'triumph', because craft of the highest order, his biography of Elizabeth I was a 'failure' because he 'treated biography as an art', flouting its limitations. Art conferred immortality on its subjects, she believed, something craft could not do. Falstaff, she said, would outlive Dr Johnson. Pearl Buck, the American writer who won the Nobel Prize in 1938 for her 'rich and truly epic descriptions of peasant life and for her biographical masterpieces', was even more brutal. 'Fiction is painting,' she said, 'biography is photography. Fiction is creation, biography is arrangement'.

From a modern perspective, the distinctions drawn between art and craft, painting and photography and, by inference, between fiction and fact, are surely misleading, if not spurious, at least in any discussion of biography and autobiography. (And, for that matter, photography, while it undoubtedly has its limitations, could scarcely be dismissed as 'arrangement' or 'craft' these days.) I would certainly like to think that, while I may not be able to offer my readers much unalloyed fiction, I can and do offer art.

In other words, I believe that to be worth reading, the biography or autobiography of an Australian who is not a celebrity, who has no honoured place in history and whose life, while not uninteresting, is hardly marked by any towering achievement or swirl of incident, must be a work of art. *To be worth reading, to seduce the reader.*

After all, whatever else it is, art is performance—and I think back here to what the man Jorge Luis Borges wrote about his famous double, the writer Borges, 'the one things happen to', as he put it, the one in the biographical dictionary, the one people write letters to, the one who shares *his* preferences for coffee, Stevenson, hourglasses and maps, but 'in a vain way that turns them into the attributes of an actor'. An actor—that's the point. For those of us who are not Borges—or Bogart or Boyd or Baryshnikov—the performance of our storytelling is all we've got.

A writer with a keen sense of how spurious the banishment of art from biography can be is the British playwright David Hare. Hare's plays tend to be about current events: Bush and Blair planning the invasion of Iraq; Foreign Office complicity in torture; and in his most recent play, *The Power of Yes,* the role played by the banks in the global financial crisis. They're firmly rooted in verifiable facts, in other words. But that's not why audiences flock to see them. 'Art is life with the mystery restored,' Hare said last year in his punchy Garrick Lecture for the Royal Society of Literature in London, contrasting art not with craft but with journalism, which, he said, is 'life with the mystery taken out'. He ridiculed the notion that his imagination should be limited to 'the facts'. His plays were not 'journalism'. They were art because they had a metaphorical dimension. Unlike a Rolls-Royce aircraft engine, for instance, which Norman Tebbit declared on the BBC to be not only art, but more beautiful than most things artists created, his plays offered metaphors for other things. Iraq in Hare's play was not just Iraq. Unlike a documentary about Iraq, where Iraq just stands for itself, his plays are about war, betrayal, humanity, power. He has transformed Iraq. The artist's only obligation is to make it clear that the work is a work of art—an exercise in transformation; to make it clear, in Hare's words, that he or she is asking questions *of* us, rather than *for* us, as a journalist (or John Howard in his memoirs, say) might do (a telling distinction, I think), to make it clear that the aim is to give facts shape and meaning for the pleasure of the reader or viewer, and not just to record 'clumsy Life … at her stupid work' (to quote Henry James). It's not the only thing you can do with facts, but it's what an artist does.

Some writers are tempted to go even further than Hare. Fiction 'frees us' from mere facts, according to Romesh Gunesekere, the prize-winning Sri Lankan novelist, moving us into the realm of the imagination. It is 'playing with the interface between fact and fiction' that excites readers and writers alike. Gunesekere is, of course, a fiction-writer, so he's approaching this interface from the other direction from a biographer, just as Beryl Bainbridge was doing in saying:

'when I write a novel, I'm writing about my own life. I'm writing biography almost always. And to make it look like a novel I either have a murder or a death at the end'. But I think he's right about the excitement.

Now for a touch of voodoo. The Lenins, Koestlers, Mandelas and Betjemans amongst us have an attribute that most of us don't at first glance have, and finding the right words to describe it can leave even the most rational amongst us sounding a little like shamans or mediums. According to the Yale psychologist Paul Bloom, a researcher in what he calls the new science of why we like what we like, celebrities (Obama, Kennedy, Mahler, Lady Gaga, Susan Sontag—take your pick), anyone we apprehend as irreplaceable in either the public or private sphere (Mary McKillop, Hitler, your grandmother, your beloved), are perceived to have an inner essence, a kind of hyperreal presence, a soul, as we once said, that transcends the 'facts' of their bodily existence in the world. The mere proximity of the Dalai Lama, say, or Kylie Minogue is experienced by many as emanating a power invisible to the senses. It always did, of course—hence all those saintly relics from the Middle Ages and pieces of the True Cross onto which essences are believed to have rubbed off. We don't go on pilgrimages so often any more to feel touched by this mysterious life-force that our reason tells us cannot exist. Instead, we get onto eBay. 'Authentic sock Britney ran over' reads a recent post on eBay. 'The actual sock worn by a TMZ cameraman Thursday when Brit drove over his foot. Tire tread guaranteed authentic.' Marilyn Monroe's billowing white dress fetched over four million dollars last year, John F. Kennedy's golf clubs sold for nearly $800,000, a bid of $10,000 was made for Obama's half-eaten breakfast, a copy of Mahler's Third Symphony with corrections and revisions in his own hand recently went up for auction for between £100,000 and £150,000. On a private level, you might prize paintings by your children or your grandmother's sewing-case beyond anything a dealer would be likely to offer you for these objects. We think we're far too sophisticated to believe in essential presences in objects or bodies, but Blooms's statistics demonstrate that we're still half under the old spell. A perfect replica of an object touched by a celebrity, by the way, will not do: nothing adheres to it, no mana, aura, essence or what I can't help thinking of as 'fairy dust'. If you want to be rational about it, you might say that such an object has no history of its own.

Similarly, when we're invited by a writer inside a celebrity's life, we enter—irrationally or not, it doesn't matter—an enchanted realm. Even Hilary Spurling has spoken of 'finding the essence of a person' in writing her biographies—not quite the same thing as finding the essence of Marilyn Monroe in her dress, but it's evidence of how hard it is for us to avoid this kind of language. An article by Lee Tulloch in *Portrait* magazine from the National Portrait Gallery about the photographic portraitist Stuart Campbell is titled 'The Essence of You'—that's the word that sprang to mind to describe what Campbell captured with his camera. Invited inside my life, on the other hand, you would not find yourself in an enchanted realm. To coax you inside my realm, and keep you there, I must trick you with art. I must offer you an intimacy with your own stylised essence, as I've said, and, through voice and language, give you a sense of a focused presence you can converse with.

Not actually believing in these essences or manas or auras, or at least not in *inherent* essences, I am constantly aware that what I am doing is legerdemain, not real magic.

This awareness—that in some metaphysical sense there is nobody there, just an effervescence—is, I think, part of the void at the heart of my writing, the emptiness I swirl around, spinning tales. In just a moment, I will try to give the void my writing corkscrews around a more definite name, but not quite yet.

Does intimacy have anything to do with the kind of seduction techniques I'm talking about? I tend to think it does. Perhaps seduction always promises intimacy of one kind or another—an enticingly deep knowledge, the unashamed disclosure of what to others is veiled, an access to innerness. It's this kind of intimacy that the unknown autobiographer or memoirist can offer the reader—intimacy with the narrator. It is not the same as the intimacy of the blog, which is no more genuinely intimate than striptease is. The intimacy that the unknown writer must strive for—through cadence, rhythm, register and the illusion of physical presence—feels more like the intimacy of two close friends talking trustingly with each other. The writer must seem to be saying, 'Only you and I will know this'. It won't be true, but no seducer relies on the truth to lure the object of desire.

Real intimacy with grand historical figures—with Catherine the Great or Che Guevara—will be an illusion, although it's an illusion that a skilled memoirist or biographer might succeed in weaving. I felt oddly intimate with Manoly Lascaris, I must admit, as I read Vrasidas Karalis's *Recollections of Manoly Lascaris* recently—a series of conversations with Patrick White's companion—not only because I could hear Manoly's voice (and hearing a voice always helps, as Frances Spalding mentioned in her Seymour Lecture two years ago), but also, I think, because Karalis slowly teased me into feeling intimate with *him*, the writer. In the end, I felt deliciously led astray. And I also felt oddly and unexpectedly intimate with Rimbaud in the Graham Robb biography I mentioned earlier; there it's the quality of the light Robb throws on certain things in Rimbaud's life. These illuminations seem so individually chosen, so targeted, carried out by torchlight, as it were, not all-encompassing. Seduction is much harder to achieve in the full light of day.

And so I come full circle to the nub of what I wanted to say today. It is, as I hinted at the beginning, about light. 'I was bringing things that had been hidden out into the light,' I said about my first book. 'I was lighting a flare.' Now, that is true. But why was I doing that? It's not as if the world was waiting with bated breath for my revelations. Who cared about my hidden selves?

To be honest, I was actually casting another kind of light. Through language, the only torch I have. In E.M. Forster's phrase about Virginia Woolf's language, I was 'pushing against the dark'—not just the dark that certain hidden selves were crouched in, but a more powerful dark, the dark that, as we grow older, we all feel stealing over us, blotting out inch by inch what we have loved and who we have been—the dark my gleaming spirals circle around.

The act of writing is an act of resistance against the mortal condition—not mortality, but the mortal condition, and not in the sense of winning the writer immortality of the clichéd kind, the immortality we might speak of in connection with Homer or Shakespeare, but in the sense of deepening and magnifying the lived moment while writing. Every syllable I coax from my mind is a push against the dark, a small beam of light that dares the dark to snuff it out. I write to stave off time, to stave off nothingness.

'In such-and-such a town … lives Pyotr Ivanovych Bobchinsky. Just say that …'

Investigative Reporter of the Spirit: The Search for Five Women

Professor Jeffrey Meyers
2012

The American poet James Dickey once called me, in his down-home Georgia accent, an 'Investigative Reporter of the Spirit'. Then, well pleased with his vivid phrase, he said, 'I like it. It's real good. You can keep that one'. He meant that I had to be a relentless detective as well as a literary critic, someone who could bring the dead back to life. I suggested this view of biography in two paintings I chose for my dust jackets: Luca Signorelli's *Resurrection of the Dead* in Orvieto Cathedral, in which the corpses, with straining muscles and ecstatic expressions, struggle out of the earth and recapture their bodily form, and Giovanni Battista Tiepolo's allegory *Truth Unveiled by Time*, in which the truth, through the biographer's quest, is finally and inevitably revealed. I've been pleased to discover relationships that were either unknown or discounted as insignificant or completely suppressed in a great writer's life. Finding out about these obscure figures was a challenge. To experience the thrill of the chase, to use all my knowledge and skill to discover what I wanted to know, have been for me among the keenest pleasures of biography.

In my work on Joseph Conrad, Wyndham Lewis, Scott Fitzgerald, Ernest Hemingway and Robert Frost, I was fascinated to learn that each of these mostly older, married writers had an intriguing but elusive lover. Attracted to their young admirers, these writers eagerly seized the sexual rewards for literary fame and inspiration for their work. As I found out about their background, appearance and personalities, these five mysterious minor characters, who revolved around these celebrated suns, took on for me an independent existence. They had extraordinary lives and were themselves worthy of a full-length study. In most cases, I met their descendants and discovered the effects of their lives on other people. I learned not only about these women, but also a great deal about the personality of the main subject, his social milieu, the range of his friendships and the models for his fictional characters.

Sexual secrets, often suppressed in print, are usually found in unpublished papers and interviews. Beyond the thorough search in the authors' archives, in the letters, manuscripts and diaries, a biographer has to follow every lead and be doggedly persistent. Four of these women had children and I interviewed all of them. With experience and luck, a passion for detection and the generosity of many people who value his work and are willing to help, the biographer can illuminate the subject in a new way. As the fragmentary evidence begins to cohere, these vague figures move out of the shadows and into the spotlight, take on colour and distinctive shape, grow solid and spring into being.

I Jane Anderson (1888–1972)

Previous writings about Conrad made very brief mention of a dashing young American woman called Jane Anderson, who came into his life during World War I. I wondered how such a bold and colourful character fitted into Conrad's staid existence. I began my search with scholarly articles by my former teacher and Conrad scholar Ian Watt, in *Conradiana* and by John Edwards in the *Atlanta Historical Journal.* Edwards mentioned Jane's connection to the American critic Gilbert Seldes and to the novelists Rebecca West and Katherine Anne Porter. I returned to Gilbert's sprightly 99-year-old brother, George Seldes, whom I'd interviewed for my Hemingway book, and he gave me his clear recollections of Jane, enhanced by his autobiography. West described Jane as 'very beautiful, with orange hair, a slender figure, a ravishing complexion and great charm'. Porter portrayed her as the predatory Condesa in *Ship of Fools*—beautiful, seductive, high-strung and addicted to drugs. Porter's biographer sent me many pages of biographical material and a photograph of Jane, which I reproduced in my life of Conrad. In the photo, she turns her strikingly attractive face towards the camera as her tawny hair cascades onto her shoulders from under the canopy of an enormous black hat. I also found 35 articles by Jane, who was a courageous war correspondent and frequently visited the battlefields of France.

I wrote to the Georgia Department of Vital Records for her birth date; to the Arizona Historical Society for information about her father, who'd been Town Marshal of Yuma, Arizona. Three other obscure sources were the most revealing: the private papers of her college roommate Kitty Crawford; the private papers of her first husband, the composer Deems Taylor; and the 446-page FBI file on Jane. Crawford provided information about Jane's colourful background, striking appearance and college life both in Georgia, where she was expelled, and in Texas, where she was forced to leave. Virgil Thomson suggested I write to the American Society of Composers, which forwarded my letter to Deems Taylor's daughter. She answered my questions about her father and Jane, and travelled from New York to her summer home in Massachusetts to show me his papers. Jane had had a bizarre childhood in Georgia and Arizona: her genteel mother had been involved in a murder trial, and she joined her wild father, who'd twice deserted his family, in a wild frontier town. Intelligent and beautiful, Jane went to New York, married, became an enterprising journalist and the mistress of several rich and powerful men.

When introduced to Conrad at his home in April 1916—he was then 59, she was 28—the Georgia girl 'played and sang Negro songs of the cotton fields and plantations. Conrad listened, spellbound by the plaintive melodies of the South'. But that summer, Jane, exhausted and ill from her wartime reporting, had a nervous breakdown. Conrad, who cultivated a romantic attitude towards women, played the chivalrous gallant and invited her to recover in his house in the Kentish countryside. The well-born and well-connected Jane—young, exotic, independent and adventurous—was the very antithesis of his maternal and domestic, obese and crippled wife Jessie. Powerfully attracted to Jane and alluding to the charming heroine of *The Mikado*, Conrad confided to a friend that she was 'quite yum-yum'. He also told his agent, while trying to advance her literary career, that she was 'as frank and open as a woman can be, I believe, and all her instincts are rather generous ... You will find her a most amenable creature.'

Conrad believed that passion between an older man and younger woman was potentially destructive. He had no wish to become involved in a squalid and embarrassing scandal, and felt the need to preserve appearances. But there are many indications that he had an affair with Jane. She adored Conrad, had unconventional sexual attitudes and willingly slept with great men to make her way in the world. For his part, Conrad led a quasi-celibate life with Jessie and took his last opportunity to delight in the 'generous instincts' of the 'amenable creature'. In the summer of 1916, they had secret meetings in London, and photographs taken during Jane's visits reveal their closeness. His invitation to convalesce in his house was extraordinary and their close proximity inevitably caused quarrels with the jealous Jessie. He tacitly admitted his guilt when she discovered his love letter to Jane, and acknowledged his 'back-sliding'.

Jane, an emotional tornado, was a bright ray of light in a dark period of Conrad's life. She distracted and rejuvenated him when he was depressed by the war, and inspired him to join the propaganda effort by going on sorties in planes and ships, and by writing about his experiences. Jane disturbed Conrad's emotional life in other ways. She flirted with Conrad's son Borys, who fell for her in Paris during his leave from military service. She also became the mistress of Conrad's young Polish friend Joseph Retinger, broke up Retinger's marriage and, by arousing Conrad's jealousy, damaged the friendship of the two men.

Jane inspired the liveliest character in the first novel Conrad published after the war. In *The Arrow of Gold* (1919), she's the exotic, seductive Rita de Lastaola, mistress of the autobiographical hero. Both Jane and Rita have blue eyes and rust-coloured hair. Conrad's description of Rita suggests his strong attraction to his magnetic model. She was:

> a woman formed in mind and body, mistress of herself, free in her choice, independent in her thoughts … All that appertained to her haunted me with the same awful intimacy, her whole form in the familiar pose, her very substance in its colour and texture, her eyes, her lips, the gleam of her teeth, the tawny mist of her hair, the smoothness of her forehead, the faint scent that she used.

Jane's intoxicating 'familiar pose' is the same as Rita's. Jessie wrote rather acidly, 'Miss A— seated herself before the fire like an idol'; in *The Arrow of Gold*, Rita is seen 'sitting cross-legged on the divan in the attitude of a very old idol'. Jane's free-wheeling style, her flirtation with Borys, her liaisons with the press magnate Lord Northcliffe and the politician Sir Leo Money, her connections in 'all the right places' and political influence with high-ranking officials are all clearly portrayed in the novel, which ends as Rita abandons the autobiographical hero.

After she drifted out of Conrad's life, Jane went to Spain and then to Germany, and her pro-Fascist activities aroused the interest of the FBI. Their report described Jane's second husband, the Marquis de Cienfuegos, traced her propaganda career in America, England, Spain and Germany, and threw considerable light on her personality. I wrote to the historical institutes in Munich, Koblenz, Bonn, Potsdam and Frankfurt for records of her wartime activities in Germany. (Germans always answer letters.) I spent a lot of time searching for the descendants of Cienfuegos in Oviedo and Madrid until the trail went cold. I finally realised, after comparing the facts in the FBI file with those in the archives of the Spanish nobility, that Jane's husband was a bogus marquis.

The idealistic Conrad would have been appalled to know the history of the last 30 years of his enchanting mistress, who descended into espionage, alcoholism, drug addiction and abject poverty. She was tortured in a Spanish Loyalist prison, made propaganda speeches for the Spanish Fascists and treasonable broadcasts for the Nazis. Jane charmed and impressed the Nazi Minister of Propaganda, Joseph Goebbels, who recorded their meetings in his *Diaries*. In July 1943, Jane, along with Ezra Pound, was indicted for treason for broadcasting wartime propaganda from Germany to the United States. After the war, she evaded the military police for two years, was arrested in Salzburg in 1947 and released for lack of evidence to convict her. She then disappeared into Franco's Spain and died in Madrid. Jane's tragic life exemplified the classic Conradian themes: divided loyalties, imprisonment, degradation, treachery and betrayal.

II Iris Barry (1895–1969)

The talented and attractive Iris Barry, Jane Anderson's contemporary, lived for three years with the artist and writer Wyndham Lewis. A bohemian figure, utterly lacking in Conrad's tender gallantry, Lewis treated her very badly. He and Iris had curiously parallel lives. Both disguised their obscure backgrounds and, with considerable wealth in their families and many rich friends, remained poor all their lives. Both were separated from their fathers at an early age and educated partly in Europe. They had sharp tongues and quick tempers, and many love affairs. Ambitious and confident in their ability, they both made their mark in the world of art. Desperately striving to make a living in the hard times between the wars, they both emigrated to North America.

I consulted Lewis's archive at Cornell University and Iris's papers at Boston University, and was able to meet her son, her last companion and seven of her friends including Rebecca West, Peter Quennell, Julian Symons and Alistair Cooke. These interviews enabled me to recreate Iris's life before she met Lewis and after she left him. She was born in Birmingham, with the unromantic name of Iris Crump, into a dreary and impoverished family. Her father, a Sheffield brassfounder, was divorced by her mother after she contracted gonorrhea from him. Her mother, as dark as a gypsy, styled herself Madame Pandora, and told fortunes in Bognor Regis and the Isle of Man. Iris was quick-witted and intelligent. Her wealthy grandparents paid for her education in Birmingham and at the Ursuline Convent in Belgium. She was a slim, tiny woman, with searching and sceptical blue eyes, and black hair cropped close to her shapely head. Though she had little money, she always wore striking clothes. She had a clinical precision of speech and listed her recreation as 'talking'. She laughed easily, especially at pomposity; and could be very amusing or quite truculent, always long on mockery and short on tact.

She met Lewis through Ezra Pound, who had a keen eye for talent and was living in London. In April 1916, Pound spotted Iris's verse in *Poetry and Drama*, which she'd sent to the magazine while she was working at the Post Office in Birmingham.

He praised her poetry and urged her to move to London; she followed his advice and Pound introduced her to Lewis, just returned from the war front. She was strongly attracted to the handsome, mysterious and exciting artist, and seems to have been good for him. Notoriously negative and saturnine, Lewis allowed Iris to draw out the lighter side of his nature. Iris recalled how 'Lewis, ghastly pale under his black hair and after silences that seemed, at least, to denote some suspicion of his fellow-creatures, proved full of inimitable conversation, riotous song, and an unequalled play of humour'.

Iris lived with Lewis—the only man, she said, who never bored her—from 1918 to 1921, while ordering machine guns for the Ministry of Munitions and working as a librarian at the School of Oriental Studies. Lewis worked hard to secure portrait commissions from clients whose wealth he often resented. After posing for Lewis and hiding from his friends, she learned to sit anywhere without moving. When patrons came to see him, she stayed obediently in the back room, not making a sound. They had two children—through carelessness rather than intention—a boy, Robin, born in June 1919 soon after Lewis left the army, and a girl, Maisie, in September 1920. Lewis already had three other illegitimate children. He and Iris led a poor, unsettled, erratic existence, thought the infants would burden them and interfere with their careers, and didn't want to keep them. He loftily told a friend, 'I have no children, though some, I believe, are attributed to me. I have work to do'. He left Iris with the children but without money to support them and, like Pound's offspring, they were given away. When she once mentioned the children to Lewis, he said with calculated coldness, 'Oh, was there more than one?'

Iris once bitterly told a friend that when she returned from the hospital with her baby girl, Lewis was having sex with Nancy Cunard in his studio. She had to wait outside on the steps, holding the baby, until he was finished. In April 1921, Iris wrote Lewis a poignant and disillusioned letter that expressed her uneasiness about abandoning the children and suggested that their relationship was coming to an end: 'We never had any peace of mind, ripe, tasty hours together, Lewis, except those stolen from my domestic cupboard, leaving a skeleton here … Write quick & say you miss me & that you are well & your plans thriving'.

Their daughter Maisie was adopted by a prosperous family and had a happy childhood. Robin had a much harder time. He lived with Iris's mother till he was four, and spent the next six years in a dismal orphanage in Essex. A friend once accompanied Iris to visit the six-year-old child, who called her Auntie and didn't know she was his mother. Clearly cold and miserable, he suffered from chilblains. He begged to be taken away, and his obvious illness and cruel neglect naturally hurt Iris and made her feel guilty. Lewis, who had been abandoned by his own father, never saw his children, and they didn't know he was their parent until they were adults.

Maisie, more resentful about her background than Robin, once owned a valuable oil painting by Lewis but threw it in the dustbin. Neither of them really knew Iris until she returned from America in 1950 and, rather late in the game, made embarrassing attempts to be motherly. The letters of Lewis and Iris revealed that she remained emotionally attached and loyal to Lewis long after he'd lost interest in her. There's an exquisite irony in the two phases of their relationship. In the early 1920s, the impoverished Iris wrote a long series of despairing letters pleading with Lewis to send the money he'd agreed to pay her and the two abandoned children. Iris sometimes had no food to eat and no shoes to wear to work. But Lewis evidently shared her bitterness. When she sent him one of her novels and asked for a kind word to be used as publicity, he coldly replied, 'Our relationship was an unfortunate disaster. I don't want to have anything more to do with you.'

In a savage but stylishly written letter of 11 April 1930, Lewis played the injured party and made what he hoped would be the final attempt to rid himself of a desperately clinging woman:

> I have received your further letter. The endearments that you think fit to employ I confess disgust me, and I cannot at all make out what causes you suddenly to indulge in them. The lapse of so many years may have effaced from your memory the fact, but it has not effaced it from mine, that my acquaintance with you was of a most unpleasant nature. Why then in heaven's name these epistles? Your book is not, as you may guess, of any interest to me, and I am returning it to you.

This letter reveals the worst side of Lewis's character. Iris made emotional demands he could not meet. Poor himself, he would not or could not pay. He was then living with his future wife, Froanna, wanted to sever all ties with Iris and extinguish all guilty memories of their unwanted children. Iris also had difficulty finding a job during the Depression. In November 1931, despite Lewis's hard-hearted cruelty, she sent him another moving letter, when she was in truly grim circumstances, asking for help with a fine mixture of tenderness and pride.

> I wonder if after all this time I might ask something of you? I wouldn't unless it were really quite desperate … I wondered whether you could possibly scrape up a few pounds and send them to my mother? ... Of course I know I've no claim on you at all—but I thought maybe if you happened to be able to put your hand on £10 you might just this once help me over a rather bad patch … If I make this plea so simply, it is perhaps because I hope that now, at this late date, I may have earned your confidence.

We don't know what reply Lewis made, but hope that he helped Iris's mother, who'd brought up his son.

Ten years later, in the early 1940s, when Lewis and his wife were marooned and destitute in wartime Canada and Iris was well employed at the Museum of Modern Art in New York, their situation was ironically reversed. Now it was the proud Lewis's turn to write begging letters. In December 1941 and March 1942 Lewis pleaded,

> On Monday morning (yesterday) I had seven cents left … Five of the above seven cents I had to keep for the telephone to reach a patron to borrow money when he gets back … It seems I must remain here indefinitely, waiting for *somebody* to take pity on my condition and rescue me from this truly awful plight.

Fortunately Iris, more adaptable in her new country, was more responsive to Lewis's needs than he had been to hers.

After Iris spun out of Lewis's vortex, she published several novels, became a founder of the Film Society of London and was film editor of the *Daily Mail* from 1925 to 1930. She divorced two husbands—a minor English poet and an American financier—and became a librarian at the Museum of Modern Art. Three years later, she founded its film library and was the pioneering curator until her retirement in 1950.

Two of Iris's close friends, the film maker Ivor Montagu and the television magnate Sidney Bernstein, were reluctant to discuss her, but I had a fascinating interview with her son, Robin Barry. Following up every vague lead, I phoned a man I thought might be her son—a very delicate situation indeed. He eventually agreed to meet me at his home in Vincent Square, London. The first thing I saw when I entered his sitting room were two superb and entirely unknown drawings by Lewis of Iris Barry. Robin was a tall, slim, handsome, kind and cultured architect, who'd never known Lewis. Still angry and bitter at the way he'd been mistreated, he couldn't understand my interest in what he called his boring, second-rate writer and quite rotten father. But we became friends; I dined with him several times while writing the biography in London. He told me all he could about his mother and introduced me to Iris's French companion.

After her retirement, Iris moved to France to live with Pierre Kerroux, a handsome man, 30 years younger than she, who used his boat to smuggle olive oil from Corsica. They remained together for 20 years in a farmhouse in Fayence, near Grasse in the Maritime Alps, on her tiny pension and the money they earned by growing vegetables and roses for perfume. Pierre told me about her final years and how her papers—including letters from Lewis and drawings by Picasso—had been stolen from their house. After an operation, Iris died of cancer of the larynx in a Marseilles hospital in 1969 and was buried in Fayence.

In his novel *Tarr* (1918), Lewis made a fleeting reference to Iris in his description of 'the painted, fine and inquiring face of Prism Dirkes'. His main artistic tribute to her was the painting *Praxitella* (1921), which depicts a massive Amazonian figure in a voluminous and billowing black dress with wide brown stripes at the bottom of the skirt. Seated in front of a pale green background, she has heavy boots, metal hands and spidery fingers, wide shoulders and a blue-tinted, crimson-lipped, Cubist-faceted, mask-like face. Her expression is grim, her eyes are downcast and she's crowned with a sharply cut, horseshoe-shaped headdress, topped with a heavy knot of black hair. It's ironic that Lewis portrayed the tiny, gentle and devoted Iris as a monumental, severe and threatening figure.

III Bijou O'Conor (1896–1975)

My next candidate for best supporting actress, Bijou O'Conor, was a contemporary of Iris Barry and a very different sort of woman. Upper-class and hard-drinking, she played a brief but resonant role in the life of Scott Fitzgerald. He met the sophisticated and scandalous Bijou at the Grand Hotel de la Paix in Lausanne in the fall of 1930, when his wife Zelda was seriously ill and confined to a mental asylum. Bijou, almost as alcoholic and self-destructive as himself, was far more reckless, a true bohemian without Fitzgerald's conscience and capacity for remorse. Their affair was brief, and provoked Fitzgerald's uncontrolled drinking and wild behaviour. But it also, during one of the darkest periods of his life, alleviated his tormenting guilt about Zelda, provided precious affection and gave him sexual reassurance in what she described as their 'roaring, screaming affair'. He found her utterly fascinating and enshrined her in his fiction.

In 1975, the eccentric old Bijou, who lived near Brighton with a Pekinese, gave a taped interview about her affair with Fitzgerald. The husky upper-class voice intrigued me, and I wondered what had brought them together and how Fitzgerald fitted into Bijou's life. I've often discovered that someone who seems obscure, dead and forgotten can be brought to life once I tapped into the institutions that survived her: an Oxford college and the Foreign Office, who put me in touch with her family.

I began with the *Who's Who* entry on Bijou's father, Sir Francis Elliot. A grandson of the second Earl of Minto, he rowed for Balliol College, entered the diplomatic service, and served in Sofia and Athens. I telephoned the present Earl of Minto, whom I imagined wearing a deer-stalker and pacing the armour-lined corridors of his crumbling castle in the Highlands. Instead of the servant I'd expected, the earl himself answered the phone. Though he hadn't heard of Bijou, his curiosity was aroused by my questions about his family. We had a leisurely talk and he suggested various lines of inquiry.

My first breakthrough came from the librarian of Balliol, who was interested in my query about Sir Francis and rang me up at once. Though Sir Francis had no sons, his grandson, as I suspected, had gone to his old college. This grandson, Captain William Elliott-Young, had been killed in World War II, but *his* son, the tenth baronet, Sir William Neil Young, now lived in London. I phoned him at Coutts Bank, which put me right through to him. Sir William was in the midst of his work but, like the Earl of Minto, was fascinated by his great-aunt and disposed to chat about her. He described her extravagance, her alcoholism, her mythomania—and her wooden leg. Most importantly, he put me in touch with Gillian Plazzota, the former wife of Bijou's son. Gillian told me more about Bijou's unusual appearance and bohemian character, and about Bijou's son, Michael O'Conor. She gave me his phone number, but suggested I 'be gentle with him, and ask about photographs and letters before requesting information about Bijou'.

Though slightly suspicious at first, Michael O'Conor was curious about why I was so interested in Bijou, amused by the circuitous trail I had followed to find him, and eager to hear what I knew about Bijou and Fitzgerald. He agreed to see me the following morning in Surrey. He'd been educated at Radley and Oxford, become a petroleum engineer, and worked in Kuwait and Venezuela. He showed me a photo of Bijou's Pekinese but did not have one of his mother. Michael said that the most important of Bijou's numerous lovers was a Russian photographer, Vladimir Molokhovets, whom I searched for but couldn't find.

When I rang Sir William Young the next day to thank him and ask if he had a photo of Bijou, he promised to send me one and suggested I see her first cousin, the elderly art historian, Sir Brinsley Ford. As Sir Brinsley was telling me family stories and personal memories of Bijou, his spritely granddaughter made a dramatic appearance and greeted him with a kiss on his bald dome. She was delighted to learn that her distant cousin had been Fitzgerald's mistress and that her highly respectable family included an eccentric rebel.

In 1920, Bijou married Lieutenant Edmund O'Conor, a professional naval officer, and accompanied him when he was stationed in China. She acquired an expert knowledge of Chinese and developed a lifelong passion for Pekinese dogs, the first of which had been given to her by the Chinese empress. Lieutenant O'Conor had been infected with tuberculosis during the war and died of that disease in Australia in 1924. Though widowed at 28, Bijou never remarried. She then lived on a small naval pension and on whatever cash she could extract from her unwilling father. She spent some time in a tuberculosis sanatorium in Davos and was also treated for alcoholism in Switzerland. Bijou looked like Edith Sitwell, thin, chic and *jolie-laide*, with fine features and soft brown eyes.

Very social, a bit intolerant and rather snobbish, she had rare charm and an air of mystery. An amusing *raconteuse*, who kept her circle of friends riveted by her lively conversation, she smoked heavily and enjoyed drinking binges.

Fitzgerald portrayed Bijou and her friend Napier Alington as the widowed Lady Capps-Karr and Bopes, the Marquis of Kinkallow, in his story 'The Hotel Child' (1931). 'Practically the whole damn story is true, bizarre as it seems,' he said. 'Lord Alington and the famous Bijou O'Conor were furious at me putting them in.' In real life, in about 1918, Bijou, careless with a cigarette and possibly drunk, had burnt the ceiling of the guest room in her uncle's house. She must have told Fitzgerald about this embarrassing incident, for in his story Lady Capps-Karr and the Marquis of Kinkallow are ejected from the Swiss hotel for starting a fire while attempting to fry some potato chips in alcohol. Fitzgerald's satiric caricatures of Bijou and Alington seem to have been inspired by his powerful reaction against Bijou after their stormy affair had ended.

More significantly, Bijou reappears in Fitzgerald's greatest novel, *Tender Is the Night* (1934), set on the French Riviera. Bijou appears as the fragile, tubercular, decadent Lady Caroline Sibley-Biers, who, Fitzgerald writes, is doing a dance of death 'as the Sepoys assault the ruined fort'. This picturesque phrase and Lady Capps-Karr's favourite expression, 'After all a chep's a chep and a chum's a chum'—Fitzgerald's bizarre notion of quintessential upper-class English speech—occur both in the story and the novel, linking his fictional characters to their common model, Bijou O'Conor. At the end of the novel, Lady Caroline and Mary North dress up as sailors and are arrested after picking up two French girls. Though the hero Dick Diver has been insulted by Lady Caroline, he rescues both women from an Antibes jail. As the French police express their disgust, Dick observes that Lady Caroline lacks any sense of evil and bitterly concludes that she represents the 'concentrated essence of the anti-social'. Fitzgerald died of a heart attack at the age of 44 in 1940. Most of Bijou's possessions, including the letters he wrote her, were stored in a London warehouse and destroyed during the Blitz. One dark night, after she was knocked down by a bus, her leg had to be amputated and she was fitted with a wooden one. She sued London Transport for reckless driving and was awarded substantial damages, which (like the replacement) supported her for many years. One of her louche friends once persuaded her to smuggle contraceptives into Ireland in the hollow of her artificial leg. During the war, Bijou—notoriously indiscreet but a highly gifted linguist in French, Russian, Polish, Greek and Chinese—worked for the Russian Department of military intelligence at the War Office.

After the war, she resumed her luxurious but parasitic life in Monaco. She planned but never wrote her autobiography, to be called *Interlude in Attica*.

After an adventurous life, she finally settled into a squalid and near-penniless existence with a circle of old-age pensioners on the south coast of England. She died, shortly after the taped interview was made, in the fall of 1975.

Despite her brief appearance in Fitzgerald's life, Bijou was more important to Scott than he was to her. Though he reacted against her arrogant attitude and reckless way of life, and satirised her in his fiction, he desperately needed her companionship and enjoyed her wit and charm. Fitzgerald was one of Bijou's more interesting lovers. She recognised herself in his works, made him the subject of her own amusing stories and survived to have the last word about their affair.

IV Jane Mason (1909–1981)

Ernest Hemingway condemned Zelda for interfering with Fitzgerald's writing. Yet I discovered that he, too, had been in love with an attractive and volatile woman. I always visit places where my subject has lived, and was duly impressed by Hemingway's home in Key West, at the tip of the Florida Keys, which had a catwalk from the main house to his separate study. It was set in a superb tropical garden, with a pool and tennis court. He lived there with his second wife, Pauline, and two young sons, and it seemed a perfect place to live and work. I wondered why he was always crossing to Havana to 'write' in the Ambos Mundos Hotel.

In those far-off days, when crossing the Atlantic was a pleasure trip, Hemingway sailed to New York on the *Ile de France* in September 1931 with a pregnant Pauline and met Jane and Grant Mason. At 22, Jane was as stunning as Grace Kelly, as sexy as Hemingway's heroine Duff Twysden and as wild as Zelda Fitzgerald. A tall woman with an athletic figure, she wore her smooth strawberry-blond hair parted in the middle. She had classic, delicate features, large blue eyes, a fresh complexion and a bearing that suggested refinement and distinction. Vivacious and amusing, Jane was a hard drinker, a daring driver and a crack pigeon shot, perfectly at home in the exclusive company of men. She was also high-strung and temperamental, moody and emotionally unstable. Though Jane had apparently amiable relations with her husband, she was bored with his stolid personality and looked for sexual adventures. Grant worked very hard and travelled frequently; he neglected Jane, could not control her and left her free to behave as she wished.

Suspecting that Jane had been Hemingway's lover, I set out to trace her. Her fourth husband, the late Arnold Gingrich, had been Hemingway's editor at *Esquire*, but the magazine could not help me. After following a false lead and calling everyone named Mason in Bergen County, New Jersey, I finally found out that Jane had died in 1981 and that her son Antony lived in Tuxedo Park, a wealthy suburb north of New York City. During a weekend at Antony's house, he helped me reconstruct Jane's early life. Her mother, Betty Lee, was a singer from Syracuse, New York. Jane was born Jane Welsh in 1909, grew up on an estate in Tuxedo Park, and adopted the name of Kendall when her mother remarried. Educated at Briarcliff, a school for socialites, and in Europe, she had two debuts in Washington in 1926. The following year she married Grant Mason, a tall, good-looking, well-born but unassertive graduate of St Paul's School and Yale University. Grant, a founder and Caribbean manager of Pan American Airways, was heir to a great fortune.

At the time they knew Hemingway, the Masons lived in splendour at Jaimanitas, 30 minutes west of Havana, had nine servants including an English governess, owned a large yacht and gave lavish parties. They adopted two young English boys in the early 1930s, but Jane was an erratic and irresponsible mother and let the servants take care of her children, who resented her neglect. I looked at Jane's photographs, scrapbooks and clippings, and saw home movies of Jane and Hemingway on his boat, the *Pilar*. Jane's date book for the summer of 1934 recorded that when Grant went on a business trip to Venezuela, she spent every day swimming, fishing, lunching and dining with Hemingway. He later bragged that Jane liked to climb through his hotel room window for their rendezvous.

Hemingway blamed the subsequent failure of his marriage to Pauline on their sexual problems. After her second Caesarean birth, her doctor thought it would be dangerous to have another child, Pauline would not allow birth control and Hemingway was forced to practice coitus interruptus. Pauline later confessed, 'If I hadn't been such a bloody fool practicing Catholic, I wouldn't have lost my husband'. With Jane, who was unable to conceive and had adopted two children, there was no fear of pregnancy or need for birth control. Pauline felt extremely threatened by Jane, who was 14 years younger, came from a socially prominent family and was far more athletic, exciting, beautiful, talented and wealthy.

Jane's son Antony told me that she was accident-prone and often unwell, that in the course of her life 'she broke every bone in her body and had every conceivable illness'. The ironic inscription she wrote for her own tombstone read, 'Talents too many, not enough of any'. In May 1933, driving her large Packard with Antony and two of Hemingway's sons, Jane was forced off the road and tumbled down a steep embankment. The boys were unhurt, but she was severely bruised and became desperately depressed. A week later, in an apparent suicide attempt, she jumped from the second-storey balcony of her house outside Havana. Grant Mason callously described the tragic incident as a play for sympathy and remarked, 'in case she tried another such stunt I arranged for constant nurse attendance and then shipped her to New York on a Ward Line vessel with special bars on the portholes'. Hemingway, more sympathetic, said Jane was a damned beautiful woman and it was no fun to break one's back at the age of 24. In May 1934, when Hemingway returned from his first African safari and acquired his fishing boat—both expensive presents from Pauline to bind him to her—he sailed alone to Cuba to spend July through October with Jane.

While in New York, Jane began extended psychoanalytic treatment with Dr Lawrence Kubie. In 1934, Kubie was commissioned by the editor of the *Saturday Review of Literature* to write a psychoanalytic interpretation of Hemingway's work. Eager for a sensational coup, Kubie didn't seem to realise that it would be unethical for him to write such a piece. Hemingway was outraged by Jane's revelations of their intimate talks and sexual life and naturally hostile to the doctor's public analysis of his psychological conflicts. He alerted his lawyers, sent a ferocious note to Kubie warning that he could not libel an author with impunity and suppressed the damaging article. I wanted to find it. After searching through Kubie's collected works, I contacted one of his colleagues who put me in touch with the doctor's daughter. She kindly gave me copies of the article as well as his correspondence with the *Saturday Review* and his lawyers, with Hemingway and his publisher Charles Scribner. She also gave me permission to publish it, with an introduction, in the spring 1984 issue of the psychoanalytic journal *American Imago*.

In the summer of 1935 when Jane returned from *her* hunting expedition in East Africa, where she had an affair with Hemingway's dashing friend Colonel Richard Cooper, Hemingway invited her to go fishing with him in Bimini. He found it difficult to break with her completely and their separations made him all the more keen to see her again. He saw Jane frequently while writing his great African story 'The Short Happy Life of Francis Macomber' (1936). When he spoke of sailing the *Pilar* from Key West to Cuba, Jane volunteered to cross the Straits with him.

Hemingway had a violent and bitter break with Jane in April 1936. She may have said or done something to antagonise him; they may have had an awkward sexual encounter; she may have rejected him for Richard Cooper, who was fishing with her in Bimini; Pauline may have put pressure on him to return to married life in Key West. One friend noted, 'The air's all charged up because Hemingway's been caught playing hanky-panky and Pauline comes rushing over to Havana to protect her interests. They probably had a terrible fight over that woman'.

Hemingway's quarrel with Jane led directly to his satiric portrayal of her as Margot Macomber, a beautiful but bitchy woman who goes on safari in Africa, sleeps with the white hunter and shoots her husband. Hemingway describes Margot as:

> an extremely handsome and well-kept woman of the beauty and social position

> which had, five years before, commanded five thousand dollars as the price of endorsing, with photographs, a beauty product which she had never used … She had a very perfect oval face, so perfect that you expected her to be stupid. But she wasn't stupid.

When Margot torments her husband after he's run away from a charging lion, the white hunter thinks that wealthy American women like Margot are 'the hardest in the world; the hardest, the cruellest, the most predatory and the most attractive and their men have softened or gone to pieces nervously as they have hardened'. Hemingway recalled that Jane, ignoring the condemnation of her character, was 'flattered when people took her for Mrs. Macomber'.

Hemingway's portrayal of Jane and Grant Mason as Helene and Tommy Bradley in *To Have and Have Not*, published a year later in 1937, was even more hostile. In the novel, Bradley opens the door of his bedroom and observes Helene and the hero Richard Gordon making love. When the distracted Gordon turns around to look at Bradley, Helene, with a desperate desire for sexual satisfaction, exclaims, 'Don't mind him. Don't mind anything. Don't you see you can't stop now?' And when Gordon is unable to continue after this fictional coitus interruptus, she says, 'Haven't you any regard for a woman?' and slaps him twice across the face. Helene's bizarre behaviour helps to explain the end of Hemingway's affair with Jane.

Though Jane dazzled Hemingway and inspired one of his greatest stories, he did not have the means to satisfy her luxurious tastes, disliked her emotional mood swings and never seriously thought of marrying her. She was exactly the sort of dangerous woman—beautiful, elegant, rich, sporty and daring—that both attracted and frightened him.

V Kay Morrison (1898–1989)

My last example of an unknown relationship in a writer's life had been hidden in plain sight for years. As an undergraduate at the University of Michigan, I had seen Robert Frost, vigorous and handsome at the age of 84, give an impressive reading of his poems. His wife Elinor had died when he was 65, and I didn't think the energetic and attractive Frost would have been ready at that time to abandon his sex life. After Elinor's death, he had published some lyrical love poems, and the received view was that he continued to write about his late wife. But I wondered if there was someone else at the centre of his emotional and sexual life during his last 25 years.

The most likely candidate was Kay Morrison, the wife of Ted Morrison, a tenured lecturer in the Harvard English department. Kay was Frost's secretary and manager when he taught at colleges in New England and went on lecture tours. My suspicions were confirmed at the University of Virginia when I read the papers of Lawrance Thompson, Frost's authorised biographer, whose deletions were far more interesting than his published book. Apparently unglamorous and efficient, in her plaid skirts and wool sweaters, Kay had a varied and reckless sexual life, made possible by a complaisant husband and a prim social code.

I found out about Kay's early life from her sister, her daughter and her college archives. Born in Nova Scotia in 1898 and 24 years younger than Frost, she was the daughter of a clergyman, grew up in Scotland and graduated from Bryn Mawr College in Pennsylvania. Frost's devoted mistress, astringent amanuensis and affectionate muse was refined and stylish, with a slight build and bright auburn hair. After his wife's death, Frost exaggerated his helplessness, Kay's maternal quality and his own rejuvenation:

> I owe everything in the world to her. She found me in the gutter, hopeless, sick, run down. She bundled me up and carted me to her home and cared for me like a child, a sick child. Without her I would today be in my grave.

Intensely puritanical but with a strong sexual impulse, Frost—like Conrad—dreaded a public scandal. He was astonished that Kay, who behaved so conventionally, could be so wild sexually and felt, 'Here's a lady who's willing, why not let go?' He talked brilliantly to Kay, describing his family tragedies, the illnesses, deaths and suicides, and he loved her that she did pity them. One day, walking in the woods, they came to a place that Frost thought sufficiently secluded 'for either rape or murder'. As they sat on the warm earth and continued their intimate talk, Frost began to make love to her. All he had to do was take off her drawers and consummate the urge that seemed mutual. But Kay brought out the cruel as well as the tender side of his character. For many years, he punished her—quite irrationally—with harsh criticism and unreasonable demands, for sleeping with him, for taking his wife's place, for refusing to marry him and for the guilt he felt about betraying her husband.

Frost's relations with Kay were complicated by her surprising involvement—like Jane Anderson's—with at least three other men who were close to him. Stafford Dragon (whose very name is irresistible), the hired man on Frost's Vermont farm, played the lusty Mellors to Kay's Lady Chatterley. She was also involved with Ted's 'best friend', the porcine *littérateur* Bernard De Voto. The Virginia papers revealed that the 'incredibly attractive' Lawrance Thompson, on the scene and eight years younger than Kay, was Frost's sexual rival. In an extraordinary and volatile situation, he was also sleeping with the apparently strait-laced but wildly promiscuous Kay. Thompson's liaison with Kay allowed him to participate in and even change the course of the life he was writing, and he often replaced her as Frost's companion, keeper, nurse and body-servant.

I was able to confirm all this when I interviewed Kay's daughter, Anne Morrison Smyth, at her home in Amherst, Massachusetts. As Anne led me into the living room, she startled me by saying, 'I've been waiting all my life for you to come'. At last, she felt, someone at work on Frost had read the unpublished papers and knew the basic facts. She was now free to tell her part of the story. Anne remembered many journeys from Cambridge, Massachusetts, up to Frost's farm in Vermont. The 12-year-old girl would watch from the back of the car as Ted drove, staring rigidly ahead, while Frost had his amiable arm around Kay, who sat between them and leaned on his shoulder. When our long and emotionally charged interview was over, Anne exclaimed, 'I knew this would all come out some day!'

Ted worshipped Frost, tolerated the affair as long as it was kept secret and there was no scandal, and managed to suppress his volatile mixture of resignation and rage. These New England puritans had been brought up to keep up appearances, maintain superficial propriety and preserve the husband's precarious dignity—no matter what passions thrashed beneath the surface. The suppression of emotions, the preservation of decorum, the denial of intolerable reality were all reminiscent of Henry James. When I suggested this interpretation to Anne, she said she'd spent years immersed in James's novels, especially *What Maisie Knew*, about an innocent child in a treacherous world. But she had never quite understood, until that moment, why she had been so strongly attracted to them. Apart from Anne, none of the two dozen friends of Frost whom I spoke to about Kay realised that she had been Frost's lover. They were deceived by the calm surface and seemed quite surprised when I told them about it. The poet Richard Wilbur recalled that Kay 'told me once that there had never been an "affair" between her and Robert, and I believed her. When Frost "let on" to the contrary, as he sometimes did, I thought it was an old man's vanity talking'.

Frost wrote Kay about 500 letters, but she destroyed most of them and only 19 fragments have survived. In his letters and poems, he struggled between concealment and revelation. Frost wanted Thompson to tell the full story of his relations with Kay, but the biographer died in 1973. When his third volume was completed by another writer, Kay and Ted, still very much alive, excised all traces of her intimacy with Frost.

My startling discoveries completely changed the traditional view of Frost's public persona as a homespun rustic and celibate sage, and revealed the sexual themes in *The Witness Tree* (1942), the first volume to appear after he began his liaison with Kay. This book featured sexual imagery that had rarely been noted before: orgasmic waterfalls and powerful bucks crashing through the underbrush in *The Most of It.* Frost's love poem *The Silken Tent* describes with the greatest possible delicacy the conflict between Kay's bondage and freedom as she is pulled loosely by Ted in marriage and tightly by Frost in love:

> And its supporting central cedar pole ...
> Seems to owe naught to any single cord,
> But strictly held by none, is loosely bound
> By countless silken ties of love and thought.

Kay was ecstatic about this tribute, and agreed that this poem described the two men and two ties of love that pulled her in different directions.

After my book was published, I received a gratifying letter from Kay's former son-in-law, whom Anne did not want me to meet. He said,

> I was on the scene, and I was there with Ted and with Kay, the husband and wife, and I was there with Robert Frost, and I was watching it every day, and I knew something was going on, and I never understood until I read your book what was actually happening.

Kay Morrison, an unconventional and seductive married woman, stayed with the widowed Frost till the end. Frost spoke for all five authors in this essay when he observed with characteristic wit, 'If I had a beautiful studio, I'd never paint. I'd have ladies visiting. Might as well be candid'.

All these women were attractive, even stunning. All were talented, unconventional, rebellious and sexually promiscuous. Three of them successfully competed with men and had distinguished careers: Anderson as a writer and war correspondent; Barry as a film critic and archivist; O'Conor as a linguist in the war office. Anderson and Barry divorced their husbands, O'Conor was widowed, Mason and Morrison remained married. Anderson and Morrison not only slept with the author, but also with his close friends. The first four women broke with their lovers; only Morrison stayed with the writer till the end of his life. The high-strung Anderson, O'Conor and Mason had nervous breakdowns and ended badly. All five extraordinary women were not only lovers, but also muses who inspired important works of literature and art: *The Arrow of Gold*, the painting *Praxitella*, *Tender Is the Night*, 'The Short Happy Life of Francis Macomber' and *The Witness Tree.*

The Informed Imagination

Drusilla Modjeska
2013

In July 2009, two artists from Ömie, high on the slopes of Mt Lamington in Papua New Guinea, were in Sydney for an exhibition of their barkcloth art. Early in their visit, their sponsor David Baker, the then director of the now-closed New Guinea Gallery, drove them and me, and Alban Sare, the Ömie man who'd come down with them, to a shopping mall to buy shoes and warm clothes. To Alban, who'd been to Sydney before and had spent time in Port Moresby, the mall was not so strange—just larger and shinier; he liked it. For Pauline Rose Hago, the younger of the two artists, familiar only with the town of Popondetta on the plain below Ömie, the cars in the carpark were enough to give her a headache. But Dapene Jonevari, a senior artist and a *duvahe*—rather inaccurately translated as chief—went into a state of shock when bad spirits congregating on the escalators stole all her strength. I do not tell this as a comic story. I mightn't believe in bad spirits on escalators, or not entirely, but I don't doubt that Dapene, one of the strongest women I have encountered here or in PNG, was assaulted by the force of a world of which she'd never seen the like. What nature of beings were the 'new people' she'd seen often enough down on the plain, and of whom she'd heard stories, though none to prepare her for this?

Back at my house later that day, Dapene was still limp, her expression glazed. Two cups of strong sugary tea didn't seem to help. I looked to Pauline for guidance—as I had when I was in Ömie. She had been alongside me on every path, in every village, in the forests where Dapene led the women to cut the trees for their bast, in the houses where the women paint, in the rivers where we washed. Always Pauline; certain, strong-voiced Pauline. And here we were, in my place, in my house, and I was asking her for help.

'Where is your ground?' she asked.

Where indeed?

At the oval at the end of my street, they poked at the hard earth with toes in new shoes. Yes, they supposed it was ground, of a sort.

Your gardens? Pauline asked. They are where?

In the cities we have no gardens; we have shops, I said, and Pauline translated for Dapene; a murmur, all I had to interpret was tone.

We walked along the edge of the inner harbour to a park on the next bay, and as we walked Dapene regained something of her stature; by the time we returned to the oval, she and Pauline were singing Ömie songs. It was dusk, joggers were jogging past, the lights were coming on, as they sang to a rhythm I'd heard every day of my stay in Ömie.

Back at my house, they wanted to sleep—while in the kitchen I brooded on Pauline's question, and my inability to protect them here, as they had me when I was on their ground. When they came downstairs for dinner—sweet potato and pork that didn't convince them as pig—Dapene's strength had returned. Pauline took my hand and leaned into my shoulder. Sister friend, she said, the name she'd called me in Ömie.

Sister friend. It was a kindness, and I liked it, but in truth, was I, am I, sister and friend?

These were not academic questions. I was in the depths of yet another draft of *The Mountain* at the time, struggling with the post-colonial complexities of how to write as a white outsider of a country I first encountered in 1968 when I was 21 years old. After Dapene and Pauline returned to their mountain, I returned to my desk with Pauline's question reverberating in me. Where was our ground: ours in the sense of a highly asphalted world, and ungrounded culture? Where was my ground? Mine in the sense of the book I'd waited a long time to write, knowing it would be hard, knowing I'd need experience as a writer, and yet here I was with two decades of publishing under my feet (so to speak) and I was as uncertain as I had ever been. More, probably, because, unlike at the start—as many a writer has lamented—there was none of that magical innocence that can carry one through a predicament before you know enough to know you're in one.

The ground I thought I had for the book that was not yet *The Mountain* was an approach to the writing of lives that had begun with *Poppy*, a 'biography' of my mother. It had been there that I'd found a voice that felt authentically my own, and during the 1990s I had became an advocate for the first person singular—the 'I', and the 'eye'—as a way of uncovering, or re-covering occluded feminine experience. With *Stravinsky's Lunch*, I articulated this use of the first person as a 'method', if that's the word, that could draw together the imagined and the informed in the lives of two women artists. It was by bringing the imagining self to the gaps in the record that the writing self could reclaim the overlooked and under-recorded lives of women. Imagination—and fictive methods—could thereby meld with the biographical and autobiographical to give shape to lives for whom the record was fractured and uncertain. The 'informed imagination' of the first person had become, in a sense, the ground of my writing and I took it unquestioned into writing about PNG.

In this lecture, I am going to talk about why that ground proved unstable, and why in writing *The Mountain* I came to reconsider the meanings of the informed imagination. So I hope I haven't lured you here under false pretences, for under the rubric of the biography lecture I am going to ponder my recalibration of that borderline ground, my journey into the land of fiction. I still consider myself a writer of lives, but to write of lives in that particular place required a different form of biographical knowledge.

1.

I will start by taking you to Ömie in March 2004. The barkcloth artists of Ömie are now recognised, in the words of Nicholas Thomas, as 'the most brilliant living exponents' of a 'great world art tradition' that once stretched across the Pacific from New Guinea to Hawai'i. But in 2004, the Ömie, a small group of less than 2,000 people, were impoverished and demoralised; only the oldest women were still painting. I was there with David Baker, who had been shown their art and invited by a small group of young men who wanted to start a business that would bring status and pride, as well as cash, to this marginalised group. David Baker was there not as a small gallery owner, but as a sponsor, or potential sponsor, for he recognised that this was art that should be in major gallery collections. I was there—apart from my own interest (which was considerable)—to write of what turned out to be a critical visit. This I did in a catalogue essay for *The Wisdom of the Mountain*, the exhibition of Ömie barkcloth art at the National Gallery of Victoria that opened in November 2009, four months after Dapene and Pauline's visit to Sydney. By then Ömie Artists was a community business registered in PNG, money was returning to Ömie from sales of their art, including to most of the major state galleries in Australia.

In the catalogue, I described the long, steep walk up to Ömie: the ridges, the forests, the gateways to the villages. I described the day I sat with my notebook while David Baker met in a formal meeting with the *duvahe*. I wrote of the tension between the responsibility felt by the *duvahe* to safeguard their traditions, and the community's need for money—for school fees, for lamps, tarpaulins and nails, maybe even a tin roof and a tank. I wrote of sitting with the women *duvahe*, Dapene among them, as they spoke of the young women who no longer saw the value of learning the exacting art of the cloth, of young men who needed purpose if they weren't to drift into town and find trouble. Even through the processes of translation, I could understand that well enough. And I knew very well the onerous responsibility faced by David Baker. Did he do nothing, in which case the young men would try selling the cloth to tourists on the Kokoda Track, and if that failed, would the art of this exceptional but marginalised group fade away as the art of so many neighbouring groups had done? Or did he step in as sponsor, another white 'saviour'—there's a long history to that particular trope. Could he/we avoid the sorry path too often trod by good intentions? Could we safeguard the art, and the interests of the Ömie? Or was that, too, part of the whiteman fantasy?

A lot was at issue, and at risk, for the Ömie, for us outsiders, and—as it turned out—not only for the Ömie of the high villages who had maintained their art, but also for the Ömie lower down the mountain, who'd given up their cultural practices, including their art. Was this how they were to be rewarded for their move to the missions? We hadn't even left the last village when trouble showed itself. Naivety and good intentions walked us slap into a 'shake down', a demand for money in the form of an arrest that stretched over two days.

Good material, you might say. An excellent predicament for someone wanting to give a lived shape to a post-colonial experience. But apart from the fact that I had undertaken to David not to write about the details of the shake down—at least not then, and not in the book I was ostensibly writing—had I tried to write of these events by using my usual approach, was my imagination sufficiently informed to write of what all this had meant to the Ömie, to the *duvahe*, to the young men, indeed to those who felt slighted and aggrieved? The answer, obviously, was no. To write of it only from our perspective, would I not be falling into the worst trap of outsider writing about PNG: placing myself, or 'us' the white outsiders, in the centre of the frame? I'd read enough colonial memoir and fiction, to know the dangers of that trope: the white adventurers deep in the interior of Papua, suddenly endangered, rescued by their own resourcefulness, and the good office of locals who take their side to defeat, or outwit, angry tribesmen. It wouldn't take much of a twist to have a story straight out of the NSW Bookstall melodramas and romances of the 1920s and 1930s that were among the first to commercialise the uninformed imaginations of Australian writers and their readers. Colonial memoir and fiction cast a long shadow.

In a catalogue essay I could distance myself—the narrating 'I'—to a role of observer, reporting on the varying points of tension as the question of the cloth leaving the mountain was debated: every meeting, every conversation recorded in my notebook as it was translated from Ömie to Tok Pisin to English. An inadequate research method, an anthropologist would say, but adequately observed, I hoped, to the task of reporting the decision—if decision is the word—that brought the cloth to the National Gallery of Victoria five years later.

Were I to have attempted an (auto)biographical account of that visit to Ömie, it could have had a lot to say about the post-colonial complexities faced by David Baker and me—and by the other Australian who was there with us and felt that David was making the wrong move, and subsequently withdrew. With the barkcloth carrying esoteric meanings for the Ömie, could its integrity survive sale and the temptation of commercialisation? A question to which—as with more or less everything in this story—there was no one, clear answer. An anthropologist, or a philosopher might make something of it, but I was neither. Even if I steered off dangerously personal terrain, the same question arose: how could 'our' story be told without the view from the Ömie becoming ever more occluded? What did these great changes mean for them? How, on the basis of a month's visit, was I to represent that without appropriating, or projecting, or sentimentalising, or mistranslating the un-translatable?

The problem, I hope you are beginning to see, was the inequality between the white narrator and the post-colonial subject.

2.

The first intimation that I was moving towards fiction came with the character of Milton, the young Papuan writer who appeared on the page with a raised fist and a gift for language. He took me by surprise. He arrived unheralded and sat uncomfortably with the imagining 'I' that was trying to wrest some control over the mess on my desk. I mightn't have expected him, or known what to do with him, but I knew exactly where he came from: those early years at the University of Papua New Guinea back before Independence, when, in the words of the great Samoan writer Albert Wendt, indigenous writing across the Pacific began, and 'gained its first euphoric power and *mana* alongside the movements for political independence'.[1]

I had the good fortune to arrive there with my young anthropologist husband in 1968 as this surge of creative energy was beginning. While Nick tutored, I enrolled in classes with young men—mostly men—who knew that theirs would be the generation that would take this complex country of many languages into nationhood. For someone not long out of an English girls' boarding school, that was extraordinary enough. More significantly, I found myself in classes with students who were writing. They were writing plays in which plantation labourers rose up, and Papuan girls ran from the altar of white betterment; poems in which copra workers threw down their sacks and *kanakas* spoke back; short stories that lampooned missionaries and traders; and essays in the student newspaper that called administrators and colonists to account.

As a writer of lives, that was what I wanted to write about.

It may be in the nature of memory for experiences that come to us when we are very young and not yet equipped to interrogate them remain the most vivid. It is, I think, for this reason that Milton arrived on the page so readily. He is a student when we first meet him. A play he's written is about to be performed at the university. Rika, the young white character onto whom I could split some aspect of my learning and unlearning—though not my autobiography—takes her camera to rehearsals. 'Publicity shots', they called them, a grand term for a play to be put on in the canteen, but why not? When the *South Pacific Post* censors the photos, she and Milton stand firm together. The old-timer whites might call the university a Mau Mau factory, and condemn girls like Rika as traitors to their race. But right then, at that moment, Rika and Milton are united in the belief that the radical changes that were coming—literature for him, love for her—would eliminate prejudice, even render them the same people under the skin. There would be painful reckonings to come, for them as characters, and for me, writing, trying to write the lives of those who lived through that time of hope and optimism.

Over my desk, I pinned these words from Albert Wendt: 'The post in post-colonial does not just mean after; it also means around, through, out of, alongside and against'.[2]

Looking back, and speaking personally, those years in PNG from 1968–1971 changed almost everything about the my life—and lived on in me as a core to the book I was to begin 30 years later. The impulse was frankly autobiographical—vanity I admit—though it was also more, for there was something about that country and that time that had entered my blood and I wanted—vanity again—to bring PNG back into 'our' imaginative consciousness. For over the decades between the cultural surge of those years leading into political independence and the century's end, it seemed to have seeped from fictional view. Once, Australian journalists had flown up to investigate Black writing; Australian publishers had published writers from there, as well as from here. Randolph Stowe's *Visitants* and Trevor Shearston's *Something in the Blood* were both published in 1979, when 'alongside' could join with 'against'. Even these novels, have fallen from our collective memory. While more and more sophisticated work came from the pens of anthropologists and historians, fiction seemed to revert to old ways of seeing. Well into this new century, the pygmy and the naked tribesman still make their appearance, and Highland girls, though no longer dressed in grass skirts, are as prey to the fantasies of young white men as were the fictional girls of nearly a century ago. This despite the great post-colonial novels of world literature. A weird disjuncture between the acute awareness of academia, and the remarkable obliviousness—it seemed to me—among our few novelists who ventured into PNG territory, sometimes without even going there, or, if they'd been there before, without returning. When a reason was given, it was that it was 'too dangerous'; or the wish to leave the imagination unencumbered, as if there was something about Papua New Guinea that, despite everything that had happened, could still offer a blank canvas to the outsider writer.

Hadn't Beatrice Grimshaw complained 80 years ago or more, of Australian journalists who came to Port Moresby, found a 'cannibal queen' within a mile of Government house, exchanged her story for a twist of tobacco, and caught the next boat home?

The persistence of the uninformed Australian imagination might have surprised me, but it didn't surprise Regis Stella, the writer and critic teaching in the literature department of UPNG in the 2000s. When I went through Moresby, I'd see him and his colleagues, Russell Soaba and Steven Winduo. At first, on my returns, our conversations were not always easy. Regis Stella, a stern critic, was suspicious—and why would he not be—of this white woman reappearing after so many years, with all the resources of an Australian research grant, wanting to write about a time that had formed her, while they struggled with meagre resources to produce a literary magazine and publish small anthologies with no grants, no publishing industry, few bookshops. Regis Stella was writing *Imagining the Other* then—it was published in 2007, just five years before he died, much too young, at the beginning of 2012. In it, he argued that the first task of the post-colonial indigenous writer was to understand and refuse the projections that have accumulated over the history not only of colonial but also—too often—of post-colonial biography, fiction and memoir. It was a distorting lens through which Papua New Guineans had come to see themselves, a distorting lens that perpetuated the misconceptions of others. He was not about to let me forget that 'we' outsider writers too often place ourselves as the point of reference to the known, unquestioning modern, leaving the equally unquestioned residues of the unknown and unknowable non-modern to the Papua New Guinean—especially those living in villages, or other situations 'we' do not recognise as modern. The uninformed imagination was a habit of mind, Regis pointed out, that was not confined to Australia's writers.

He and Steve Winduo were part of the tiny group of second-generation writers; if anyone knows it's tough, they do. PNG 'has forgotten its early writers', Winduo has written in a recent essay.[3] Those one-time student writers of the late 1960s and early 1970s had moved on to bigger and better things and, once in government, literature was not among their priorities. Perhaps they remembered how those student plays could be used 'against'. Writing and publishing was not an easy path in the years after Independence, and certainly not profitable. Which was why, to Regis and Steven and Russell, it was all the more important that the flame be kept alive. A flame against the corruptions and inequities we hear a great deal about; a flame around, through and out from the hard work and successes we don't hear about: the conservation workers and environmental lawyers; the children's libraries and water collection projects; the work that is containing the spread of HIV.

There was a role, I could see, for 'alongside', and it's not as if there wasn't rich material. But I was stuck somewhere between the failings of a method that had once served me well, and the daunting land of fiction I was creeping towards. It's a rigorous form, the novel, far from easy, and there are those who question the relevance for the Pacific of a European form in which Western ideas of subjectivity are deeply imbricated. Regis Stella preferred the short story and the polemic as better suited to Melanesian forms of oral story telling and rhetoric. But Steve Winduo, who has just this year finished a novel, was far from pessimistic. For him, the novel is a flexible form, with its own language; look what they've done with it in Africa, in South America, in Samoa. Why shouldn't the novel make the transition into Melanesia; isn't it part of the inheritance of world literature? Hadn't I heard of hybridity, the shifts in literary form, he'd say when my anxieties showed. And besides, he'd say, look at Russell Soaba, who'd be sitting there, inscrutable and benign, the one writer from those early days who has written his way through the intervening years, and is writing still. I salute him. His novels *Wanpis* and *Maiba*, two great post-Independence works of fictive life-writing, should be on every post-colonial literature course in this country, but they are not even published here. Steven Winduo and Regis Stella, fine writers both, have published out of Hawai'i or the University of the South Pacific. Or they publish themselves. Australian publishers have long since lost interest in writing from PNG. It doesn't sell, my publisher told me when I told her I wanted to write the book that would become *The Mountain.*

'Russell Soaba often reminds me,' Winduo says, 'that the life of a Papua New Guinean writer is a difficult one because the society itself is a difficult one'.

Shame added to the white baggage that sat with me at my desk.

By the time Dapene and Pauline visited Sydney in 2009, all I had was a shaky draft of a book without a title that was still teetering somewhere between an insistence that was autobiographical and a hope that was not yet fiction.

My strategy had been to create characters from the stories I knew, blending and amalgamating and inventing as one can't in memoir, or biography. I also fictionalised myself, if that's the right way of putting it, distancing the narrating 'I' onto a character 20 years my senior, a narrative intelligence I thought I could use to tell the story, letting her be the one to comment on the characters of my generation and the vexed politics of post-colonialism. What I was doing with this book didn't, then, strike me as so different from anything else I'd written. As a writer of lives, hadn't I always worked in that contested zone between the fictive, the autobiographical and the biographical? Was I not still exploring that rubbing point between the personal and the political, the small experience of lived lives and the washing tides of history? All that was different, I thought, was that this time I was coming at it with characters who were semi-fictional, whereas before I'd come from the other side, so to speak, with characters who had left a paper trail, however fractured or incomplete.

'It's not working,' I was told. 'You can't shift it all onto a narrator 20 years older. She sounds like you're trying not to be you.'

Around, through, out of, alongside and against. I was nowhere near, trapped in the outer reaches of my own vanities.

3.

Philip Roth, a writer I admire, has said that it can take a crisis for a work to find its shape.[4] For me with *The Mountain* that crisis began with Pauline's question: where is your ground? Then, four months later, in November 2009, within days of the Ömie exhibition opening at the National Gallery of Victoria, their sponsor David Baker died suddenly—by which I mean overnight, without warning. As a result, his sponsorship of the Ömie ended, and students whose fees he was paying, not only there but across PNG, could no longer continue at school.[5] This, to say the least, added to the destabilisation of my own sense of ground and changed a great deal about the way I continued my own relationships in PNG. Never again would I be the observer who could watch, make notes with her clean, writerly hands, then go home and fret about how to write it. What was going to happen to Ömie Artists? That alone was a big enough question. Three people came down from Ömie for the opening, and none had been further than Popondetta before. What had caused this disaster? Had bad spirits entered into him, or into them? There was dispute, as well as dismay, in their villages.

And in the fjords of Cape Nelson, where I had visited with David Baker, what would happen to the coastal villages where they done so much to move between the 'old' and the 'new'. What would happen if they could no longer get their students past year 8—when the fees are too high for village families—with the loggers already nearby, in Collingwood Bay? I could speak for an hour about what was involved in all these questions, and what I learned of the politics of Aid and Development—and of the logging, much of it illegal, which now affects over five million hectares of customary land. I had spent time with an elder at Uiaku, in Collingwood Bay, where the land-owners had won a long court case against the loggers, only to have them return in another guise. I've been back to the area since, and I know the cost, in every sense of that word, to that man, to that community.

It was not only in the villages that my relationships changed. In Port Moresby, the talk with my writer colleagues also changed as I struggled with these non-writerly questions. Russell Soaba and Steven Winduo and Regis Stella were wise interlocutors, and I thank them for it, and for the comradeship that grew between us. There was the practical help, introductions to environmental lawyers and educationalists, which I will not elaborate here other than to say Ömie Artists continues in renewed form. As to the book I was struggling with, the message I took from them was write it. Every voice is needed. This time, when I wanted to say but how, another voice in me said get over yourself. 'Hybridity', Steve said again, 'Aren't we all, in our different ways, existential *hapkas*?', and though at first I was reluctant to use it, he gave me the word from Tok Pisin which has shrugged off the negative connotations of half-caste to embrace complex cultural identities—and forms of writing.

And all the while, there was Russell Soaba still writing, producing a blog, teaching students that their stories, and the stories of their place, and of events they see around them, matter.

Witness was the word Regis Stella used, and I came to see it applied—in some small measure—to me as well as to the writers there whom he was addressing.

When Janet Malcolm, another writer I admire, faced a crisis of a very different kind in her writing life, she said that it took her 'out of a sheltered place and threw (her) into bracingly icy water. What more could a writer want?'[6] Icy is hardly the word for anything to do with PNG, and no writer would want a disturbance caused by the death of a friend. But she has a point.

I finally returned to my desk sometime in the Australian winter of 2010 with very different mental settings. The memories to which my vanities had been in thrall, slid back; I stopped looking for signs of the past. The present had claimed me. The post-colonial policeman who'd been standing duty over my desk vanished; I didn't have to batter him as Virginia Woolf had the obstructive Angel in her House. I was angry, and bruised, and no longer afraid. The effect was indeed bracing. I sat down and rewrote the manuscript that was not yet called *The Mountain* in the third person. Martha, no longer narrator, lost a lot of her story, most of her point of view, dropped in age by 20 years and became a character in the ensemble of characters who at last had room to stretch and breathe—to look at each other, and look back. Ensemble, that was the word that came to me: they, all of them, not me, not 'I'. Milton sighed a sigh of relief.

As to the result, well, it's out there in the world, and though I probably know its faults and failures better than anyone, it's not my job to lay them out, nor, indeed, to consider its virtues, if virtues there are. What I will say is that out of that period of radical doubt, the ground of my writing changed. *The Mountain* gives voice to the predicaments underlying all I'd experienced, and seen, and known in that magnificent, heartbreaking country. It is as personal as anything I have written since *Poppy*, but it is not autobiographical. The lives of people I have known may hover above it, but it is not biographical. With *The Mountain*, I crossed the borderline from a biographical form that might be called literary non-fiction, into the strange and mysterious world of fiction. At some profound level, the process remains mysterious to me, and I don't know how I did it. When I say 'mysterious', I mean it. It is not belittling the intellectual work of fiction to say that it may be that it needs to be written from the corner of the eye. What I can do, in conclusion, is to tell you, looking back, what I have learned about the 'informed imagination' and why my old methods failed me.

4.

Fiction writers often talk of empathy as the task, even the technique of fiction. Hilary Mantel talks of getting behind her character's eyes, and every writer will know what she means. As I say, it's what I had tried to do through the 'informed imagination' of the narrating self in my previous books. But Mantel also warns that we cannot proceed on the assumption that historical characters—in her case—are like 'us'; we can't hop behind the eyes of those who lived in profoundly different times and look out with 'our' eyes. Somehow the eyes we have to get behind must be theirs: and that's the paradox. We must do what is not possible.

It was this point—on the limits of the empathic imagination—which Inga Clendinnen took up in her 2006 *Quarterly Essay*, 'The History Question'. Triggered by the debate over Kate Grenville's *The Secret River*, she notes that Grenville did not attempt to enter the minds of her Indigenous characters for a number of good reasons, including that there's been 'enough appropriation already', and because she, Grenville, recognised it as an empathic move she was unable to make. Clendinnen has no quarrel with this. What she questions is that Grenville saw no impediment to imagining herself into the minds and experiences of settlers on the Hawkesbury. For Kate Grenville, as a novelist, the question to ask was, 'What would I have done in that situation, and what sort of a person would that make me?' Clendinnen, as a historian, counters that 'we' people born of modernity cannot imagine ourselves back even 200 years, when people 'really did think differently'. For her, the challenge of writing history—and the same could be said for biography—is to understand and represent this difference. For Grenville, the challenge of fiction is to make her characters 'real' to her audience, which, by its nature can only be of now.

I don't want to reprise a debate that has been divisive and painful, other than to say that through it I came to understand that the 'informed imagination' does not only mean qualifying 'informed' with 'imagination'; it also requires us to bring an informed intelligence to the nature—and limitation—of imagination itself. It would have been a grave error on my part to think that 'I' could sit in a village in PNG and 'imagine' myself into a village person. What would it be like for someone like me to be a village woman? Well if I were a village woman, I would not be the 'I' that writes this from the asphalted world of escalators. Even the briefest acquaintance with psychoanalysis alerts us to the deep structures of selfhood laid down from infancy, so that while we might all bleed, and do, our sense of ourselves and our understanding of self in relation to others and society can radically differ. This is a matter much debated by anthropologists. My task as a writer of lives, I came to see, was not as some kind of inadequate faux anthropologist. So it's perhaps fitting that the point made itself, and a certain emotional sense, when I encountered the Ömie image of the tree as a metaphor for the clan. Whereas in the anglophone West we draw a family tree from the top of the page with each individual marked along horizontal generational lines, the Ömie draw their tree upwards. The roots represent the Ancestors, the trunk the members of the clan, all in together, and the branches are symbolic of the strong and wise—the *duvahe*—who stretch the clan into the future. This does not mean that everyone in the trunk is the same—you only have to be an hour in a village to know that—or that they think of themselves as the same. But it does mean that their taken-for-granted sense of who they are in relation to each other and their society is markedly different from the way we in the West, each with our place on our horizontal lines, take for granted the nature of self.

That is what my character Rika, who wants only to be the same, has to learn. She has to learn it in her professional life with her camera, and that is hard enough. In her personal life, in her deep love for Aaron, it is harder still, coming to understand how she is seen and, in a sense, can only be seen, by the older members of the fjord village where Aaron was born and grew. She might be called sister friend by his younger women kin, she might refuse all difference, and does, in the name of race equality; are we not all the same under the skin? She might wish to be the same, ache to be the same, but she is not the same. Her marriage to Aaron looks very different to the villagers than it does to the cosmopolitan young in Port Moresby. To them, their marriage can symbolise the changing tide of history, the new day coming, but to the older women in the village, the *aya*, whose task it is to hold the ground steady, it is a turbulence in the order of things. To the young women in the village, her sister friends, who have a greater sense of the changes that are coming, Rika's IUD—a piece of metal inside her to stop the making of babies—is as incomprehensible as it would be to a woman in contemporary Australia that there are indeed certain springs where a woman should go if she wishes for a baby. The point I spell out here is that to dismantle the 'other' does not mean to replace 'other' with 'same'. Like so much in life, movement between the two depends—to use the camera metaphor—on what lens you use, what focus and exposure, and who is behind the camera.

From the first page of the first draft of *The Mountain*, Rika came off the plane with a camera. And from the first page of the first draft I didn't understand why—and had several attempts at getting rid of it. On top of everything else, its presence meant I had to learn more about photography. But my unconscious, or the unconscious of the book it hadn't yet become, was ahead of me—for the camera proved central, even essential—not only in its literal use by characters who are white, but as a motif, a device, though I hope not too obvious; an analogy for the writing lens as it moves in and out, onto and among the lives of the characters. By pulling myself right back, I was able to frame and reframe the various stories and perspectives and predicaments I had for so long wanted to give voice to. It's an obvious point, but worth saying, that a novel does not have to inhabit every character in the same way; empathy can go quite a distance, and it can also rein back in and let language and imagery do its work of conjuring the unexpressed and letting us glimpse the different as itself.

The point I came to see is that fiction does stand on different ground from biography and history. There might be scope for play along the borderlines, and there surely is, but there is also a ravine, to use Inga Clendinnen's word for it, that we should respect. While I am not foolhardy enough to speak for the historian, or even the biographer, there is an epistemological necessity for the biographer or historian—however far forward or back they project themselves—to act as the lens through which we can trust the selection, presentation and interpretation of the lives put before us. Fiction, as an imaginative act, allows a different form of knowledge. It might contain argument, but it is not an argument; it involves interpretation, but does not depend on any one character to make it. The intellectual work of a long, fictional narrative stands on the ground of perspective and patterning, voice and language, metaphor and image.

There's a great deal I could say about the novel as a form, but that's a topic for another occasion. I will say in conclusion only this: that by leaving that border zone where the fictional and the biographical can meet, I could bring a polyphonic perspective to the moral predicaments in which this book had entangled me, and to the tide of events that had gathered us all in—all the people I have spoken of in this lecture, and more—and changed us all, whether cosmopolitan or villager or cultural *hapkas*, in ways we may have tried to control, but invariably could not. But by crossing into the ground of fiction, and by creating characters who do not equate in any simple way, or even at all, to myself or to the many lives I've bumped up against in my rich experience of PNG, I had confronted myself with a possibly greater challenge.

For while the best of biography and memoir also depends on the skill of the writer to use the conventions and writerly devices of biography without them appearing conventional, for the novelist the stakes are higher. For a novel that cannot conjure lifeness, life on the page, has nothing in the annals to fall back on. If its characters do not move us, if we do not believe in the world they create, the writer cannot then fall back on biographical veracity and say that these people, or people like them, really did exist. A poor biography might still tell us something historically worthwhile, and hand the baton on. A bad novel tells us nothing, and if it does not allow us to glimpse 'that blue river of truth, curling somewhere', as the critic James Wood calls it, there is little left behind.

That's the rub.

1 Albert Wendt, Introduction to *Nuanua: Pacific Writing in English since 1980* (University of Hawai'i Press, 1995), p3.

2 ibid., p3.

3 Steven Winduo, *Transitions and Transformations in Papua New Guinea Literature and Politics* (UPNG Press and Bookshop, 2012), p41.

4 Philip Roth interviewed by Hermione Lee, 'The Art of Fiction No. 84', *The Paris Review* (Fall 1984, 93), theparisreview.org/interviews/2957/the-art-of-fiction-no-84-philip-roth.

5 Colin Filer, 'The Political Construction of a Land Grab in Papua New Guinea', Australian National University, Pacific Discussion Paper, September 2011.

6 Janet Malcom interviewed by Katie Roiphe, 'The Art of Nonfiction No. 4', *The Paris Review* (Spring 2011, 196), theparisreview.org/interviews/6073/the-art-of-nonfiction-no-4-janet-malcolm.

How Can I Be a Logician before I'm a Human Being? The Role of Biography in the Understanding of Intellectuals

Professor Ray Monk
2014

My theme today is the understanding of intellectuals. I've written three biographies—of Ludwig Wittgenstein, of Bertrand Russell, and then a slight departure, of a physicist, J. Robert Oppenheimer. And my interest in all three biographies has been to interweave an account of their thought with an account of their lives. I thought I'd begin with an account of how I got into biography.

My background is not in biography. My background is in philosophy, and a branch of philosophy that you might think is as removed from biography as possible: the philosophy of mathematics. I want to begin with an account of how I got from there to biography.

I started to specialise in Wittgenstein's philosophy of mathematics—this was in the 1980s—and that involved looking at some of the dominant interpretations of Wittgenstein on mathematics. And the two most dominant interpretations, by Michael Dummett and by Crispin Wright, it seemed to me misunderstood Wittgenstein's work, but misunderstood Wittgenstein's work in a particular kind of way—which was, it struck me, that they'd misunderstood Wittgenstein. Michael Dummett interpreted Wittgenstein's philosophy of mathematics as being what he called 'full blooded Bolshevism', and Crispin Wright interpreted it as what he called 'strict finitism'—and both of these positions are positions in the philosophy of mathematics. But they're not positions it seemed to me that Wittgenstein could possibly have taken, and that in order to attribute those positions to Wittgenstein, it's not a case of misunderstanding, as it were, the words on the page. It's a case of misunderstanding the spirit in which Wittgenstein was writing. It's a question of misunderstanding Wittgenstein. And it occurred to me that nobody who understood him, who understood the man, could possibly think that he espoused this or that position. And so I got interested in the idea of writing a biography of Wittgenstein that would seek to make clear the spirit in which he wrote, and that's quite a subtle sort of thing to attempt to do.

It seemed to me that, just like with ordinary human intercourse, when you understand somebody you're better placed to understand the tone of their voice, for example. One of the marks of understanding somebody is that you can tell when they're being sarcastic, or you can interpret the facial expressions that they're making. It seemed to me that was what was required here for the interpretation of Wittgenstein. It wasn't an explanation of Wittgenstein's work. It wasn't that I sought to explain what he wrote in terms of his life. It was more that I was hoping to give an account of what kind of person Wittgenstein was, so as to enable people to, as it were, understand the tone of voice, the spirit in which he wrote.

And so I conceived this project of writing a biography of Wittgenstein. Now at that time I didn't know anything about biography as a form, and so I started to look at biography as a form, going right back to the beginning—going right back to Plutarch with his *Lives of the Roman Emperors*, *Life of Alexander*, *Life of Caesar*. And you'll notice that all those lives are lives of people with political and military importance. So what Plutarch set himself to do was to write biography in the service of history. Why was Plutarch writing about Alexander or Caesar? Well, in order to understand that particular period of Greek or Roman history.

The narrative was not driven by thoughts but by events, by decisions, by actions. The first person that I know of to write biography of thinkers is Diogenes Laertius with his *Lives and Opinions of Eminent Philosophers*, a multi-volume work. On the whole quite short biographies of thinkers, giving an account of their lives and a very brief, in most cases, account of their thought, and with no real attempt to integrate the two—and with some quite sort of randomly chosen details about the lives of these people. One detail that sticks in my mind is in his biography of Zeno, Diogenes writes that 'they say he was fond of lying in the sun and eating figs', which is quite a nice thing to know about Zeno, I think. Whether it's going to help in interpreting his work I don't know, and Diogenes doesn't do much of that except in his much more extended treatment of the life of Plato, where he is trying to give an account of Plato's thought as well as his life. What he's not trying to do is integrate the two.

What I discovered, and I didn't know this until I did some research into biography, is that there's an enormous hiatus in biographical writing between the ancient period and the relatively modern period. Throughout the medieval period, there's very little biographical writing. There's the *Lives of the Saints*, there's the lives of this or that important emperor or king or prince or whatever, but these are not really biographies. For the most part, they're hagiographies. For the most part, they're written in order to achieve a certain purpose, the purpose being to present a person as an exemplification of a certain virtue, or of a certain kind of type, a personality type. In terms of biography, the first person who really, I felt, had something to teach me was James Boswell and his marvellous *Life of Samuel Johnson*. And if you haven't read it, I really urge you to do so. It is a fantastic piece of literature, and remains to this day, I think, one of the best biographies ever written. Virginia Woolf, who wrote entertainingly and insightfully on biography, captured, I think, what was great about Boswell's *Life of Johnson*, when she said this:

> So Boswell spoke. So we hear booming out from Boswell's page the voice of Samuel Johnson. 'No sir; stark insensibility', we hear him say. Once we have heard those words we are aware that there is an incalculable presence among us which will go on ringing and reverberating in widening circles however times may change and ourselves. All the draperies and decencies of biography fall to the ground. We can no longer maintain that life consists in actions only or in works. It consists in personality.

I think in those words Virginia Woolf has captured what's great about Boswell's *Life of Johnson*. And what was instructive for me, having made this decision to write a biography of Wittgenstein, one of the great eye openers was the value of direct quotation. One of the things—the thing, I think—that makes the *Life of Johnson* the great work that it is is that on every page you hear, as Virginia Woolf said, the voice of Johnson himself. Johnson comes to life, and he comes to life because Boswell spent so long with him, and Boswell recorded his conversations with Samuel Johnson and reproduced those conversations. So you have the words of Johnson himself, the voice of Johnson himself, so you hear that voice, as Virginia Woolf says, booming out. You get to know Johnson. You get to know his tone of voice. You get to know what kind of things he says, what kind of things he likes, what kind of person he is, and so, as Virginia Woolf says, now we've got a new kind of biography—a biography the point of which is to give us the personality, to give us the person.

It's not an account any longer of what he did. It's giving you an understanding of him. That's the wonderful thing about Boswell's *Life of Johnson*: that when you read it, having read it, you feel that you understand Samuel Johnson in something like the way that you might understand your brother, or your wife, or your husband, or your lover. You feel as if you're close to Samuel Johnson, that you sort of can predict how he's going to react to something. And then when you read Samuel Johnson himself, you're better placed to understand what he's written.

Now Johnson, of course, himself was a biographer. He wrote a biography of his friend Richard Savage, he wrote a collection of lives of the poets. But more to the point from my point of view—because Johnson as a biographer is much less important to me than Boswell as a biographer—Johnson was one of the first people to reflect on biography, and he did so to great effect. In the eighteenth century, you had literary journals like *The Rambler*, *The Idler* and *The Spectator* and so on, and Johnson wrote for most of them. And there are these very short essays that he wrote on biography, but they've really set the tone for subsequent reflection on biography as a genre. Johnson identified five questions to ask about biography, and they remain, I think, five of the most important questions to raise about biography.

The first is, what's the relation of biography to other genres, in particular to history and fiction? And remember this is the eighteenth century. As well as being the time when biography—in the persons of Johnson and Boswell—was making its mark, so was fiction. This was the age when the great foundational works of novel-writing were produced: *Robinson Crusoe*, *Moll Flanders* and so on. And I've seen it suggested that these two forms, fiction and biography, have a common origin, which has much to do with the coffee house, funnily enough.

You've got people sitting there drinking coffee, and so what do they talk about? Well, they talk about people. They gossip. And biography is a kind of higher form of gossip, and so is novel-writing, because most of the novels that were produced were fictitious accounts of people. So you have this tripartite development: people meeting in coffee houses, discussing other people, discussing literature, which involves discussing *Moll Flanders*, *Robinson Crusoe*, and then discussing biography. So you have this great flowering of biographical and fictional literature. One of the questions that Samuel Johnson asked was, what is the relation of biography to, on the one hand, fiction, and on the other hand, history? And his answer retains a certain kind of truth, which is this: what biography shares with history, importantly, is a concern with fact.

You can't, as a biographer, just make things up. You are responsible to documentation, to the truth. What you say in a biography, like what you say in a work of history, has to be true. But, like a work of fiction, what you say in a biography has to have a kind of narrative drive. The biographer has to develop some of the skills of the novelist, the skill of holding your attention, and particularly, Johnson emphasised, the emphasis, which a historian doesn't have, on the lives, the opinions, the experiences, the emotions, of an individual. That's what biography is all about. It's all about the individual in a way that history is not. So Samuel Johnson said that biography holds this unique place between, on the one hand, history, where you have to be answerable to the truth, to the facts, on the other hand, to fiction, where you're compelled to construct an engrossing and engaging narrative centred on an individual.

His second question was, who deserves a biography? Who should we write biographies about? And in particular Johnson was concerned, like Virginia Woolf was, to counter the idea that only those people who've achieved great deeds, who've been involved in great actions or great works—you know, the Alexanders, the Caesars, those people—should have biographies written of them. Johnson says no, we can also have biographies of literary people, of intellectuals, of philosophers, of poets, of people whose claim to our attention is not that they've led a campaign, a military campaign, not that they've been in charge of a country, but that they've written an interesting poem, that they've written a great novel, that they've had great thoughts. In other words, like Virginia Woolf says about Boswell and Johnson, now we see a kind of narrative that's driven by personality, by what we would call, but Johnson didn't, the inner life—the attempt to understand the thoughts and feelings of another human being.

Then his third question was, what details should a biographer include? And from my point of view, interestingly, he responds to that by saying, well, we can't give a general answer to that—we can't, as it were, give a theory of biography about what you should include and what you shouldn't. It will vary from case to case. So his answer to question three brings into play his answer to question one, which was that biography shares with the novelist the concern with an individual human being, and because it's an individual human being, there is no general answer to question three, what details should the biography include. It will vary from person to person. Should you describe how they walked? Should you describe what they ate? Should you describe their voice, their height, how they related to other people? It will depend on the person. It may be that how somebody walks—this is an example that Samuel Johnson himself gives—it may be that if somebody walks in a brisk, impatient kind of manner, that that's worth including in a biography because that might be indicative, expressive, of a certain kind of personality. You're trying to get across a personality, a character, and character can be expressed in any number of ways, and those ways are so varied, and so multiple, that no general account of them can be given. And so Johnson says what details should be included will be dependent upon those details that give us some idea of the personality of the person involved.

Then a different kind of consideration: the moral responsibilities of the biographer towards first of all the subject, and then the public, and then the truth. And Johnson here directs his readers' attention to a tension, particularly between the first and the third. It may be that as a biographer you have access to truths, to facts about your subject which will not do them any credit. And so which moral responsibility should take precedence: your responsibility to the good name, the good reputation, of your subject, or your responsibility to the truth? And on this question Samuel Johnson says the moral responsibility to the truth overrides that of other responsibilities.

I had this issue myself with Russell. My biography of Russell was criticised by a lot of people because they felt that I was putting Russell in a bad light, that I was showing him to be reprehensible in all sorts of ways, and I was aware of that when I was writing this biography. It was huge. It was a two-volume biography. I spent 10 years writing this biography, and I read 40,000 letters of Russell's. Russell didn't throw away anything. He kept everything and then he left it all to McMaster University in Canada, and I spent a lot of time at McMaster weeding through these documents. And some of them are heartbreaking, the way he treated other people. Then as part of my research I went to meet people who were close to Russell. And this is a strange thing about biography, that unlike other kinds of research, it involves one's own emotional engagement. So I became a good friend of Russell's daughter, and of his granddaughter, and they became friends of my family. They came and they got to know my kids and so on, and I got to know them very well.

What struck me in this research was, to get to know the people who were close to Russell was to pick one's way through a kind of history of emotional wreckage. Russell had a disastrous effect on a lot of people who were close to him, and it followed a certain kind of pattern, which was that he would withdraw from the people close to him, often with disastrous effects. His son had a nervous breakdown, two of his granddaughters, whom he took charge of, ended up in psychiatric institutions, his daughter disowned him, he married four times and two of his wives suffered from acute mental problems. I think in many of these cases, it's to do with this fact that he withdrew what they had become dependent upon, which was the emotional support that he gave them.

I'll give you one detail that I found particularly distressing when I was reading through these letters, because he kept all his legal correspondence too. In the course of divorcing his second wife, Dora—it was a particularly nasty divorce and they argued bitterly about the custody of their kids. They had an open marriage and so while they were married, even while they were happily married, they had affairs with other people and they were quite open about it. In the course of the divorce, Dora had an affair with a man called Paul Gillard—and she became totally besotted with this man and completely in love with him—who then died in very mysterious circumstances. Dora was utterly distraught, and she wrote a very long, rambling, heartfelt letter to Bertrand Russell, explaining the history of her relationship with Paul Gillard and how his death had affected her. She said in this letter, look, I know this is strange, we're divorcing and here I am writing you this intimate letter, but I feel that you are the one person in the world who will understand how I feel about Paul, and what I'm going through at the moment. A heartbreaking letter to read. When he received this letter, Russell sent it on to his solicitor with a very short note saying, 'Please look through this letter to see if there's anything that could be used to our advantage in the coming court case'.

And it's that kind of attitude. It's not that Russell is the worst person in the world. It's not that he's Hitler. He's not Goebbels. But it's the strange ability he had to emotionally distance himself from those close to him that, going back to Johnson's question about the duties one has to the truth and the subject, it seemed to me I had a greater obligation to portray and describe this because it was true—and because it was an important facet of Russell's biography—than I did to preserving the image of Russell as a benign and cheerful soul.

Then the fifth question is a different question altogether because this question is kind of a general philosophical question. It's a version of what philosophers call the 'other minds' question. Samuel Johnson asked, 'Can one know the inner life of another person?' And he answered this question by saying, 'by conjecture only can one man judge of another's motives or sentiments'. So he says autobiography is at an advantage to biography because if you're describing your own motives or sentiments, if you're describing why you did something, or how you felt about something, you're in a privileged position compared to somebody who's not you.

I'm very sympathetic to Samuel Johnson's answers to one, two, three and four, but more or less totally unsympathetic to his answer to number five. It seems to me the one thing that biography has to teach us is that Samuel Johnson's answer to number five is not true. It's not true that we have to rely on conjecture when we attribute a motive or a sentiment or a feeling to another person. And this is something that Wittgenstein actually discusses in his later work. And Wittgenstein says this: 'Just try in a real case to doubt the feelings of another person'. For example, when faced with the crying of a baby, is it possible to say in a Johnsonian spirit, I don't really know that this baby's upset—I have to guess it, I have to conjecture it. No, you know that that baby's upset as well as you know anything else at all.

In fact, this distinction that Johnson wants to make between the motives and sentiments of other people and, as it were, the external, the actions, the appearances of other people—this distinction, it's a natural one to make, and all sorts of people have made it. Virginia Woolf makes it in her novels, and in her writings on biography. But if you reflect in a Wittgensteinian sort of way about how we describe other people, we often describe somebody's appearance, somebody's external aspect, by attributing to them an internal view. So somebody might say to me, how did your daughter look on her first day of school? And I would say, she looked apprehensive. How did your son look when he'd finished the computer game that he's been playing for the last month? He looked triumphant. We habitually describe how somebody looks by attributing to them what Johnson would call a sentiment.

This is important, I think, both for novel writing and for biography, that if you want to get across what somebody's feeling, you don't have to do it in a Virginia Woolf kind of way. You don't need what the philosopher Gilbert Ryle called 'privileged access' to somebody's thinking, in order to describe what they're feeling. You can describe what they look like. And this is the genius of Boswell's *Life of Johnson*, that Boswell doesn't have to have access to Johnson's, as it were, interior monologue. We sometimes think that—Virginia Woolf thought that—in order to understand somebody really you would need to get inside their minds, but we don't. We can quote them, we can describe them, we can give instances of how they react to things, and this in itself tells us cumulatively what kind of person they are, and something about their inner life. It's a mistake to think that access to somebody's internal monologue would necessarily give you a better understanding of them. That assumes that they understand themselves.

It's as common as anything, I think, to understand something about oneself through one's relations with other people. It happens very often, I think, that you're brought to understand why you reacted in a certain kind of way because somebody else has some insight into you. This happens all the time with me and my wife. My wife will say to me, look, you don't really mean that, you know. Because she understands me, because she can see what I blind myself to—various motives and reactions and so on. This also happens, of course, in therapy and analysis. The person that we're speaking to has insight into our motives, our thoughts, that we ourselves don't have. So it seems to me that Johnson's answer to question five is not only wrong; it's at the heart of a lot of mistaken thinking, not only about biography but also about what it is to understand oneself and what it is to understand other people.

One of the great merits of Wittgenstein's later philosophy is that he tried to turn this on its head, because in philosophy this takes the form of privileging, as it were, the egocentric as opposed to the public. In philosophy we're taught often that modern philosophy begins with René Descartes in *Meditations*, doubting everything, doubting everything about the external world, and trying to come up with something he can't doubt. And what can't he doubt? Well, his own existence. *Cogito, ergo sum*: I think, therefore I am. That, according to Descartes, is where you hit certainty, where you hit something that you cannot doubt. Descartes in the *Meditations* begins with that, begins with the certainty of his own existence, and then starts thinking about does he now have reason to accept the existence of other people and accept the existence of the external world.

In Wittgenstein's later philosophy he turns that on its head in a rather beautiful kind of way, through what's called the private language argument. Wittgenstein says no, it can't be that one starts with the individual and goes out to the public—it must be that one starts with the public. Why must that be? Because in order to use a language one has to be part of a community. So when, for example, we're describing our inner life—when we're describing, let's say, our dreams—nobody has access to our dreams other than us. But when we're describing our dreams we use words, and those words are words of a public language, and we've learned those words in a public context. I might have a dream. I might choose not to describe it to anybody, in which case it remains private—that's perfectly possible. But after all we have a word, 'dream', and that word is a public word, it's part of a public institution. How did we learn that word? It can't be that we learned that word from our own experience, and then we applied it to other people—that can't be right. We must have learned it from other people and then applied it to ourselves. The private can't be prior to the public. The public must be prior to the private. It must be that we are able to describe our dreams, and then it's intelligible that we can have a dream and we don't describe it. So can we know the inner life of another person? Yes.

I was thinking about biography, and I was looking at ancient biographers, I was looking at Boswell and Johnson. But a great sort of epiphany for me, when I was thinking about how I was going to write a biography of Wittgenstein, was reading Richard Ellmann, who I think is one of the greatest modern biographers. The two that I admire most are his biography of James Joyce and his biography of Oscar Wilde. His biography of Oscar Wilde is particularly good, and it shares with Boswell's *Life of Johnson* this point: that absolutely central to the narrative is quotation.

This is something that, as an academic, I had to unlearn. When you write as an academic, what you tend to do when you quote somebody—often the quotations are in a smaller font than the rest of it. It's as if, well, you can gloss over this bit if you want. And then as an academic you quote something, and then you describe what it is that you've just quoted as if it was in a foreign language or something. The worst example of this I can think of is a biography that I was sent to review, of Virginia Woolf, of all people, by a professor—people think I make this up, this is actually true—he quoted a letter that Virginia Woolf wrote to Leonard Woolf in which she says, 'I feel no sexual attraction towards you'. And this man then began his next paragraph by saying, 'Here Virginia Woolf is saying she feels no sexual attraction towards Leonard'.

What I learned from Richard Ellmann on Wilde is, quote your subject, move on. You don't need to explain what it is that you've just quoted. What you just quoted is not something to be analysed and discussed and so on. It is part of the narrative. That's what you get in Boswell on Johnson, and that's pre-eminently what you get in Ellmann on Wilde. Of course, it helps if you're writing a biography of a subject like Oscar Wilde who is just incapable of saying or writing anything dull. So anything that Oscar Wilde says is worth quoting. And Richard Ellmann understands that all too well, and his biography is structured around that, and it's a beautiful piece of work.

But a particular model for me, for writing a biography of Wittgenstein—where after all I'm interested in trying to get across Wittgenstein as a thinker, as an intellectual—a particular model was this rather great biography by Andrew Hodges of Alan Turing, which came out about a year before I started work on my Wittgenstein book, and was a huge influence on me. I remember telling my publisher, what I really want to do is I want to write a book on Wittgenstein that does for Wittgenstein what Andrew Hodges has done for Alan Turing.

Until Hodges wrote this book on Alan Turing, Turing would seem to be a very unlikely subject for a biography. He was a reclusive man, he wrote some extremely difficult work on mathematical logic, and then he did some impenetrable and secret work in decoding the Nazi code in the Second World War, and then he was prosecuted for immorality, just as Oscar Wilde was, because he was gay, and he ended up committing suicide. Now Andrew Hodges is a perfect fit as a biographer for the subject. Andrew Hodges is a mathematician, he's gay and he's been actively involved in the politics of the gay movement. Hodges brought all that beautifully to bear on this book about Turing. What Hodges did in this book that was such a revelation for me is he didn't shirk from describing Turing's mathematical work, his work on computable functions, which is not easy. Hodges did a great job of explaining that work, and explaining what it had to do with the building of computers, and therefore one is ready for Turing's computerised solution to the decipherment of the Nazi code.

But interweaving with that, Hodges described Turing's love life, his love for another man, his emotional suffering from having to hide that love for the other man, and then his persecution by the authorities. The horrible thing that happened to Turing is that, when he was prosecuted for being gay, he was forced to undergo hormone treatment. It's a very weird thing about 1950s British life, when forcibly injecting people, men, with female hormones was supposed to be some kind of solution to being gay. Hodges describes all that, and then describes the extraordinary suicide of Turing. Turing committed suicide by injecting an apple with cyanide and then biting the apple. Hodges is very good on the symbolic significance of that, and the evocation of various fairy tales and so on.

But what was a revelation for me was the way Hodges didn't try to reduce Turing's intellectual work to various facts of his biography, but neither did he gloss over the intellectual work. In some kind of subtle way, he brought all those things—Turing's political work, his intellectual work, his emotional life, his homosexuality—into a single narrative. That was what was important to me, that it was a single narrative. It wasn't reductive.

A friend of mine, James Conant—a philosopher—has written on the relationship between philosophy and biography, and he's distinguished two different positions: reductivism, which seeks to explain a person's philosophical work in terms of their biography; and compartmentalism, which says that the details of somebody's life have nothing at all to do with what they thought. Conant, to my mind quite rightly, says one has to resist both of those positions. It seemed to me that that's what Hodges did in his biography of Turing. He didn't reduce Turing's intellectual life to the details of his biography, nor did he keep the two apart. In a very skilful and insightful way, he brought them all together, in a single narrative. So that's what I tried to do in my biography of Wittgenstein.

I was also helped by a notion of another biographer, Lytton Strachey. Lytton Strachey, you may know, was the inaugurator of the movement called New Biography, which is a reaction against Victorian biography. The tomes that Strachey derided were detailed and laborious and respectful. Strachey said this: that the qualities that make a good historian or biographer are a capacity for absorbing facts, a capacity for stating them and a point of view. A point of view. That was, for me, the key in Strachey's view of biography, that what a biographer does is present a way of seeing somebody, which isn't just an accumulation of facts. What Strachey was reacting against was the Victorian view of biography where the biographer just accumulates the facts and puts them before the reader. Strachey quite rightly derided that because it doesn't lead to any insight, it doesn't lead to you understanding the person involved.

Boswell's method sometimes looks haphazard or random. You don't know why he's suddenly talking about Samuel Johnson talking about actresses or whatever, but there's a method to his madness. You realise at the end of the book that what you've been given is not just a haphazard collection of facts; you've been given a way of looking at Samuel Johnson, a point of view of him. Samuel Johnson now makes sense, and that making sense is not just an accumulation of facts, it's an arrangement of those facts. And that, it seems to me, is the art of the biographer. The art of the biographer is to arrange the facts without theorising, without analysing, but arranging them so as to present not just what happened but a way of seeing a point of view of what happened.

And this relates to something in Wittgenstein's later philosophy, which he discusses in part two of *Philosophical Investigations*. The duck/rabbit—his famous ambiguous illustration. You can see it as a duck or as a rabbit. You can at will switch between one and the other: you can see it now as a duck and now as a rabbit. But now ask yourself, well, what changes? What changes when you see it now as a duck, and now as a rabbit? The illustration doesn't change. You might be tempted to think, well, okay, that doesn't change, but something in the mind does change. Wittgenstein says no, that can't be right either, because whatever is in there is going to be just as ambiguous. It's not some thing that is different in each of those cases: it's the way you look at it. You're looking at it now as a duck, and now as a rabbit. In some sense, you're seeing the same thing. In another more subtle sense, you're seeing something different, or rather you're looking at it differently. That, Wittgenstein says, is what the philosopher is trying to achieve. The philosopher is trying to get you to see things differently and that leads him to this notion of the understanding that consists in seeing connections, which was a crucial notion for Wittgenstein.

Wittgenstein had a Galtonian photograph composed. It's made up of four photographs: there's Ludwig Wittgenstein on the bottom right, and his three sisters, Gretel, top left, Helena next to her, and on the bottom left is Hermina, 'Mini', superimposed on one another. You look at it to begin with, and it looks like one person—a rather strange-looking person, of indeterminate sex. Then you look and can see the necklace, and also you can see the open neck shirt. The point that Wittgenstein had in mind in making this picture was to see the connections between himself and his sisters. In superimposing one on another, you can in a quite literal sense see the connections. You can see the family resemblances—between their eyes, between their noses, the structure of their faces.

The notion of a family resemblance plays a key role in Wittgenstein's later philosophy, in this way. Wittgenstein says in traditional philosophy—like Plato's works—in a typical Plato dialogue, what happens? Socrates asks a question, and it's usually a kind of 'what is' question. What is truth? What is justice? What is knowledge? And then the people that he asks this question to will give examples of knowledge, or truth, or whatever. Then Socrates will say, no, I don't want examples. I want to know what is the essence of truth, or of knowledge, or whatever. And at that point Wittgenstein would say, no, resist that; examples are all you've got, and if you want to understand our concept of truth, or knowledge, or whatever, look at the examples and see the connections between them. It's not that—and Wittgenstein says this is a common source of philosophical confusion—it's not that there is one single thing that is in common with all the instances of knowledge or truth or whatever, rather there is a multiplicity of things that we call truth, a multiplicity of things that we call knowledge, that we call piety. An acquisition of that concept involves seeing the connections between them. And just like with the members of the family, it may not be that there's one single thing that all family members have in common. Rather there will be a series of overlapping similarities and dissimilarities. You take all the members of the family together: some of them will have the same eyes, some of them will have the same nose, some of them will have the same chin. There won't be, as it were, an essence that every member of the family has in common. Rather there will be this series of similarities and dissimilarities, and to see the family connection is to see those connections.

So what does this have to do with biography? Well, it struck me that in my quest to write a biography of Wittgenstein that would get across what kind of person he was, so as to enable people to read him, as it were, in the right spirit, what I had to do—in a way that harks back to Boswell on Johnson, Ellmann on Wilde, Hodges on Turing, and Wittgenstein's own later philosophy with the importance of seeing connections—was not to theorise about Wittgenstein but to describe various things that he wrote and that he said. And the art of the biography is to structure those things, so that the reader now can see the connections, just like somebody looking at that composite photograph can see the connections.

A revelation for me was Otto Weininger and his book *Sex and Character*, which is a terrible book. It argues that women are not really people, and neither are Jews because Jews are a kind of woman, and neither are homosexuals, because homosexuals are a kind of woman. Now Weininger himself was both Jewish and homosexual, and so when he finished publishing this book, he committed suicide—as it were, to say, well, this is the conclusion of the book. Absolutely balmy book but Wittgenstein cited it to various people as an influence, and he used to give it to people in Cambridge, and they used to be very puzzled as to why he was giving them this balmy book. And I read this book, and it seemed to me that one thing that was really important was not all this nonsense about women and Jews and homosexuals, but this: the idea, he says, that logic and ethics are fundamentally the same; they are no more than duty to oneself.

This is why I called my biography of Wittgenstein *The Duty of Genius*. The duty of genius is to realise the duty to oneself, and to see that this has two aspects: logic and ethics. What I tried to do in my biography of Wittgenstein was to draw together the extraordinary personality of Wittgenstein. Wittgenstein's life is dominated by two things: one is the determination to be, as he put it, *anständig*, decent—to be a decent person; and the other thing was to think honestly and deeply. At the heart of my attempt to get across Wittgenstein's spirit was to show that those two were two sides of the same coin. So here I had what Strachey would call my point of view, that logic and ethics are fundamentally the same; they are two aspects of the single duty, the duty of genius. This is how I try to describe Wittgenstein in all his manifestations, in all his thinking and his relations to other people, to show that his concern to be a decent person was the other side of the coin to his concern to think clearly, and this is how I try to draw together his logic, even his mathematical logic, with his personality.

Who, Me?

Robert Drewe
2015

I've called this lecture 'Who, Me?' because I thought that encompassed memoir-writing as well as anything else. Fish or fowl, just an autobiography with a more melodious name, a cry for attention, a woe is me self-portrait, a form of revenge, an onanistic confessional exercise, a truth-twisting jaunt closer to fiction? Worse, complete fakery? And why does it make critics cranky? No-one seems to know what to expect from a memoir, or from an autobiography for that matter, and those who write them are as uncertain as those who publish them.

The Polish Nobel Laureate, Czesław Miłosz, subtitled his memoir 'A Search for Self-definition', and I dare any Australian writer to put that on their book jacket. Jean-Paul Sartre stressed that his autobiography was nothing but words. Patrick White insisted that his publisher play down his memoir, *Flaws in the Glass*, by stating on the jacket that it was merely a self-portrait in the form of sketches. When they can be bothered to treat it with any seriousness, the critic's most charitable view of the memoir is that it's an extreme case of self-absorption. I beg to differ, but sort of—they're only partly right. Memoirs are as diverse as the people who write them. In his wonderfully irritable *Harper's* essay, 'The Art of Self: Autobiography in an Age of Narcissism', William Gass systematically dismembered the memoir 21 years ago.[1] The distinguished American critic began by stating, it's an odd activity: 'I imagine a blotter soaking up its own absorbency and disappearing like a Cheshire cat by slow degrees'. Well after that rather complicated metaphor he really went to town. He wondered rhetorically whether there were any motives for the enterprise that aren't tainted with conceit, or a desire for revenge, or a wish for justification. 'To halo a sinner's head,' he said, 'to puff an ego already inflated past safety'. He went on to say, 'history is now a comic book, and autobiography the confessions of celluloid whores and boorish noisemakers whose tabloid lives are presented for our titillation by ghosts still undeservedly alive'. Phew.

Now we note that Gass, like many modern critics, preferred to call all writing about oneself autobiography, and to never mention the word memoir. Even while attacking a literary genre or subgenre that had been around for a millennium and a half, he couldn't quite bring himself to acknowledge its separate existence. Incidentally, although they've definitely had a hand in it, the memoirs of history's winners are not solely to blame if history does resemble a comic book. Take the King Richards I and III, for example: history has it that the former was very good, the latter very bad, when it was probably the other way round. It wasn't memoir that turned the vicious, misogynistic King Richard I, who spoke only French and in whose adulthood visited England only twice, into the beloved, iconic figure, Richard the Lionheart. With him, military victories led to mythologising. Drama should take some of the heat. After four centuries of brilliant Shakespearean agitprop, it turns out that Richard III was neither a wicked tyrannical leader, nor a nephew murderer, not even a Machiavellian hunchback. Since his recent emergence from a municipal carpark, he's been reassessed as a brave and thoroughly decent chap with scoliosis.

As it happens, William Gass's scathing view of the memoir was hardly a new one. Jean-Jacques Rousseau's *Confessions* scandalised Paris in 1782 with the author's frank accounts not only of his masochism and enthusiastic masturbation of the non-literary kind, but his shameful blaming of a young servant girl for the theft of a ribbon he'd stolen himself from the family they'd both worked for as adolescents. Apparently ribbons were worth stealing in the eighteenth century. Decades later, the only way the renowned philosopher could relieve his youthful guilt at this double sin was to write about it. As he said, 'this burden then has lain unalleviated on my conscience until this very day, and I can safely say that the desire to be in some measure relieved of it has greatly contributed to the decision I've taken to write my confessions'.

Following Rousseau's *Confessions*, Edmund Burke criticised the new sort of glory Rousseau had obtained for bringing to light the obscure and vulgar vices which we know may sometimes be blended with eminent talents. But for better or worse Rousseau had begun the movement of confession into the literary arena: he got a shameful secret off his chest and redemption theory was born.

But the confessional memoir had had its beginnings long before, in Roman north Africa, in the village of Figasti in what is now Algeria, in 371CE when a 16-year-old boy raised in a mixed Christian and pagan family of Berber, Latin and Phoenician blood and with a background of delinquent behaviour, pinched some fruit from a neighbour's tree. As adolescent transgressions go, pilfering unripe pears is hardly evil. As he recalled 30 years later, he'd been neither hungry nor poor and he didn't particularly want to eat the pears. He stole them simply to be bad. 'It was foul and I loved it,' he wrote. 'I loved my own undoing.'

As Daniel Mendelsohn, the American memoirist and memoir scholar, wrote in a 2010 *New Yorker* essay, 'But Enough about Me', however trivial a crime and perverse its motivations, this bit of petty larceny had enormous consequences for the boy's future, for the history of Christianity and Western philosophy. To this day it even affects the shelf layout, the separate memoir section in your local bookstore. For although the boy eventually straightened himself out and converted to Christianity, the man he became was tortured by the thought of this youthful peccadillo. His desire to seek a larger meaning in his troubled past ultimately moved him to write a starkly honest account of his dissolute early years. He was as disarmingly frank about his prolific sex life as he was about his teenage scrumping, and also honest about his stumbling progress towards spiritual transcendence, right up to the climactic moment when by looking inward, with what he called his soul's eye, he saw the light, an 'immutable light higher than my mind', and decided to write everything down. The man was St Augustine, and his book was also called *Confessions*. At least one famous quotation from his *Confessions* is still considered by today's would-be memoirists: 'Lord, make me chaste but not yet'.

The guilt of two naughty teenage boys, thieves of ribbons and pears, could be said to be responsible for the advent of the confessional memoir. While there had been a long tradition of publishing biographies of famous men's public endeavours and military derring-do, St Augustine was the first writer to make the accomplishment an interior enterprise and the road to salvation a spiritual one. According to Mendelsohn, the arc from utter abjection to improbable redemption, at once deeply personal and appealingly universal, is one that writers have returned to and readers have been insatiable for ever since. From the Middle Ages and through the Renaissance, the memoir—from the French word meaning memory or reminiscence—was popular with French writers in particular. Two more ancient forerunners of the twentieth-century war memoir, a popular subgenre of its own, were Julius Caesar's *Commentaries on the Gallic Wars* and his *Commentaries on the Civil War,* in which he describes events during his many battles.

Military leaders especially have been writing their memoirs ever since and, from the First World War at least, so have the lower ranks. And so have military prisoners including our own David Hicks, whose memoir, *Guantanamo, My Journey*, details his arrest on terrorism charges and his five and a half years in the Guantanamo Bay detention camp.

'All autobiographies are lies,' pronounced George Bernard Shaw. 'I do not mean unconscious unintentional lies: I mean deliberate lies.' Shaw went on to say no man is bad enough to tell the truth himself during his lifetime, involving as it must the truth about his family and friends and colleagues. And no man is good enough to tell the truth in a document which he suppresses until there is nobody left alive to contradict him.

Clive James, author of *Unreliable Memoirs*, agrees with Shaw. James, by the way, is one of the top three bestselling Australian memoirists, the others being those most incongruent authors, Albert Facey, author of *A Fortunate Life*, and Errol Flynn, author of *My Wicked, Wicked Ways*. Amusingly frank as ever, James declared that all attempts to put oneself in a bad light are doomed to be frustrated: the ego arranges the bad light to its own satisfaction as indeed did he, beginning with the leeway granting title of his *Unreliable Memoirs*.

I'm reminded here of a quotation credited to John Cheever. When asked by an earnest interviewer, 'I suppose you're your own severest critic', he replied, 'Not at all, I'm forced to say I have many fiercer critics than myself'. Speaking of ego, when Sigmund Freud was invited by an American publisher to write his autobiography, he replied with customary serenity, and fairly disingenuously, quite an impossible suggestion: 'outwardly my life has passed calmly and uneventfully, and can be covered by a few dates'. Maybe outwardly, but the Freud life story was a little more complex within. In a letter to a relative, Freud said that the $5,000 advance the publisher offered him—$70,000 in today's money—was a hundredth of the sum he'd need—$7 million in today's money—to entice him into such a reckless project. Such a huge publisher's advance wasn't forthcoming, enabling Freud to take the high ground and declare that 'a psychologically completed honest confession of my life would require so much indiscretion on my part as well as that of others about family, friends and enemies ... most of them are still alive ... that it's simply out of the question'. What makes all autobiographies worthless, he went on, 'is their mendacity'. Clearly his life wasn't just a matter of couch dates crossed off his appointment book.

Already we've noticed that most of these eminent people refer to autobiography rather than memoir. A case could be made for autobiography being the overarching genre but, if not a separate category, memoir is a definite subgenre. In fact, it predated the autobiography as we know it, and the novel for that matter, by hundreds of years. So how does a memoir differ from an autobiography? The line between them might seem blurry but put simply, an autobiography tells a story of a life whereas a memoir tells a story from a life. An autobiography tells a life story from go to whoa, or certainly right up to the back stretch. It's a chronological telling of the author's entire existence, often even before conception to the moment of the book's publication. It includes the phases of childhood, adolescence and adulthood, and can often begin a generation or two before conception, often going right back to the subject's grandparents—and it's expected to include all the major details of his or her public and private life.

A memoir on the other hand, with its narrower, more intimate and dramatic focus, describes selected memories of benchmark events, emotions and turning points in the author's life. With a memoir, the author has questioned what happened and has come to some sort of understanding about how he or she now sees the world. Memories are typically less formal, less encompassing, less obsessed with factual events, and more concerned with the emotional truth of a particular portion of one's life, whereas autobiography is focused on detailed chronology, events, places and people that have inhabited the life of the subject.

Now I must admit that when I see or hear the word autobiography, my mind turns immediately to the writing of retired politicians and test cricketers, and I think not of literature but of Father's Day—as do publishers who time these books' release accordingly, a couple of months ahead of the usual pre-Christmas general release, thus putting the books in the same retail category as a new tie or a nice bottle of red, and even displayed in David Jones alongside them.

Interestingly, there's also a female counterpart of Father's Day memoirs. In April, in time for Mother's Day in May, publishers release female memoirs which are known in the publishing industry as WOTOs: women overcoming the odds, a very popular genre. WOTOs typically record the memoirs of widows left to look after a struggling cattle station in the outback, or who've sailed singlehandedly around the world or climbed Everest, or saved endangered species or of celebrities whose men have dumped them, sadder but wiser, they're all the better now the bastard has gone.

In the case of politicians' books, dull titles like *Afternoon Light* (Sir Robert Menzies), *The Good Fight* (Wayne Swan), *Cabinet Diary* (Gareth Evans) and *Battle Lines* (Tony Abbott) spring to mind. Solemn titles that not only tell me this politician has fought the good fight but make me feel I've read the book many times already. Only one of these books however, Mark Latham's turgid-sounding but explosive memoir, *Diaries*, threw that idea out the window.

On the memoirs of cricketers, I find myself wondering if they or their editors can possibly come up with a new pun involving both cricket and retirement. *At The Close of Play*, *Over but Not Out*, *Standing My Ground*, *Over to Me*, *Line and Strength*, *To the Point*, *Bowled Over*, *Crossing the Boundary* and *Time to Declare* have all been recent popular cricket book titles. Incidentally, as *Time to Declare* has been used as a title three times already by Mark Taylor, Michael Vaughan and Basil D'Oliveira, it really is time for time to declare to declare.

In a recent *Meanjin* article, the go-to publisher for Australian politicians, Louise Adler of Melbourne University Publishing, shed an intriguing light on contemporary political memoirs.[2] She reveals that these books are rarely produced without considerable 'editorial support, the unacknowledged ghost writer, the credited co-author, advisors, researchers, fact-checkers and a legion of loyal staff'. She reminds us that the memoir is the last opportunity for politicians to secure a 'place in history. Delusional perhaps—but this is the last chance to seize the microphone to record their achievements for posterity. As Winston Churchill is believed to have opined, "history will be kind to me for I intend to write it"'. And he was right. In spades. In 1953, his version of history won literature's Nobel Prize for his mastery of historical and biographical description, as well as for brilliant oratory in defending exalted human values.

Anyone who 'imagines a political memoir to be objective, fair or even accurate is naïve', Adler says. 'The political memoir is unabashedly myopic, subjective and reflexively partisan.' All of this suggests to me the words of Mr Dye in Anthony Trollope's, *The Bertrams*:

> in politics one should always look forward, he said, as he held up to the light the glass of old port which he was about to sip. In real life it is better to look back if one has anything to look back at.

Gore Vidal gave his definition of the two genres in his own memoir, *Palimpsest*. A memoir is how one remembers one's life while an autobiography is history requiring research dates and facts double-checked. So a memoir is something a bit livelier, with secrets revealed, and a more intimate focus—and there in a nutshell we have what it is about the memoir that bothers the veracity squad. Memory is a flawed thing, they grumble. At best it's a slippery slope. Unless you've carried a recorder around with you for your whole life or have a photographic memory, there's no way that the dialogue in your memoir can be factual. How to answer that? And does it matter, or change the essence of the book, that Hunter S. Thompson might actually have taken fewer tabs of acid the weekend that prompted *Fear and Loathing in Las Vegas*? Or that due to forgetfulness, Errol Flynn's tally of starlets, waitresses and boarding school maids was a few score short of the true mark? Or that in her memoir, *The Story of My Life*, Helen Keller described in great detail becoming deaf and blind at the age of 19 months—a stage at which neurologists and psychologists say it's highly unusual for us to retain memories?

Of course, there are plenty of examples of so-called memoirs that have completely departed from the truth: the literary hoax from Ern Malley to Helen Demidenko, via a string of other writers who have faked either their race or their story, has a long tradition in Australia, perhaps topped off by the memoirs of the ex-criminal Mark 'Chopper' Reid who wrote 13 of them, with help. We remember Demidenko—then actually Helen Darville and now Helen Dale, a Queenslander of English parentage—alternately embarrassing, then infuriating the local literary establishment in 1994 with her novel *The Hand That Signed the Paper*. This was the multi-prizewinning, supposedly autobiographical knowledge of a student's discovery of her family's bleak wartime history as peasants in Ukraine under Stalinism, and their so-called liberation by Nazi invasion. Here the criticism wasn't so much for the writing but for the author's Ukrainian masquerade including wearing national costume to receive Australia's biggest literary prizes, including the Miles Franklin and the Australian Literature Society's Gold Medal—plus the book's perceived antisemitism. I have a vivid memory of her at the winner's table dressed in a peasant blouse and brushing her long, pale blonde hair while being presented with the Australian Vogel Literary Award.

A more recent scandal centred on the international bestseller *Forbidden Love* by Norma Khouri, the supposed story of her relationship with Dalia, her best friend in Jordan, who fell in love with a Christian soldier, Michael. When Dalia's Muslim father discovered the chaste relationship, he stabbed Dalia to death in a frenzy in a so-called honour killing. Khouri wrote of her lifelong friendship with Dalia in Jordan, how her own life was in danger under the patriarchal Muslim system that protected Dalia's male relatives, and how she had to be smuggled out of Jordan to become a standard bearer for oppressed Arab women. Her book became a template for a rush of similar stories. Her hoax was uncovered after long investigation by *Sydney Morning Herald* reporter Malcolm Knox, who revealed Khouri—real name Norma Toliopoulis—had lived in Jordan only until the age of three, was an American citizen and had lived in Chicago ever since.

No matter how lame it sounds, all the writer can do is stress the first rule of memoir: that you shouldn't lie. And the veracity squad then say yeah, yeah, but we all know memory is flawed. For example, just picture a family Christmas dinner with several generations present and notice that everyone around the table has a different perspective on a particular incident in the past. And the serious memoirist will then say, a little self-righteously, 'but I tried to accurately and ethically reflect the intention of what was said and done', and the veracity squad will stomp away unconvinced. But what's the alternative? Have the memoirists and their families wear wires to ensure their lives are recorded with 100 per cent accuracy? Transcribe everything into a public record with nothing edited or crafted? Never dramatise a particular person into a standout character even though in your mind they were? No abusive priest or brutal former teacher would ever feel threatened under such a boring documentation procedure.

No creepy uncle, unfaithful ex-spouse or alcoholic father would ever feel betrayed. However, as long as writers have the desire not to simply record real life but to transform it into literature, this scenario seems highly unlikely.

Another difficulty for critics is that while memoirs might strive for the art of fiction, they're not believed capable of achieving the meaning found in novels. But there's an irony here, when novels are often dismissed for the sin of being memoir dressed as fiction. However, I think there's one excellent reason why a writer might choose to present something in memoir form rather than in fiction: it's because the story is better that way. This was definitely the case with four standout Australian memoirs: Raimond Gaita's *Romulus, My Father*, Sally Morgan's *My Place*, Timothy Conigrave's *Holding the Man* and Albert Facey's *A Fortunate Life*. They achieved meaning as true stories, as memoir rather than fiction, and our national culture would be infinitely poorer without them. On the other hand, a little fiction in Danni Minogue's memoir, *My Story*, in which she reveals the truth behind her divorce to Julian McMahon and her arguments on the panel of 'The X Factor', might have done the book no harm at all.

In 2000, I felt I should record certain chaotic events that occurred in my Perth suburban community and in our family home in the 1960s, and I began writing my memoir, *The Shark Net*. I certainly wasn't a writer keen to rush into a memoir, or to write a factual story for that matter, but for 35 years while I published novels and short stories, these events seemed both too powerful and too confusing to fully disclose. They didn't need to be transformed into something more artful, or with more meaning, or with more attention given to the writer. If anything I thought the way to deal with and understand the chaos of that time was not to emphasise ego, as memoirists are accused of doing, but to minimise it as much as possible and in doing so to reproduce the dazed confusion of the 18-year-old boy who was unwillingly near the centre of big events, but at the farthest remove from controlling them.

The encompassing story in *The Shark Net* was the five-year rampage of a serial killer, Eric Cooke, who is still embedded in West Australian folklore for killing eight complete strangers—including a friend of mine, John Sturkey, while he slept. The police were out of their depth looking for eight different killers because Eric Cooke killed in so many different ways: by gun, hatchet, knife, scissors, blunt instruments and motor vehicles. He was a murderer who worked for my father and was a regular visitor to our home—officially by day and unofficially, as a masked and gloved prowler, by night. Meanwhile, the community panic he caused—my father and I were among many adult and teenage males fingerprinted as potential murder suspects—was mirrored in our household by a simultaneous domestic chaos that culminated in the sudden death of my mother.

Now I doubt that the story in *The Shark Net* would have had more meaning if I'd turned it into a novel. It was already exuding meaning from every pore. In fact, I found it difficult to keep the meaning restrained. Some true stories are best kept true. Having said that, there are a couple of chapters in the book that are clearly fiction. In one, I reimagined a real incident in Cooke's pre-murdering days when, as a young show-off rejected at a dance by posh girls because of his hare lip, he dived fully clothed into the Swan River and swam across it. In another, I imagined his reaction, while on death row in Fremantle Prison, on hearing the news relayed to him by warders that his first son, Michael, a mentally delayed boy, had walked into the river and drowned. They were fictionalised fact because I had no way of checking with Cooke—he'd been hanged in 1964—but they were fiction based on what I gathered about his life and behaviour from long interviews I conducted with his widow and second son. It was important to me to show him as a human being and not just as a grim headline, a hare-lipped serial killer. As it happened, nothing I'd written before or have written since has had such a big reader reaction. About once a week, and more often when I'm in Western Australia, someone still either writes to me about the book or collars me in person to discuss it.

This brings up the two questions most asked about writing a memoir. How do you remember things that happened so long ago? And what's the reaction of people you've written about? All I can answer is that I've got one of those memories that easily recalls trivia and emotions and incidents from childhood but forgets passwords and the name of someone I met only yesterday. But what I recalled in *The Shark Net* and in the second memoir, *Montebello*, was so emotion-charged there was no chance I'd ever forget it. Having said that, of course I check dates and names and important events to make sure I've got them right because there's always someone who will rush in to correct you.

There is no one quite as self-righteous as a pedantic reader, especially an amateur historian—a burgeoning retirement occupation, as I found when the newspaper files in Perth's Battye Library provided the name of the cox in the Scotch College rowing crew who was killed by a bull shark in the Swan River in 1923 as Charles Robinson. Not at all, said my complainant, beginning a correspondence between us that lasted several years, during which he continued to demand the book be withdrawn from sale and pulped. He insisted the name was Charles Robertson.

As for my relatives' reaction to being named in a memoir, this potential problem didn't come up; an important facet of my memoirs (lucky for the memoirist, deeply troubling for my youthful self) being my parents' untimely early deaths. Frankly this underlines one common feature of the memoir:

I'd say that in 99 per cent of memoirs, the writer waits until the parents are dead. In the case of *The Shark Net*, I should mention there was one very well-known complainant: the American evangelist, Billy Graham. In the book, I recalled attending his crusade in the Perth Showgrounds with my mother in 1959. She was swept away by his charisma. I remained firmly in my seat. For some strange reason the Graham organisation denied he'd ever been to Perth. I supplied newspaper cuttings and photographs that show him on stage in the Perth Showgrounds, and of the 40,000 people who turned up, and the complainant went away.

There was one other conceivable problem I thought in mentioning, in unusual circumstances, the name of my closest childhood friend. One day when we were nine years old, he remarked to me thoughtfully that he wished he could remember what it was like to suck his mother's breasts. I didn't take much notice. He was always saying things like that. Next day he said, 'Well, I found out'. What? How? He'd asked his mother to remind him. 'You're nine years old,' I said. 'So what?' 'And she's old.' 'So?' There was a fairly long silence, then I asked, 'Well, what was it like?' He thoughtfully examined a wart on his thumb. 'It was okay. No milk, of course.' Anyway, I wrote about this highly unusual conversation, changing my friend's name in the book to Nick Howell to save him embarrassment and save me a potential libel suit. *The Shark Net* was duly published. I was on the publicity tour and speaking about the book at a reception at Perth Sheraton Hotel. At the end of my spiel, the chairperson invited questions from the audience. To my shock, a frowning middle-aged man shot to his feet, and in his mature face and heavier body I discerned the former nine-year-old boy whom I'd called Nick Howell. 'I have a question,' he said sternly, his voice echoing around the hotel reception room. 'In the book, you wrote about me sucking my mother's breasts when I was nine. That's right, you got that right. Why didn't you use my real name?'

While most stories enjoy the freedom of fiction, some stories need limitations like the overarching first person voice from the past, and the pressure of truth and the unique byplay that occurs in a memoir between the present and the past. In his essay *Reflection and Retrospection*, the distinguished American critic, Philip LaPorte, sees these so-called handicaps as advantages. In writing memoir, 'the trick it seems to me', he says, 'is to establish the double perspective which will allow the reader to participate vicariously in the experience as it was lived'. The author's retrospective employment of a more mature intelligence to interpret the past is not merely an obligation but a privilege, an opportunity. And the critic, Sven Birkerts, in *The Art of Time and Memoir*, adds that memoir begins not with event but with the intuition of meaning, with the mysterious fact that life can sometimes step free from the chaos of contingency and become story.

Now here's a case where I agree with the critics about a literary memoir not matching the author's fiction. Many, like me, found Salman Rushdie's memoir, *Joseph Anton*, a disappointing semi-failure. Rushdie's alias while he was on the run from the Iranian fatwah was chosen from the combination of the names of his illustrious literary heroes Conrad and Chekhov. Despite this little conceit, *Joseph Anton* didn't—perhaps couldn't—match the literary magnificence of his two prizewinning novels *Midnight's Children* and *Shame*, as the critics rightly complained. *Joseph Anton* was as pompous as it was intermittently gripping, with Rushdie referring to himself throughout in the third person like a rugby league footballer and a TV interviewer. Perhaps this was his delayed reaction to the grim events that turned him into the world's biggest literary celebrity. Perhaps, unfairly, we expected more meaning from such a long-running human interest news story that had already supplied just about everything that drama had to offer.

And perhaps we felt mildly queasy that Rushdie's ego was so obvious and so ordinary as to be delighted by such things as his cameo appearance in the chick flick *Bridget Jones' Diary*. We expected more of him. As he wrote of himself, acting was his unscratched itch. But the lack of intuitive reflection isn't the only point. It's not that I think his story of living under the Ayatollah's fatwah, of being on the run from a death sentence for more than a decade for offending Islam with *The Satanic Verses*, should only have been dealt with as fiction: it's about as powerful a story as one could imagine. I just think his memoir should have been a better memoir.

As it is, *Joseph Anton* succeeds as an insight into Rushdie's considerable self-esteem under extreme pressure, and I must say, who of us could have withstood similar tensions and for so long? It's indicative of *Joseph Anton* that some reviewers passed quickly over the intense human drama and concentrated on the frivolous revelations of his affairs and those of his allegedly wayward wives. And on the juicy literary gossip. For example, the first morning of the fatwah is also the day of Bruce Chatwin's funeral and in the church Rushdie sits next to Martin Amis and Paul Theroux who says, 'I suppose we'll be here for you next week, Salman'.

Rushdie is hardly the first enormously gifted novelist to have his memoirs shafted by the critics. Patrick White still gets a pasting in some quarters for *Flaws in the Glass*, published in 1981. According to Richard Davenport-Hines in *The Spectator* in 2012, 'his spiteful bestseller *Flaws in the Glass* must rank as the most inadvertently self-diminishing memoir since Somerset Maugham's'. Davenport-Hines urged new readers of White to go instead to the masterpieces of his mid-career. These are thunderingly powerful, full of emotional depth and grandeur, epigrammatic and ironic with brilliant scrutiny of human characters and motives. In contrast, *Flaws in the Glass* is an ugly book.

Another English literary magazine sulked because White hadn't written enough about being homosexual. The South African Nobel Laureate Nadine Gordimer entered the fray declaring, 'I should have been disappointed if he'd written more about being a homosexual than about becoming and being a writer'.[3] She went on to wonder: is autobiography the story of a personality or the work that has made the subject an object of sufficient public interest to merit writing about him or herself? 'If the subject is an artist,' she went on, 'and in particular a writer for whom the act is performed in the medium of his own art, what one wants and expects is a revelation of the mysterious incest between life and art'. Maybe there was some consolation for White in that, according to his biographer David Marr, *Flaws in the Glass* outsold all the famous novels proving, as if we didn't know already, not only that many readers prefer nonfiction but they prefer nonfiction full of vengeful waspish gossip.

But for every Rushdie and White accused of failing to imbue their memoirs with the same meaning as their novels, there are of course hordes of famous examples of fiction writers who did. Here's a few random examples—Nabokov's *Speak, Memory*, George Orwell's *Homage to Catalonia*, Graham Green's *A Sort of Life*, *I Know Why the Caged Bird Sings* by Maya Angelou, *De Profundis* by Oscar Wilde, *The Diaries of Samuel Pepys*, Hemingway's *A Moveable Feast*, Robert Grave's *Good-Bye to All That*, Tobias Wolff's *This Boy's Life*, Joan Didion's *The Year of Magical Thinking* and Paul Auster's *Winter Journal*. And, of course, there are famous entirely meaningful memoirs, never out of print, from previously unpublished writers like Anne Frank's *The Diary of a Young Girl* and T.E. Lawrence's *Seven Pillars of Wisdom*.

Twenty years ago, James Atlas in the *New York Times* asked, why this pull towards the anatomy of self?[4] He said it reflected a phenomenon pervasive in Western culture: people confessing in public to an audience of voyeurs. The notion of privacy, of a region beyond the reach of public probing, had become a foreign concept, he went on, and the culture of narcissism had been replaced by the culture of confession. It was a phenomenon that transcended high and low. The media revelled in the sexual peccadilloes of magnates and movie stars. Why should aspirants to literature be immune to this climate of unbridled candour? Writers no longer needed to furtively disguise their transgressions as fiction. Famously, Atlas wrote that if Proust were writing today about his penchant for observing handsome young men sticking hat pins in live rats, he wouldn't hide behind the narrator of his novel, *Remembrance of Things Past*. The book would be a memoir. Would that necessarily be wrong? As Robert Lowell, the American poet, put it, 'Why not say what happened?'

What can lie behind the critical disapproval of memoirs is the literary theorist's resentment that a genre exists that encourages the author not to sit anonymously and invisibly behind the text, but to stand centre stage in full light. To have the audacity to choose which portions of his or her life to emphasise also gives offence. Who do you think you are? What do you think you're doing? These are not the parts the critics would have chosen. Any novelist can be downcast by an inept review that marks him or her down for not choosing a subject that interests the critic more. Sheltering behind his review, the critic yawns dismissively, 'I like chess, Carlton Football Club and inner-city living, and you've gone and written a novel about fishing in the Arafura Sea. Sorry'. They can't grant the writers their material. It's clear that they want them to have written a different book. How much worse than for a memoir writer when those sort of reviewers want the writer to have lived a different life?

In their reviews of my second memoir, *Montebello*, a couple of critics, who I've never met, vigorously suggested they knew more about me than I did, and corrected me on this shortcoming. They went on to accuse me of only writing about myself to which I confess yeah, you got me, my memoir's about me.

1 William Gass, 'The Art of Self: Autobiography in an Age of Narcissism', *Harper's Magazine* (April 1994), harpers.org/2017/12/the-art-of-self.

2 Louise Adler, 'Political Memoirs', *Meanjin* (2015, 74(3)), meanjin.com.au/memoir/political-memoirs.

3 Nadine Gordimer, 'Mysterious Incest', *The New York Review of Books* (April 1982), nybooks.com/articles/1982/04/15/mysterious-incest.

4 James Atlas, 'Confessing for Voyeurs; The Age of the Literary Memoir Is Now', *The New York Times* (May 1996), nytimes.com/1996/05/12/magazine/confessing-for-voyeurs-the-age-of-the-literary-memoir-is-now.html.

Here I Stand

David Marr
2016

One afternoon in 1988, I had a call from Martin Road. Patrick White seemed to have had a stroke, and they needed my help, and would I come around? The drive from my place to White's, from one world to another, only ever took a few minutes, and I found the whole household mustered in Patrick's attic bedroom. His agent was there and so was the actress Kerry Walker, a great friend of Patrick's. And for the umpteenth time in his life, Manoly Lascaris had packed Patrick's hospital bag. The whole cast and crew was waiting for the ambulance to arrive.

Patrick lay silent. Kerry was reading to him, and he ignored her. He wasn't there. In the few days since I had last seen him, he'd shrunk. His hands gripping the blanket were knots of bones and veins, and his teeth were out. Once or twice in a soft, clear voice he said, 'Oh dear'. Outside, the birds were making a racket, the garden smelled of jasmine. It was a perfect spring afternoon. In the four years I'd been working on his life, I'd come very close to this man. I was learning things. He was lifting me up. Despite his impatience—'When are you ever going to finish that fucking book?' he would demand on the phone—he was, I knew, backing me entirely. And now, as far as I could see, he was dying.

I was poleaxed. But even as I stood there in the attic, I was asking myself, how will I write this? And I knew then that I would not be putting myself in the scene. It belonged not to me but to a dying man, his household, and the sweet angels of the New South Wales Ambulance Service who now came up the stairs. Wendy, a New Zealander, walked in asking the perfect question: 'What's the story?' Manoly began to explain. She ignored him. Behind her came a big bloke called Troy, who held Patrick's wrist very gently as he took his pulse. They didn't hurry—everything was calm and orderly. The stairs were too narrow for a stretcher, so they lifted Patrick between them in a bosun's chair. I wrote, he was breathing very heavily, and his arms kept dropping.

Wendy said, 'No, Patrick, mate, hold me 'round the shoulders'. They gave him a spell at the head of the stairs and then began to manoeuvre him down, pausing to rest every few steps. It took five minutes, perhaps more, for them to reach the hall. The back door was unbolted and in the light that streamed into the house, White looked like a sack of bones. His face was blank but his eyes were full of fear. They carried him through the garden, and down to the ambulance waiting in the lane.

I was invisible there. I was invisible in the two or three pages I wrote about Patrick's near-death experience and his recovery, after spending 36 hours on what he called the brink. Readers would be in no doubt if it crossed their minds to wonder that I was present at these events. There are no footnotes for pedants to track through my sources. I'd interviewed no-one. I was an eye witness. An oxygen mask, I wrote, was kept strapped to his face, and he was fed through a green tube in his nose. Pads on his chest connected him to a monitor in the corridor. His heart was on television. Forgive me: even 25 years later, I'm really proud of that joke. Patrick so loathed television.

He gave me his medical records with a survivor's pride. He knew the biographer needed them. They showed pneumonia, glaucoma, pulmonary fibrosis—his lifelong curse—a collapsed spine, chronic wheezing and rheumy eyes, but no sign of a stroke. As it turned out, he had two more years to live. In that time, I would witness one or two more heart-stopping crises at Martin Road. They are, like the first, all in the book, but I am not. I'd made a decision, I'd made a promise to myself: I would remain invisible. Of course, I'm also everywhere, as a biographer must be. My judgement is at play in every corner of the text, I wrote the words, it's my book, but David Marr—awkward, stumbling, occasionally charming David Marr—is nowhere in its pages, pulling focus from Patrick White.

Five years ago, Frances Spalding, speaking in this room in this series, wisely remarked it would be foolish to try to establish a set of rules for biography as it's a hybrid and fluid genre, always spilling out of neat packages, and persistently reshaping its enquiry as the questions that interest each generation change. This is one reason why there can be no such thing as a definitive biography. I agree with her, even as I stand here about to lay down the law.

After 30 or 40 years of reading, and once or twice writing biographies—lately, sharp little biographies of political players, men like cardinals and prime ministers and leaders of the opposition—I believe there are rules biographers should follow. I know these rules are personal. I know writers will come along, great writers, and break them with impunity, and even distinction, but these rules make sense to me.

My partner dreads me bringing a biography to bed. Novels he can live with, history causes no interpersonal problems, but when I have a biography in my hands I'm soon muttering, you can't do that, no, you can't do that, that's not the way to do it, no, you can't, oh no, no, that's completely impossible. I say this tonight, Sebastian, by way of apology.

My key rules are: one, the voice of the subject must always be clear in the text; but, two, the biographer must command the life. Three, we must not muck around with time—we must always be moving, as in life, into an unknown future. Four, spare readers your homework; and, five, biographers should remain as much as possible out of sight. Each of these rules is worth a Seymour Lecture, but I'm here tonight to commend only the last, to make a case against current fashion for the invisible biographer—to argue that great biographies work by establishing an intimate relationship between reader and subject, a relationship that does not need, and may be doomed, if chaperoned by the biographer. Biographers write, and we should leave readers to get on with it.

I'd been a journalist for 10 or 12 years when I sent Patrick what I know now to be the most tortured letter I have ever written in my life, warning him that I was planning to write his biography. I didn't think for a minute the news would please him. I did not expect cooperation. All I was asking from the laureate of Centennial Park was a truce. I wanted to get on with the project without being sabotaged.

There's a reassuring cliché that biographers spout, that we need no-one's permission to write their lives, none of us owns our own life, every life is available for a biographer. That's true but mighty obstacles can be put in our path. I'd already been run ragged by the Chief Justice, Sir Garfield Barwick, as I worked on his life in the aftermath of the Sacking. Barwick received me cordially in his old chambers at Taylor Square but didn't, on reflection, much like what he saw, and made certain over the next three years that none of his friends spoke to me. I worked around the problem.

The second method, not available to Barwick, was to forbid access to papers. A forceful Russian who became by marriage Lady Maria St Just, invented for herself, after Tennessee Williams's death, the role of protectress of his reputation. She blocked access to his papers for a generation, killed off at least two biographies, brought scholarship on Williams's work to a standstill, and made life hell for producers of the plays. John Lahr's much acclaimed (but I think unsatisfying) biography of the playwright was only made possible by St Just's death.

She was also a ruthless exponent of strategy number three for sabotaging biographers: the withholding of copyright consent. I'm torn about this. As an author, I welcome the fact that my copyrights will remain in force, funnelling a fortune to my nephews and nieces for 70 years after my death. But in solidarity with frustrated biographers, particularly biographers of writers, I would wish they expired on death. When families inherit copyright, reputation becomes a family matter. Widows are terrible, sisters are worse. They operate on the principle that what was hidden in life must remain hidden in death. When we read a biography that tiptoes round the truth, particularly difficult truths of the heart, pause before condemning the biographer and ask, who owns the copyrights?

Cavafy kept biographers at bay for nearly 70 years with a unique fourth strategy, essentially laying a curse on biographers as a class. In 1908, living alone above a brothel in Alexandria, his work unknown except by a few Greek connoisseurs in that city, Cavafy knew with absolute certainty that fame would come one day—fame and biographers—and he wrote these staggering lines: 'From all the things I did, and all the things I said, let no one try to find out who I was'. Aren't they fabulous? 'From all the things I did, and all the things I said, let no one try to find out who I was.' He was not declaring himself off-limits forever, but he demanded that the times be right before biographers wrote. In this poem, *Hidden Things*, a kind of sonnet that might usefully be pinned over every biographer's desk, the poet explained.

> An obstacle was there transforming the actions and the manner of my life.
> An obstacle was often there to silence me when I began to speak.
> From my most unnoticed actions, and my most veiled writing,
> from these alone will I be understood.

Clearly, in 1908, Cavafy had no idea how candid his poetry would become over the next couple of decades. He was not in the end, I believe, remotely silenced. Still, that curse, or perhaps magisterial direction, that Cavafy delivered at this early point in his career sets a standard for all biographers, that there may be times when we have to wait until we can see, and the times allow us to write, what lies in most veiled writings and unnoticed actions.

The first biography of Cavafy didn't appear until 1974. It's not very good. It was written by a man called Robert Liddell. Manoly Lascaris knew Liddell in Alexandria during the war, and gave him a copy of Patrick White's *Happy Valley* to check whether this man he'd fallen so deeply in love with was indeed the writer he seemed. Liddell reported that the novel was terribly good, but warned Manoly he might end up strangled like one of the residents of Happy Valley, Mrs Moriarty. Lascaris decided to take the chance. This might be the end of me, he thought, but it has to be.

When I knocked on Patrick's door, I feared every kind of obstruction would be put in my way, the whole lot of them: silenced friends, closed archives, forbidden copyrights, bans and curses—particularly curses. But instead he asked me in.

By sheer luck, I'd come along at precisely the right moment. Having no longer the energy to tackle big novels—he'd just abandoned a novel which is in this Library somewhere in handwritten form—and he abandoned it at the one-third point. And we—meaning me and a couple of other Patrick White scholars with, of course, the cooperation of his literary executor, Barbara Mobbs—published that fragment a couple of years ago. It's one of the happiest things I've ever done.

So he could no longer tackle big novels, he just didn't have the energy. And he'd said already what he wanted to say about his own life in his memoir, *Flaws in the Glass*, and he felt he could face a biography. Indeed, he felt a biography was due to him by about this stage. And he had a secret purpose which took me years to discover. My ambitions, of course, were absolutely conventional. I was after all born in Pymble. I'd been intrigued by White's writing, the little I knew of his life since I was a child. I wanted to find out who he was, where his writing came from, how his country had shaped him, and how he had more than a little, shaped his country. But Patrick saw the biography as a last reckoning, a chance to tie up the loose ends of his life, to find what was left of the people and causes he'd discarded in his long existence. I would be his spy, bringing back to Martin Road news of his scattered world. He hoped for a last few cluster bombs thrown at the establishment, and he looked forward eagerly to being around to enjoy mayhem at the book's publication.

The next half dozen years turned out to be much more complicated than that. At first very wary, Patrick came to trust me. I was never blind to how appalling he might be, but I think it's true to say that I came to love him. He was the wisest man I have ever known well, but I never saw myself as a player in his story. As Auden says of poets, I made nothing happen.

My determination to stay out of sight in the biography was in part, I know, simply good manners. There's Pymble again, I suppose. It seemed to me, then and now, discourteous to elbow my way into someone else's life, but it was also truthful. I was determined not to claim a relationship with White that I did not have. Our relationship was essentially professional. I was not one of his class or circle. I was not there as a friend, a colleague, or a member of the family. I had work to do. I was an observer—privileged, but an observer.

I know if I was writing that book today my editors would be urging me vigorously to get in there, to get into its pages. They would be telling me I should be seen in there hunting down the real Patrick White. I should be writing tales of adventures in my researches. I should be writing about the way in which I tracked White's life all round the world. I should write about the night in the streets of Alexandria when I stumbled on a Nubian wedding. I should talk about the goldmine of letters that turned up by chance in Texas.

Those editors would have in mind something like Thornton McCamish's recent and in many ways splendid biography of Alan Moorehead, *Our Man Elsewhere.* After a brief synopsis of the popular historian's life and works, McCamish bears his soul on page 6. Every book lover knows the thrilling experience of discovering a writer whose work changes the way they see the world. It had already happened to me several times before I picked up (Moorehead's) *A Late Education*, in my late 20s, so I knew what was happening as I read. I'd found a writer who would forever be indispensable to my imaginative sense of the past. A few pages, later McCamish and his wife are admiring the faded splendour of Moorehead's favourite hotel in Cairo when it seems to the author that the man himself appears: 'I could almost see him drawing back the accordion grill of the elevator car, releasing a gust of big band mood music and stepping out neat and alert, tie knotted, folded cap tucked under the epaulette, I could see him dropping into a club chair right there, ready to set out on his brilliant career right there'.

This is horrible stuff on a number of fronts, not least because McCamish is such an assured biographer and shows such supple judgement of his subject, that none of this personal scene-setting, or the very many pages he devotes to his search for Moorehead, are in the least bit necessary. I'm being harsh, I know, but I don't care that the biographer is standing in a bar, or on a street corner, or on a hill where Moorehead once stood. I want everything McCamish learned by going to these places, which we must do. By doing his homework, I want everything he learned along the way absorbed in the text, and in his understanding of his subject. I don't care that McCamish is excited by this or that. His task is to excite me, and frankly I don't care about McCamish, particularly as he makes me, with such skill when he's truly concentrating on his task, care so deeply about Moorehead.

There are two fundamental difficulties with quest biographies. First, they inflict homework on readers. Biographers find research thrilling. We couldn't possibly be in the game unless we did. I have had some of the most exciting days of my life in the Petherick Room, which has, without my permission, been moved in the Library. But the thrills of research are almost impossible to convey, because the thrills come after long periods of boredom. It's the thrill of triumph, a moment of triumph, after days of defeat. You have to be there, you have to be there. You cannot inflict the boredom on the reader, to give them the thrill. It is a very personal business, research.

The second problem with the quest biography is that they bugger around with time. All biography is time travel. Taking readers to another time is very hard, and it makes it harder if, for instance, you want them to be in 1940s Cairo, if you keep shuffling between then and now, between what Moorehead and what

McCamish saw, between the go-getting war correspondent then, and the fan driven 70 years later by the thrill of the chase.

Now even as I lay down the law tonight, I must acknowledge great exceptions to my distaste for quest biography, and the greatest of these is surely *The Quest for Corvo*, A.J.A. Symons's life of the writer, pimp and religious nut, Frederick Rolfe. Rolfe wrote the novel, *Hadrian the Seventh*. It's a novel I think of every time a pope dies because it's about a character whose knock on the door … is the call to Rome—because the rule is, of course, that the cardinals can call on anybody to be a pope. Doesn't have to be a cardinal theoretically, doesn't even have to be a Christian. God can direct them to call on anyone in the world to be a pope. This is the underlying thesis of Rolfe's hilarious novel: when any pope dies, I wait for the knock on the door.

Symons's biography is an endless delight, but the point is that there's nothing much to Baron Corvo at all. The quest biography is perfectly suited to the life of a fraud. Moorehead was no fraud. McCamish would have served him better to have left his enthusiasms to a brief preface, newspaper interviews post-publication, talks at writers' festivals and one day, when he's suitably old, his Seymour Lecture. It is, by the way, a pretty good book. But I'm not saying for a moment that I've at all times kept myself out of my writing. I'm not shy. I'm not afraid to put myself out there. I'm not reluctant to use what old subs at Fairfax call the vertical pronoun.

I came into the trade in the 1970s, when something called new journalism was all the rage. It was enriching and renewing journalism by making journalists able to talk more directly about their personal response to the situations that they were reporting. In that, it was truthful. The old absolutely blank style of journalism was giving way to something more personal. But the problem was that bright beginners like me, we all believed that our response was the most interesting thing about a story, and that had to be beaten out of us.

Well perhaps it was beaten out of me a little too thoroughly by those old subs at Fairfax, because I had to fight my way back to a style of writing that was personal, perhaps even deeply personal, but it was not about me. I didn't have to keep putting me onto the page. Mind you, that has to happen from time to time, and that has to happen I've discovered in writing those *Quarterly Essays*. They're sprints, they're not the long-distance efforts of the big biography. They're not seven years and 300,000 words, as it was with Patrick White. They're four months and 30,000 words. They still have the same purpose: to make sense of this country through biography, and so I've written about Rudd and Abbott and Pell and Shorten. And the power of the *Quarterly Essay* is that they involve face-to-face encounters. The most difficult of these I had with Bill Shorten because he was so veiled, so veiled. But the most personal was with Rudd, and there was no way of me keeping myself out of the denouement of that *Quarterly Essay*.

We had at last met. It was for the interview. We'd met along the way but now was the time for the interview. Typically, Rudd said that the interview—I live and work in Sydney—the interview will take place in Mackay. So I flew to Mackay. It was to take place in the afternoon, and we walked along the beach at Mackay with only two security guards as our company. People called out to Kevin, you're the best prime minister we've ever had. He warmed to such remarks.

As we walked along, in a spirit of great candour, I warned him that the essay would begin with me quoting something he had been saying around the meeting rooms the year before in Copenhagen: 'Those Chinese fuckers are trying to rat-fuck us'. And I will never forget the sound of our feet squeaking in the sand as we walked along in silence. But we patched that over, and had an hour or so of very intimate talk, for which I'm very grateful. Then we had dinner together, and as the dinner was ending he sort of asked—he asked me, man to man—what my essay on him was actually going to be about. And I thought, well, it's an adult asking an adult a question, we've been talking frankly to one another for some hours, and so I told him. Hmm. And this is what I wrote: he lost his temper.

> He doesn't scream and bang the table as he does behind closed doors. We're in the open. The voice is low. He's perfectly composed. From the distance of the next table it would be hard to tell how furious the Prime Minister is. Indeed, some boys come over in the middle of it all to ask to have their picture taken with him. Later, he says politely and returns to his work. What he says in these angry twenty minutes informs every corner of this essay. But more revealing than the information is the transformation of the man. In his anger Rudd becomes astonishingly eloquent. This is the most vivid version of himself I've encountered. At last he is speaking from the heart, an angry heart.

Now I had to be there. I had to be on the page to pull that off.

Standing here a couple of years ago, Ray Monk talked about Boswell, and rightly declared his *Life of Samuel Johnson* among the best biographies ever written. A new kind of biography, said Monk, a narrative that's driven by personality, by what we would call—but Johnson didn't—the inner life. And my guess is that for the last half hour many of you have been muttering to yourselves, as I mutter about biography in bed, what about Boswell? Doesn't Boswell make nonsense of Marr's plea for the invisible biographer? No. I'm not demanding an absolute ban. I'm arguing for us to stay out of the way unless there is a purpose for being there in the text. Boswell had a purpose when he wrote one of the great double acts of literature. Boswell earned the right to be Boswell.

I first read the *Life of Johnson* when I was 24 years old, working in the bar of a ski hotel in Austria. I'd brought it as my winter book. There was a lot going on around me. Over Christmas, this rather Spartan hotel was an outpost of astonishing members of the aristocracy. One of the families that came was so grand that the governess they brought with them was a Habsburg. And the hotel belonged to the former private secretary of Ribbentrop, whose sons had oddly Spanish names and who it turned out had only returned from the Argentine a few years earlier. There was a lot going on around me, and what did I do? I read Boswell's *Life of Johnson*. And the other day I picked the book up again, and was reminded by how compelling it is. I took it to bed chortling.

Boswell tells us he's writing for the curious, for the curious in literature. It's a key word. Yes, it points to curiosity in people, but it also brings in the notion that the curious—curious objects, curious incidents, veiled writings, unnoticed actions—can reveal big truths. In the late nineteenth century, the word curious had a scientific flavour. Monk puts Boswell among the pioneer novelists like Defoe, but he was also one of the greats of the Scottish Enlightenment, the pragmatic philosophers and economists and scientists who were trying in the late eighteenth century to work out, with fresh eyes and sharp intelligence, how the world really worked. Boswell's world was Johnson. He gathered the evidence, and he threw it all in. That it'd show him in a bad light—him, Boswell—didn't bother Boswell a bit. He was quite abject about it. He's a kind of abject sponge, he sucks it all up and throws it in.

The account of his first meeting with Johnson is so wonderful. He'd been trying to engineer a meeting, trying and failing. All these people he'd hoped would introduce him to Johnson, you know, dropped the issue. And then Johnson one day just wandered into a shop where Boswell was, and it's all recorded in the book. Boswell tries a light sally about Scotland, and Johnson just slashes him down. He tries another sally, and Johnson once again just smashes him. It's all there, it's all recorded there. Anyway, he felt that on the basis of these exchanges, both of which he'd lost so comprehensively, he might call on Johnson, and he did. And there is this account of the first of his first proper meetings with Johnson. How can you not trust a man who humiliates himself in his own text, and then turns his eye on the subject of his devotion, really, and writes this?

> He received me very courteously; but, it must be confessed that his apartment, and furniture, and morning dress, were sufficiently uncouth. His brown suit of clothes looked very rusty; he had a little old shrivelled unpowdered wig, which was too small for his head; his shirt neck and knees of his breeches were loose, his black worsted

> stockings ill drawn up; and he had a pair of unbuckled shoes by way of slippers. But all these slovenly peculiarities were forgotten the moment he began to talk.

And for the next 20 years Boswell sat there and wrote down all that talk. That's what I mean by saying Boswell earned the right to be Boswell. He built a biography on scientific lines, with every document he could find and a couple of decades' conversation. He was an indispensable part of that to and fro. They quarrel, they quip, they test one another, they fall out, they make up, and from these exchanges emerges an often comic picture of Boswell, and a portrait of Johnson that remains, after 200 years, an unequalled masterpiece.

So my advice to biographers determined to clamber onto the stage and play around with their subjects in the limelight is, do the work. Put in the years. Entangle your lives, and then you've earned the right to walk the stage together. Even then, you will be marked down as a show-off—my mother's most cutting rebuke—unless you deal with yourself as ruthlessly as Boswell did with himself.

I know there are no fixed rules. I know what I'm talking about is a question of taste. I know this isn't a matter of life and death. I'm a grumpy old guy who hasn't found, in 20 years, another big life worth writing. I read biographies with an impatient eye, but I would wish an end to the rather tired idea that the biographer should be out there sharing our attention. Why, in the end? Because frankly we are rather tedious people. Where should we stand? In the shadows—in the shadows manipulating everything, leaving readers with the illusion that they are alone in the company of Brett Whiteley, or Wittgenstein, or Lyndon Johnson—and by the way Mr Caro, hurry up, please, with the next instalment of your life of President Lyndon Baines Johnson. I'm getting impatient. I want the fifth volume.

The potency of biography is compelling intimacy. That is why we read biography with such passion. Compelling intimacy, though, with people far more interesting than biographers.

Truth. Truthfulness. Self. Voice.

Raimond Gaita
2017

I'm deeply honoured, obviously. Who could not be to have been asked to give this lecture—though I hesitated to accept the invitation because I've not written a biography or autobiography. Nor have I reflected on these forms of writing with the depth, knowledge and literary refinement possessed by some of the previous lecturers: David Marr and Robert Dessaix, to name just two. That's partly because they are writers—real writers, writers with a capital W—which I'm not.

From the time I wrote *Romulus, My Father*, I've been called a philosopher and a writer, or sometimes a philosopher and an author. I understand why: I know I'm not here because I wrote *Good and Evil: An Absolute Conception*, or edited, with Gerry Simpson, *Who's Afraid of International Law?* But I'm not being coy when I say that I'm not a writer. I'm often appalled by the clumsiness of my prose yet when my efforts to ameliorate that are even partially successful, those efforts don't give me the kind of pleasure, the kind that writers take—by definition, I'm almost inclined to say—in a well-constructed sentence.

A dear late friend, the poet and essayist Peter Steele, wrote a wonderful essay called 'Poetry as the Mind in Love'. You can read it in a collection of his essays titled, *Braiding the Voices: Essays in Poetry*. Poetry as the mind in love could be generalised to become writing as the mind in love. In love, of course, with language. I'm not that kind of lover. It's true that I've said to my wife, Yael, and to some friends, that I wish I could write poetry, but one reason I know that I never will, or never could, is just because I'm not that kind of lover. I'd like to write poetry, not because I'd like to create poems in which I and others could delight, but because I believe if I could write good poetry, it would make me—make my sensibility—more adequate to the wondrous complexity and beauty of the world.

When Robert Manne became editor of *Quadrant* following the collapse of the Soviet Union, a collapse that made Cold War politics obsolete, I wrote over 50 columns for him. I say for him because I wasn't naturally a *Quadrant* author. Readers complained to Rob every month saying they couldn't understand a word that I wrote. One wrote a letter to the editor in which he says something like this: 'Each month I wait with masochistic anticipation for the arrival of *Quadrant*, to see what new barbarities Raimond Gaita has perpetrated on the English language'. When I read that, I was reminded of a fellow student at University of Melbourne in the late 1960s who wrote in a review of an article that I'd written, 'Gaita says that Sartre distinguishes what he calls things in themselves from things for themselves, but if you ask me the whole thing is up itself'. You'll understand, then, why, when some people urged me to write about my father and our life together in central Victoria, I replied that, while there might be a good story to be told, I was not the person to tell it. Well, I did write it, and people now call me a writer, and always I protest sincerely that I'm not, and always people think that I don't really mean it.

I don't think of *Romulus, My Father* as a biography, and still less as an autobiography, because it doesn't contain the degree of critical psychological probing that would justify being called either. This is not a distinction I'm prepared to die for, but anyway, that's the reason that I decline both descriptions. I've described *Romulus* as a tragic poem. I hope that doesn't sound pretentious. Obviously, I don't mean to compare it to the great tragedies, especially the Greek ones that so affected me. The reason that category or the genre—that is, of tragedy—came to mind is given in the book itself.

After I describe how I felt, at the age of 15, visiting my father in a psychiatric hospital after he'd gone mad, I say that as a student:

> tragedy, with its calm pity for the affliction it depicts, was the genre that first attracted my passionate allegiance. I recognised in it the concepts that had illuminated the events of my childhood. They enabled me to see Mitru [who was my mother's lover], my mother, my father and Vacek, living amongst his boulders, as the victims of misfortune, in their different ways broken by it, but never thereby diminished.

I didn't avoid psychological probing because I feared it would reveal to the reader, or to myself for that matter, things best left under cover—not consciously at any rate. Instinctively, I wrote in a genre not suitable for such probing. A friend to whom I showed the first draft suggested I put it away and later, when I was ready, write a much longer book. He's deeply and professionally interested in psychoanalysis and I'm sure wanted me to reflect on my relationship with my parents, especially my mother. I declined his suggestion because I realised immediately that it would not make for a better book of the kind that I had drafted, but instead make for a book of a different kind altogether. What informed my understanding of the kind of book I had written was my understanding of tragedy as I characterised it a moment ago, as showing a calm pity for the suffering that it depicts.

I didn't know what I was doing when I wrote the first draft of *Romulus, My Father* in three feverish weeks, oscillating between exhilaration and depression. I'd only written philosophy before and, though I instinctively wrote in a certain genre, I had no conscious intention to do so, and few other conscious intentions other than to write truthfully, and to bear a kind of witness to values by which my father lived. I think despite the book's many failings I achieved that, and I'm grateful to people like J.M. Coetzee and philosopher Jean Curthoys who seemed to acknowledge that. Coetzee writes:

> one of the features of Gaita, as a philosopher, is his interest in embodied values, in an ethical truth that lives in the world. It's not because he preaches certain values, but because he embodies certain values that the unlettered blacksmith, Romulus Gaita, came to serve as a lifelong moral compass for his son, and via his son, to us.

Reviewing a book of essays in my honour, Jean Curthoys, who taught philosophy at University of Sydney, writes—making clear that the tribute is to my father rather than to me:

> It's a mark of Gaita's persistent reminder of how much he learnt from his father that so many of the prominent writers and academics who have contributed to this collection of essays and two poems on Gaita's ethical thought accept Romulus as the ground of that thought. And are comfortable with the idea that a man barely educated, a blacksmith of peasant background, a man who once contemplated murder, and who never fully recovered from the psychosis to which he succumbed in mid-life, had a depth of understanding which when presented in the language of moral philosophy, put that profession to shame, as the endorsements to the second edition of *Good and Evil* attest.

While some people, or some critics indeed, have said that had I been ethically more critical and psychologically more probing of my father, I would have been able to enter more fully into my mother's perspective on the world, I think they missed something fundamental. They failed to see, as people often do, what is involved in understanding another person's take on the world.

I was 12 when my mother killed herself. I hadn't seen her for almost two years, and not much before that in my life. To see the world as someone else sees it, you need to be imaginatively inward with the concepts in whose light they understand themselves, others and the world. If some of those concepts are fragmented, only partially understood by the person who possesses them, as was obviously the case with my mother in regard to her illness, then you have to understand that too. Iris Murdoch said that understanding of another person is 'a work of love, justice and pity'. For it to be a work of justice you have ideally to be in conversation with a person, or at least in an imaginative conversation with them; to be able to speak to them, to ask them why they believe this or have done that and then listen and possibly respond to their replies.

Empathy, or at any rate the desire and the capacity to understand as fully as possible how another person understands things, is essentially—I mean that it belongs to its very nature—a dialogical engagement. This is how I put it in an essay about my mother, whose title is 'An Unassuagable Longing', published in *After Romulus*, 13 years after the publication of *Romulus, My Father*.

> When I drive to Shalvah [the house my wife and I built in the country] passing through Castlemaine and then Maldon on roads my father and I travelled often, or when I'm on the beach road driving to Mentone in Melbourne where Hora lived, I miss them, sometimes intensely. I don't miss my mother in that way. I sometimes also wonder what my father would think of the film or the book, or what Hora would think of the film, but I can speculate, knowing them, that they might think this or think that, or that they would be unpredictable in the way that only human beings can be.
>
> My mother, of course, had a distinctive perspective on the world. Neil Mikkelsen, who as a young farmer was, I suspect, in love or at least infatuated with her, described her to me before I wrote *Romulus, My Father* as 'a woman of substance'. Commenting on that in the book, I say that he probably meant not merely that she was no scatterbrain, but that she had the arresting presence of someone who experienced the world with a thoughtful intensity.
>
> I never knew my mother like that, not because I knew her differently, but because as a child I could not make such a judgement. She doesn't have for me the individuated presence of an adult, a distinctive perspective on the world. So I can't imagine being with her as though she did. But that's how she would have to be if I could miss her in the way I miss my father and Hora. I wish I could miss her that way.
>
> When I miss my father and Hora, I imagine them in conversation. I could miss my mother as I do them only if I could talk to her as an adult. If I could ask her why she did this or that, or if I could comfort her were she to ask for it, or to forgive her for the wrong she did me, if she were inclined to ask for that, for which I sorrow but do not judge her. But I cannot seriously conceive of any of this.

> I knew her only as a boy. Even when I wonder anxiously what she would make of the book or the film, *Romulus, My Father*, and of this book, *After Romulus*, and of me, her son, who put her under intense public scrutiny, I know that, though I can frame the question that I would put to her, it's incoherent for me even to try to imagine a conversation with her.

I read that passage at such length because I think it makes an important point about empathy, which is now such a prized virtue.

There is a deeper reason why I didn't know what I was doing when I wrote *Romulus, My Father.* For some months after I decided to write about him—a decision triggered by responses to the publication in *Quadrant* of a eulogy that I gave at his funeral in 1996—I tried, but failed, to write more than a few pages. Then in late January of 1997, I listened to a tape of music that one of my daughters had given me. On it was a song by a country and western singer, Emmylou Harris, called 'Goodbye'. 'I can't remember if we said goodbye' is its refrain. It's not a great song, but that haunting refrain suits the melody and her voice. For a week, I played it every day—loud, so loud that the glasses rattled in their cabinets and the bass rumbled in my guts. I then told my wife that I would rent a cottage near where I grew up and write the book about my father. I spent the first week, of three, writing about my mother.

That obviously provides rich material for psychological speculation, but I don't think much of it would add to an understanding of *Romulus, My Father*, or even of 'An Unassuagable Longing'. It would fill no interesting interpretive gaps, I think, unless such speculation was forced into those gaps by didactic theoretical or ideological reductionist pressure.

Peter Gay says in his biography of Freud that Freud wrote to Stefan Zweig saying, 'whoever turns biographer commits himself to lies, to concealment, to hypocrisy, to embellishments, and even to dissembling his own lack of understanding, for biographical truth is not to be had'. That's Freud at his worst. I say that as an admirer, indeed as someone who's trying to finish a long overdue essay for the *Oxford Handbook of Philosophy and Psychoanalysis.* At best Freud's comment is an exaggerated way of saying that biography and autobiography are vulnerable to psychologically motivated distortions. But anybody who took it as read—took what Freud said literally—would not read biography or autobiography. Nor would anybody who took it literally be interested in the Seymour Lectures on Biography unless they came to them only to see if someone at last had the courage to tell the truth, as they believed Freud did. Peter Gay obviously didn't take it seriously otherwise he wouldn't have written his biography of Freud.

If someone were to ask—as of course many people have—was Romulus or Christine Gaita as their son depicts them, some would answer that they were and others that they were not. Theories about my actual complex psychological state —I mean as that state was then rather than as it appears in the book—will not settle, or even help to settle, those questions. Of course, someone who believes that they were not as I described them might invoke psychological accounts of my unconscious motives to explain why I failed to characterise them as they were. Yet those accounts will not establish that they were not as I said they were.

So, though I had no idea of what I was doing when I wrote *Romulus, My Father*, I do believe I know what I'm doing in the as-yet-unfinished book of essays that express gratitude to, often love of, people I've known who have mattered deeply to me, some of whom have inspired me. I'll include part of one of those essays in this lecture. Perhaps they're better described as elegies or portraits. Some are of teachers, others are of friends. One is of my late father-in-law. Writing about him, I'll inevitably write about my wife. My publisher calls it my 'mentors' book' and I understand why he does it, but 'mentor' is not a concept that can capture adequately how some of the people I write about have mattered to me. At its deepest and most precious, they nourished in me a love of the world of a kind that's not conditional upon a weighing up of the good and the evil in it. Sometimes it was mediated by the beauty of the natural world, and sometimes by the beauty of things human beings have created.

Because, for me, the things that human beings have created extend back to ancient Greece, I live joyously in an extended continuous presence. Plato is my companion. So are Descartes and Kant, to name only a few great philosophers. Ditto for Aeschylus, Shakespeare, Dostoevsky and Bach, and of course there are others. I couldn't imagine my life without them.

The essays—I'll continue to call them essays—would be worthless, or will be worthless when they're finished, if they're not truthful in intent and achievement. In such small pieces (none is longer than 5,000 words) that explicitly express gratitude, much will be left unsaid, just as in fact much is left unsaid in *Romulus, My Father*. My hope, as it was when I wrote *Romulus*, is that what is left unsaid will not compromise the truthfulness of what is said. There will, of course, be many psychological and ethical motives urging me to write as I would wish things to be rather than as they were or are. But it's scepticism about the possibility of truthfulness of a more radical kind than the one that directs us to psychologically motivated distortions that I want to talk about this evening.

It's now commonplace to observe that if you ask seven people to describe someone they all know, they'll tell seven different stories. It's an observation that can point in two directions. Taking us in one direction, it directs attention to psychological difficulties that stand in the way of an account upon which all seven could converge. For so long as the difficulties are only psychological, disagreement is, at least in principle, likely to be resolvable and agreement attainable. But when the observation that the seven people will tell seven different stories about the same person known to them all takes us in another direction, then the scepticism implicit in it is more radical. It claims that the differences cannot, even in principle, be resolved in a way that could reveal what the person was really like, because there's nothing in this world, no facts, that amount to what someone is really like, against which we could match various narratives in order to assess their truthfulness.

What I said in response to Freud I say again now. Anyone who professes that kind of scepticism will not read biography, autobiography, narrative history or anything else that relies on the assumption that there is, at least in principle, an answer to the question, 'Was so and so really like that?' It will be asked of the portraits in my new book. I hope the answer will always be yes. How could I not hope that?

For the remainder of the lecture I want to discuss why I think that is a justified hope. I'll do it by reflecting on an extract from one of the essays in this new book. Its subject is a man whose name was Martin Winkler. He taught theology in Germany in the 1930s with the great organist and humanitarian Albert Schweitzer. When he was around 40, Schweitzer gave up his university post and concert career and trained to become a doctor. After graduating in medicine, he went to Africa where he built a hospital in order, he believed, to bring the benefits of Western medicine to one of the many places in the world where it was desperately needed.

Schweitzer asked Winkler to accompany him, but because Schweitzer worked, as Winkler put it, 26 hours a day, he declined. Not long after, however, he went to New Guinea to do there the same sort of work that Schweitzer did in Africa, though not as a doctor; Winkler trained as a nurse. When war broke out, he was arrested as an enemy alien and brought to Australia where he spent the remainder of the war in internment camps. After he was released he practised as a Lutheran pastor, and worked for some years as a labourer until he was employed to teach German at Ballarat Grammar School. Though I went to another school as a boarder, Saint Patrick's College, Winkler taught me German at the grammar school from Year 9 until the end of Year 11, when I left Saint Patrick's College to attend Melbourne High School.

Winkler was perhaps the wisest man I have known. Eccentric and a strong passionate personality, he was more than a little daunting. But in Year 11, threatened with expulsion from St Pat's, I found refuge each week in his study.

The headmaster told me that I was corrupting the boys because I had read Bertrand Russell on education, and had spoken enthusiastically to them about his attitude to sex and sex education. 'I don't like the way you think, Gaita, but I like the way you play football,' he told me, explaining why he hadn't yet thrown me out. It was a famous footballing school, St Pat's. I wasn't a great footballer, but I was called 'the tank' because I couldn't see without my glasses and so I just went through everything. The headmaster took what was in fact a disability as the virtue of courage. That's why he said, 'I like the way you play football'. He thought I had what they call character, of one kind anyway.

Winkler liked the way I thought, so when he learned about the cause of my trouble he gave me a book to read—at home, I should say, because I was about to go there on vacation. 'He's superficial, he doesn't understand what he attacks, but you might as well understand why you are in such trouble,' he told me. The author to whom he referred was Russell and the book was called *Why I'm Not a Christian*, which he took the trouble to borrow from the Ballarat City Library.

Despite reading Russell or, perhaps as the headmaster of St Pat's probably thought, because I read him, my energies at the time were more directed to becoming a juvenile delinquent than to study, infatuated as I was then by the rebellious glamour of Elvis Presley, Jimmy Dean and Marlon Brando. Why did Winkler play Bach to me when I came to him to learn German in order to read the humanities at university? Winkler more than honoured his responsibility to do that, and in the process I came to see how the love of his subject (German language and literature) and his love of Bach and Handel and of much German cultural history, were inseparable.

Without compromising the need to do what was necessary to enable me to pass my examinations, Winkler taught me what it can be to love a language—a natural language, steeped in the history of a people who shaped it and were shaped by it. For him, the study of a language was a kind of anthropology that enabled one not only to understand a people and their mode of life, but also a way of being human in their language. I'm sure that's why I've emphasised, in much of my work, the importance that our thinking about almost everything that defines the human condition should be expressed in a natural language, used creatively.

Winkler was in fact initiating me to what Plato would have called a form of pedagogical eros, initiating me into the art of loving as Socrates put it in the *Symposium*. Conscious though he was of the greatness of much of what's called Western civilisation, he was a European through and through, steeped in German culture. His knowledge of the evils of Europe, especially of Germany, lacerated his soul as much as love of its treasures nourished it. For a man like him it could not have been otherwise so soon after the Holocaust. One of the least complacent men I have ever met, he knew the dangers inherent in revering tradition. He knew that a certain kind of respect for traditiom—perhaps the most common kind—excluded and silenced voices from the past, and paradoxically, by wrapping them in the cotton wool of respectability, muted even those that it celebrated, depriving them of a power actually to shake us. He knew also that, as George Steiner put it, 'we come after'—that is, after the Holocaust—and that we cannot, having come after it, justifiably have the confidence of people who came before in the capacity of the humanities to humanise.

But he also believed that the Holocaust should not diminish his love of Bach and much else of German culture. As a human being he wanted (and as a teacher he felt obliged) to share that love with his students, hoping that they would find it worthy of their love, and nourish in them, as it had in him, a love of the world. For me in later years, thinking about the Holocaust—about how it should be characterised morally, legally and politically, about what it shows about the prospects of a common humanity and the hopes we can place in education—this was a gift.

When Gandhi was asked what he thought of Western civilisation, he said it would be a good idea. Winkler was not long out of the internment camps when the Nuremberg trials of the Nazi war criminals began. A year later, the UN passed a declaration on genocide, describing it to be, 'a shock to the conscience of mankind, as contrary to moral law and to the spirit and aims of the United Nations, and as a crime which the civilised world condemns'. Raphael Lemkin, who coined the term 'genocide' and who developed the first account of the concept, believed passionately that its establishment as a distinctive category in international law was an imperative for 'a civilised jurisprudence'.

Many people have pointed out that civilised is a word that is itself ethically compromised by association with a racist incapacity of Europeans who formulated international law to see depth and meaning in the lives of cultures that they then described as primitive, and the peoples as savages, which included of course the cultures of most of the peoples of the earth, including many who had been victims of colonial genocides. Inevitably, therefore, many of the readers of my essay on Winkler might be suspicious of a German Lutheran pastor who went as a missionary to New Guinea in the 1940s.

I first met Winkler in 1961. In 1960, the great Australian anthropologist Bill Stanner wrote that the culture of Australia's Indigenous people can express, 'all the beauty of song, mime, dance and art of which human beings are capable'. It reflected a new—in the West—capacity to see in black cultures an ever deepening responsiveness to the finding facts of the human condition—our mortality, our sexuality, our vulnerability to misfortune—and therefore to see them as cultures from which we can learn.

Winkler spoke to me in the same spirit about the people with whom he lived and worked in New Guinea. He told me often that he'd learnt more from them than they had from him, especially about what it means really to understand the connection between our humanity, and our embodiment. Or, if you like, to understand fully that we are human beings rather than only persons or rational agents, living inescapably and, if we understand its significance, fully, joyfully, as part of nature.

It would of course be natural for me to say that Winkler was an inspiration to me, but I resist doing so—any rate, doing so flatly, as it were—because inspiration is a word that is too general to describe Winkler's effect on me, covering as it does a multitude of virtues and vices. Inspiration can be corrupt, and sometimes it is merely the effect of enthusiasm—and even when enthusiasm is passionate, it'll be banal if directed towards things that are banal. Because it's contagious, enthusiasm can be a pedagogical asset but it's ethically neutral with respect to what it's directed towards.

Love, on the other hand, as Plato was perhaps the first to see, is in complex ways related to the good. One can be a passionately enthusiastic debunker, but love asks to celebrate the beloved. Even more than enthusiasm, love can be a pedagogical asset, a psychological aid to making something attractive, or energising students who are not interested in their studies. But much more important than that is the fact that love can be revelatory. It's sometimes an indispensable means to seeing the value of something. Often we see something as precious only in the light of someone's love for it.

So you see, when I speak of love, I really do mean love. If I'm told that someone is passionate about this or that, I always want to know whether the concept of love, and the distinction between what it really is and its many counterfeits, would be essential in elaboration of that passion.

With no pedagogical strategy about how to bridge my delinquent interests and ambitions, and the fine things he put in my way, Winkler never talked down to me. The quality of his attention to things that he loved made me trust their value and to trust him. We become like what we love, Plato said. It's true. Winkler's love made him the kind of person I trusted and was right to trust, though often I didn't understand until much later, sometimes many years later, the full significance of what he said.

For many years after I left school, I visited Winkler at his home in Ballarat, and for many years, he showed me love's role in teaching. In my first two years as an undergraduate, I studied psychology. Together with two friends I started a magazine, critical of behaviourism and more generally of scientistic approaches to psychology that were then fashionable in the department.

When the Beatles came to Melbourne, one of my co-editors wrote an article about the enthusiasm of young people in the audience which he called a form of mass hysteria. Mass culture and alienation were popular themes at the time. His article was an earnest, slightly prissy lecture on social responsibility. Winkler didn't like it. He listened while I defended it at length. Eventually, after midnight, he drew himself up and placed his hands on his large dining room table (he had six children) and leaned towards me and said, 'Gaita, do you know what the core of responsibility is? It's responsiveness to the needs of another in a lived encounter'. I'm quoting from memory, of course. He then said I should read Martin Buber's book, *I and Thou*.

I was humbled and moved. Though I didn't fully understand them, his words stayed with me for years. Sometimes when we don't understand everything that another person says at the time they say it, we trust what they say and allow it to enter our lives to find, in its own time, ways to engage with what we already know, and with our capacities (emotional, intellectual and spiritual) for understanding.

We often learn most deeply when we're moved by what people say or do in life or in art. And when we're moved we often claim to have understood something we had not understood before, or understood so fully before. We sometimes say we've seen depth, or even sense, where we had not seen it before. When we find wisdom in words or deeds because a particular person has spoken or done them, when the authority of someone's speech or practical example moves us to take something seriously that we hadn't taken seriously before, or that we did not fully understand, or to find depth where we had not found it before, then usually over time (and sometimes not even very consciously), we critically assess whether we are right to believe the words to be wise words. Right to have been moved in the way that we were.

Then we must try to assure ourselves that we did not yield our assent only because we are naïve or callow or sentimental, or liable to pathos or gullible and so on. For that reason, we have to step back from what has moved us in order to assess critically whether we were justifiably moved, and whether we can trust ourselves for being moved as we were. When he drew up at the table that evening, Winkler called me to a kind of seriousness, to consider a possibility that had never occurred to me, but also just to think, for he detected intellectual and moral laziness in the way I was speaking and what I said. I was touched, as I often was, by his loving severity.

Years after I first met him, when I despaired of teaching, Winkler told me that there are two ways to think about teaching. One is to dream of pulling a switch that will make a thousand lights come on. Another way of thinking is nourished by the image of passing a candle from one person to another, or of planting seeds not knowing when or where they will grow. The former, turning a thousand lights on, is a temptation to charismatic teachers. Earlier, I said that inspiration was not the most important word to capture Winkler's effect on me. It doesn't distinguish the teacher who inspires and seeks disciples, who abuses their trust by eroding their freedom to dissent—it doesn't distinguish such a person from one like Winkler who, though a forceful personality, because of his love of his subject, never abused that trust.

'Love,' Plato says in the *Symposium*—it's a beautiful line—'never proceeds by force, nor does it submit to force'. And by that he meant including the force of a charismatic personality. Truth, Plato rightly believed, is a need of the soul, but possession of it is food for the soul only if we come to it in the right way. Winkler honoured his responsibility to the world that he loved, and to his students, as Hannah Arendt put it, 'never to strike from their hands their chance of undertaking something new, something foreseen by no one'.

Winkler's advice about teaching was the wisest I'd ever received, as was his rebuke when I defended my co-editor's article on the Beatles. The seeds he planted in me were then still germinating. They grew only many years later when I wrote *Good and Evil: An Absolute Conception*, which I dedicated to him. I could have subtitled it 'responsiveness to need'. Winkler's words which, as I said, stayed with me for many years, engaged with something I knew from my life with my father. I suspect that's why they stayed so long with me.

My father showed a compassion that strikes me as wondrous towards my mother, who deserted him, and to her lover, Mitru, who had been his friend. He even paid their rent when, as happened often, they were threatened with eviction because my mother could not control her impulse to spend, sometimes twice as much as Mitru earned. That impulse—compulsion, indeed—is a symptom of manic depression from which my mother suffered from her teenage years until she killed herself at the age of 29. Mitru had killed himself two years earlier at the age of 27.

My father found it impossible to turn his back on their desperate need, which I think he believed would destroy them. My mother and Mitru responded in complex ways to my father's compassionate response to their need, but even as a boy I accepted it as a gift, though I did not fully understand why until I was an adult.

People have often asked me how I survived my childhood reasonably sane, and some believe they know the answer (some believe I'm not sane, but that's another matter) which is that I knew that my father and Hora loved me deeply, and that I never doubted it. That's an important part of the answer to be sure, but there's another part that's just as important. It's this: the fact that I came to see the world in the light that my father's goodness cast upon it prevented the pain of my childhood from becoming bitterness. It's bitterness rather than pain that corrodes the soul, deforms personality and character, and can even tempt one to misanthropy.

My father's goodness enabled me to love my mother without shame or serious resentment, though I was painfully aware of the disdain many people showed towards her because she neglected me and, later, my half-sisters; and because she took many lovers, which can also be a symptom of manic depression, inseparable in her case from her romanticism. To be enabled to love is as important as to be loved, a fact that we must constantly hold before our minds when we deal with children who have been psychologically and spiritually wounded.

Some of the barriers to loving are of course psychological barriers, but as my reference to loving without shame implies, they can also be moral, or rather as my father taught me (not by his words but by his example) by a moralistic distortion of morality. I learnt from him that the aspiration to be morally clear-sighted, which sometimes requires a morally severe assessment of what somebody has done, is never inconsistent with a need to love clear-sightedly. He never denied that my mother had wronged him. Some people find incoherent the idea that love can be morally severe and yet not be judgemental or resentful. The roots of that incredulity go deep in Western culture, at least back to Aristotle.

Winkler's love of Bach awakened the same love in me. I drew on it, I needed it, when I wrote *Romulus, My Father*. Writing about things that affected me profoundly, including my father's descent into madness when I was 14, living alone with him in a dilapidated shack in the country—writing such things, I had to resist as much as possible all dispositions to pathos or to sentimentality. That's not merely a personal remark. Anybody in similar circumstances should do the same. But in resisting these, I wasn't trying to get feeling out of the writing: I was trying to make the feeling true. I don't mean that I wanted to be sincere. Sentimentality is sincere more often than it's not. In resisting sentimentality, I wasn't so much trying to feel right but trying to see things right, to understand things right, and to be truthful, not about the facts as I told them, but about the meaning of those facts—the meaning of the facts that were fundamental to the story. To be true to the meaning of those things, I listened to Bach.

The distinction as I've just expressed it, between facts and their meaning, is simple enough if one thinks of facts in a workaday sense as we mean it when we talk about facts you get in textbooks or in encyclopedias, or as when a judge might use the term saying to an emotional witness, 'Stick to the facts, please'. In that sense the distinction between fact and meaning is, I think, pretty clear.

At the end of *Romulus, My Father*, I described a scene outside the church door, after I had given the eulogy at my father's funeral, when I caught sight of a man who I did not at first recognise because I hadn't seen him for 40 years or more. The first draft read like this:

> When I went towards him, I saw that his eyes were filled with tears. It was Neil Mikkelsen, the man who had been kind to my mother, and who had fallen from the haystack when my father worked for him. 'Every word you spoke was true', he said. 'Your father saved my life'. His presence and his words moved me. I thought again of Frogmore and my life there with my father. My father was buried in the Maryborough cemetery, not very far from my mother.

My publisher and editor, Michael Heyward, said we needed another sentence between 'I thought again of my life there with my father' and the sentence, 'My father was buried in the Maryborough cemetery, not far from my mother'. I could see he was right, so I produced one. In the light of what I said earlier about the circumstances in which I wrote the book, you'll see why I produced the one I did. I also changed the very last sentence. Now the published version reads:

> His presence and his words moved me. I thought again of Frogmore and my life there with my father. I remembered my mother laughing as she talked with Mikkelsen at the chicken wire gate. My father was buried in the Maryborough cemetery, close to my mother.

It's a fact that my mother talked with Mikkelsen on at least one occasion by a gate whose metal frame (in fact, it was a bed frame) was covered in wire of the kind to keep chickens out. It's a fact too that I remembered her laughing on at least one such occasion. It's also a fact that my father's grave is approximately 10 metres from my mother's grave. But had I written all that as I just read it, Michael would not have been pleased. The statement of those facts cannot convey their significance in the way that the sentence I produced for him does, by its rhythm and tone. But a sentence like that is of its very nature vulnerable to sentimentality, kitsch and wish fulfilment, among other vices. I worried for a long time whether—once I'd replaced 'not very far from' by 'close'—I should say 'near to' because 'near to' is still a spatial concept, whereas 'close' brings all sorts of things that I wondered whether I wished to be true, as opposed to actually being true. So, that's why I'm trying to explain the difference here between concern for fact, and concern for the meaning or the significance of those facts.

I suspect it's not an exaggeration to say that anybody who read that sentence that I wrote in response to Michael's request would also understand why I published 'An Unassuagable Longing' 14 years later, and why the essay has that title. I owe the title to Helen Garner, who wrote this about my mother:

> In her son, whom she repeatedly left in the care of his father and Hora, she inspired an unassuagable longing when she came back and lay depressed in bed all day, unable to do the work of a wife and mother. He used to creep into the bed beside her to bask in the warmth of her body.

Alex Miller writes, 'When Rai told me he had titled his essay on his mother, 'An Unassuagable Longing' … I thought of Emily Dickinson's image, "The craving is upon the child like a claw it cannot remove"'. Later in the same essay he says he believes it's not yet over, that my writing about my mother has not come to an end. Perhaps I'm right now proving him right.

In much of my work, I've written about what I've called the realm of meaning. I'd not like that to be taken as a technical expression, though the word 'realm' gives it a slightly technical, intimidating ring that I don't intend. When I coined it, I had in mind a way of thinking about the meanings of things in our lives, about what it means to love or grieve truthfully, about why it matters and the way it matters that we should suffer wrong rather than to do it. What counts as thinking well or badly about these matters is in part determined by concepts more often used in assessments of literature than it is in other more scientific disciplines, even in metaphysical philosophy—categories like sentimentality, pathos, cliché, tone deafness, for example.

Thinking about the meanings of things is necessarily answerable to such concepts because they partly determine its cognitive character. I called it a realm —I could have called it a domain or a space—because I thought of the concepts that determine the character of such thinking as constituting a conceptual space in which thought and feeling, style and content, are inseparable. They yield a distinctive content different from science and metaphysical philosophy. They yield a distinctive content to the expression 'trying to see things as they are rather than as they appear'. And also, indeed, to what it is for things to be as they are in the realm of meaning.

That the critical categories that determine this distinctive cognitive character are also the critical categories deployed in the assessments of literature indicates that reflection in the realm of meaning should never wish to distance itself too much from the natural languages that nourish it, steeped in the contingencies of history and culture that shape, and are shaped by, the lives of peoples. The point is of critical importance, not just to the assessments of narratives of one kind or another, but also (and again I learnt this from Winkler) to the formation of a critical social and political sensibility.

In 2017, the National Portrait Gallery had an exhibition called *All That Falls: Sacrifice, Life and Loss in World War I.* Amongst other exhibits, there were crude propaganda posters intended to shame young men into enlisting and especially to shame them in front of their girlfriends or wives. In an essay that I wrote for an accompanying booklet, I commented on the fact that our cultural and temporal distance from these posters might dispose us to condescend to their crudity.

In my essay, I warn against that. I thought about this again—about that kind of condescension—when recently I wrote an essay on Donald Trump. I was urging readers never to cease being incredulous that such a man could be the president of the United States. But who, I asked in both essays, who can say with justified confidence that, in the clamour that accompanies great upheavals, they will retain an ear for what rings false? It's not enough, I go on to say, to hope that one can hold onto one's reason. In such circumstances, you need to do more than hold on to your reason, In the right circumstances, everybody is vulnerable to the danger that's always present, and against which we seldom protect ourselves, or even see the need to do so—which is to develop a sensibility in which head and heart, feeling and head, and style and content, just can't be separated. It's art and narrative, including narrative in history, that are the forms that most often deliver such a sensibility to us.

Sentimentality, a disposition to pathos, a failure to register what rings true, a tin ear for irony—these things undermine lucidity far more than when emotion overcomes reason. Winkler knew that deep in his bones. He had heard some of Hitler's speeches, and seen the murderous consequences of sentimentality and kitsch in German propaganda. That's why he played Bach for me, and talked so often to me of German poetry and literature, and why he was perhaps a little neurotically fearful of romanticism.

In 'Character and Its Limits', an essay in *After Romulus*, I write of how my father's European friends criticised his compassionate responses to the needs of my mother and Mitru. They criticised it as dishonourable and shameful. I try to take the reader to a perspective from which he or she could see that his friends did not understand the conception of goodness that transformed his understanding of what fear of dishonour and shame come to.

What, however, if someone who had criticised my father's sense of honour should ask, 'Was Romulus Gaita really like his son Raimond Gaita describes him?' Suppose that he replies that Romulus did and said the things that his son said he did in the book about him, but that while his son celebrated Romulus's values, he despised him. They were, I'm supposing this interlocuter would say, the values of a man whose foolish heart led him to dishonour himself by paying his wife's rent when she lived with a man who cuckolded him. They were, he continues disdainfully, the values of someone who believed that a man who was clearly mad, who lived between two boulders on a hillside where he talked to himself while he cooked in his urine, should be treated fully as a friend. Quite clearly, someone who would say such things about my father would tell a different story to the one that I told.

Did my father pay my mother's and Mitru's rent? He did, and that's a fact. Was he therefore a good and generous man? A man of quite extraordinary goodness? Or, was he a cuckold who dishonoured himself still further? To tell a story that would show who he was, what kind of man he was, we would have to answer that second question. But there's no neutral ground, no ethically neutral ground, on which to plant one's feet when we try to do it, no ground on which reason by itself, or facts, could favour one answer over the other.

Telling and Writing the Story

Richard Fidler
2018

I've called this lecture 'Telling and Writing the Story' because I'd like to illustrate some of the differences between presenting someone's life story on the page and on the air. It's been a while since I lived in Canberra as a grubby undergraduate at the Australian National University, and I'm afraid I have written this lecture not like an essay with a thesis, and a whole bunch of tightly argued paragraphs with a compelling conclusion. Instead I thought I'd take you through some of the things I've discovered while presenting a radio program that's largely biographical, and how that work affected the writing of two books, *Ghost Empire,* based around the medieval empire of Constantinople, and *Saga Land* which I co-authored with my friend Kári Gíslason, where the action takes place around the sagas of medieval Iceland. Along the way, it's a process that's taken me through the slums of Istanbul, the remote northwest fjords of Iceland and the dank unholy confines of an ABC radio studio.

Firstly though, a warning about the dangers of biography. In April 1988, I was a young 20-something browsing through a bookshop in St Mark's Place in New York City, and I picked up a copy of *The Path to Power*, the first volume of Robert A. Caro's multivolume biography of the life of Lyndon Johnson, the thirty-sixth President of the United States. The book was handsome and pleasingly weighty in my hands, and like all good biographies it was big enough to stun a burglar. *The Path to Power* was a wholly absorbing biography for me. Caro introduces us to a Lyndon Johnson who is as oversized as Texas, tall with huge hands, long arms and ears, and a domineering, smothering personality. We meet the young Lyndon Johnson fleeing from the poverty of Texas hill country, propelling himself frantically towards significance and political power.

In Washington, Johnson becomes a congressional staffer, and then gets elected to his own seat in Congress, and he takes care to select talented staff members who are as desperate as him to escape the humiliating poverty of rural Texas. But they soon find they've exchanged one form of humiliation for another as their frantic overbearing boss comes to dominate and subsume their lives. Johnson's staff would be expected to work from dawn till late at night. Their smallest errors would be screamed at by the boss or treated with wounding derision. Even as President, Johnson would order speechwriters and stenographers to follow him into the bathroom, where he would give dictation while seated on the toilet. Robert Caro spoke to staffers who were still haunted by Johnson's domineering personality long after he died. One talented speechwriter had left Johnson's office after just six months. He told Caro he knew that if he stayed he would wind up having Johnson's portrait hanging in his living room, and he would have to name his kids after the bastard, so he got out.

I wonder if Robert Caro, though, failed to heed the warning of that staffer. I bought that first volume of *The Path to Power* 30 years ago. I bought the second volume when it came out in 1990, the third in 2002. The most recent volume, called *The Passage of Power*, appeared in 2012, and that just covered his vice presidency, the assassination of JFK, and the transition into the presidency. Earlier this year, Robert Caro said the final volume might come out in two years or ten years, he's not sure. Robert Caro is now 82 years old. From beyond the grave, it seems, Lyndon Johnson has managed to gobble up yet another man's life. There is a warning in this, I think, for biographers. If you're going in, make sure you keep an eye on the exits.

I'm relatively new to the business of presenting people's lives on the page, but I've been doing it for some years now on the radio. My program, *Conversations*, is often biographical. The life of the guest is compressed into an hour. It's really a format that lives somewhere between biography and autobiography. It's the guest telling their story, not me, but my producers and I have worked hard to shape that story and make it flow through the course of the hour.

I imagine myself, while I'm going to air, as a convenor of an intimate conversation with just three people around a tiny little café table. A very, very small café table peopled by just three people: myself, the guest and the listener. There is a heavy load of work that goes into every single show. Often the guest is unknown to the wider world, and there's very little about them on the public record. But the nature of the show is, I think, very subjective. The voice you hear is human and fallible, and I think that's understood by listeners. We do take some precautionary measures before we bring a guest on air. We ask ourselves, is the guest's version of events too self-aggrandising, too self-contradictory? Too many elisions around a tricky subject?

Presenting a life on the page though is a very different business. There are several narrative liberties, I discovered, that are afforded to the author and denied to the broadcaster. On the written page, the narrative can sprawl back and forth in time much more easily. Individual stories can run in parallel, then intersect, and then run off in different directions. Radio, however, is much more linear. It requires more narrative discipline. But it can roll forward with enormous didactic force and momentum, and it has the lustre and texture of the human voice to bring you in, to hold you in, to beguile you.

Radio narrative tends to move like a shark, knifing through the water in a linear manner, in search of blood and horror. Actually that last bit's not true—I just added that to make it sound more impressive. But the narrative of written biography seems to be more like a Portuguese man o' war, floating along in a stately manner, tangled with all sorts of bits and pieces, pulling them all along more or less at the same time.

The different exigencies of these two mediums, presenting a life through the voice and the page, were really brought home to me a few years back while making a radio documentary series in Iceland. I travelled to Iceland in the summer of 2015 with my good friend, Kári Gíslason. He and I were there to make a series for Radio National called 'Saga Land', which we later expanded into the book. Kári's lived most of his life in Australia but he was born in Iceland, and he loves the country of his birth with all the tragic passion of the exile. He and I became friends after he appeared as a guest on my radio program. I'd read his memoir and so I kind of knew his life before I even met him, which is an odd and slightly stalkerish way to begin a friendship.

Kári has a doctorate in medieval Icelandic literature. And one night while we were drinking in a bar in Brisbane, he mentioned in passing the sagas of Iceland. Now I'd imagined the sagas were tales of warriors and fantastic monsters like Beowulf and he said oh no, that's not it at all. The sagas are not fantasy, they're not Tolkien. They're the family stories of the Vikings who first came to Iceland a thousand years ago. They're about real people who actually existed.

The sagas emerged from a poetic storytelling tradition brought to us by the Norwegian Vikings when they came to settle on that remote island way back in the ninth and tenth centuries. In old Norse, the word 'saga' simply means 'a telling'. And in the frozen dark of the winter months, Icelanders would sit in their longhouses and remember dark family feuds, or the loss of a beautiful child at sea, or the revenge of a mistreated woman. These family stories were told and retold and retold and no doubt they grew in the telling.

I asked Kári that night to tell me a saga story right then and there in the bar, and this is how he began. This is what medieval Icelandic biography sounds like. This is the beginning of the saga, we call it, of Gunnar and Hallgerð.

Gunnar Hámundarson was a gifted, brave and capable young man. He swam like a seal. He was powerfully athletic. They say he could jump as far backwards as he could forwards. When he mounted his horse, he would run up behind it with his halberd and pole-vault himself into the saddle. He was slow to make friends but loyal to those who were close.

Gunnar had just returned to Iceland from Norway, where he'd won some fame as a warrior, even though he hated to kill. In the summer, Gunnar made the journey to Thingvellir, to the annual assembly. As he walked through the rift, people couldn't stop looking at him, for he seemed to have everything. He was handsome and wealthy and well-travelled. Gunnar arrived at Thingvellir wearing a fine cloak, and a golden arm bracelet given to him by the Earl of Norway. He followed the path by the stream and there he encountered the most beautiful woman he'd ever seen. Her name was Hallgerð. He sat down next to her, and they began to talk, and after an hour or so Gunnar said to her, 'Hallgerð, are you married?' And she said, 'You can't possibly want to know the answer to that question'. And he said, 'But what if I do?' And she said, 'Then you better go and talk to my father'. So he went a little further along the path and met Hallgerð's father, and said he wanted to marry his daughter. And the father said, 'Gunnar, you're a good man. We like you. You should not marry Hallgerð. She's already had two husbands, and both of them are dead'.

You can feel the momentum of narrative there, and that's just a lovely thing. Now we do know for a fact that Gunnar and Hallgerð were once living, breathing human beings. Their names are recorded in Íslendingabók, the Icelandic genealogical database which goes all the way back to the ninth century, and contains the name of every Icelander that ever lived. But could Gunnar really leap onto his horse like that? Is it possible for anyone to jump as far backwards as forwards? This historical Viking farmer was already straining at the leash of plausibility. Was this biography laced with hyperbole, or fiction based on a real person? Saga scholars are still arguing over that one.

The sagas, as they were told between family members were memorised and passed down by generation after generation until the thirteenth century when they were put to paper, most probably by Icelandic monks whose names are lost to us. Iceland was approaching a crisis at the time, which may have galvanised them into recording these tales in case they became lost. The authors scratched them onto sheets of hideously expensive calf skin vellum and, crucially, they wrote them down not in Latin, which was the scholarly language of the time, but in the Icelandic vernacular. It was intended they should be read aloud, enjoyed and passed on. Clearly the sagas were not ornaments on the fabric of their lives but part of the fabric itself. And like all biographies they spring from that deep-seated human need to understand the context of our own lives by remembering the world of our ancestors, the people who came before us. They also allow us to indulge in a bit of time travel, which I think is the real deep secret pleasure of writing and reading biography.

Today every Icelander is brought up with the sagas and they learn them like we learn Shakespeare. It's said that without the sagas, Icelanders wouldn't know how to be Icelandic. It's made them a particularly literate people. There are more published authors in Iceland per head of population than in any other nation in the world. They spend all their time essentially writing and reading each other's books. Icelanders have a saying, '*Að ganga með bók í maganum*', which means, 'Everyone has a book in their stomach'.

By the time the sagas were put to the page in the thirteenth century, Christianity was well entrenched in Iceland, and the paganism of their ancestors was somewhat abhorrent to them. But still the saga authors honoured their ancestral debt by presenting these people to us as fully human, rather than as wicked and ignorant brutes. It's an astonishing achievement. If the sagas fall short of modern standards of biographical rigour, they do succeed in illustrating larger truths of what it meant to be alive and walking around on that impossible island in the Middle Ages.

The English poet W.H. Auden admitted he was obsessed by the sagas. He used to like to say he was never not thinking about Iceland. Auden was startled by the uncompromising and violent tenor of life described in the sagas, but as he discovered there's a great deal more to the lives of these Vikings than extortion and revenge. Those of us who grew up with a caricature of the mindless Viking brute hacking and slashing his way through medieval Europe are likely to be shocked by the emotional complexity, and the intensity of feeling, which the saga authors lend to these historical figures.

Jorge Luis Borges discovered the sagas as a boy in his father's library. Borges felt compelled to make several pilgrimages to Iceland in his life. The great Argentine author made his last trip to Reykjavik when he was blind and 71 years old. Nonetheless, the awesome bleakness of Iceland stirred some deep romantic impulse, and he summoned the courage to kiss his assistant, Maria Kodama, who later became his wife and then his widow. It was the first time Borges had kissed anyone in nearly 50 years.

Borges and Auden saw the sagas as I do, as a compelling means of escape into another time and place and perhaps into an ever so slightly different way of being human. An historian whose name I can't recall once said of the ancient Romans that the ancient Romans are about 90 per cent recognisable to modern humans but the remaining 10 per cent is quite alien to us, and so it is with the

Vikings in Iceland. They share all our modern preoccupations with family and love and politics and work and status, all that stuff, but there's one aspect to their lives that seems strange—and that's the highly charged concept of honour in the Viking world.

Viking honour is not something that grows and flourishes like love or Christian goodwill. Honour is more like currency: it's finite and there's only so much honour to go around. Honour can't be earned. It must be taken from someone else, and this is Gunnar's problem at the start of his tale. He's returned to Iceland with a fine cloak and a bracelet. He's won fame as a warrior, which is even worse. Gunnar has too much honour and so he's asking for trouble. Spoiler alert—the saga does not end well for him.

The saga of Gunnar and Hallgerð that Kári told me that night was enthralling, and it held me (and the half-a-dozen eavesdroppers who were listening in as he told me this story at the bar) quite still. It was obvious to me in that moment that these sagas, these Viking biographies, would translate so beautifully into a radio program and to a podcast. There's something so pure about that oral tradition, and that's how he and I came to be in Iceland in the summer of 2015.

Now our plan was to record four stories about four people from the sagas, stories of people who lived and walked around that island a thousand years ago. And we also had a family mystery to solve, to find out if there was a blood connection between Kári and the greatest of the saga-authors. Kári and I spent our first week in Iceland travelling to the spectacular old Viking parliament site at Thingvellir, which sits in a rift between two tectonic plates in the earth's surface. And then we went to the grassy slopes of Gunnar's farm in Hlíðarendi, which is still a working farm today. The first two sagas we'd recorded adapted very easily to the radio format. They had distinct central characters, a strong narrative spine, and they sounded magical when recorded beside a trickling stream or in a field of high grass.

But then we came to the third saga story that Kári had chosen. This was the life of Gísli the fugitive. That's where we hit a bit of a snag. At this point, we were staying in a cabin in the south of Iceland. Now the coastal lands of the south of Iceland are so spectacular. On the deck of that cabin on a summer's day, I could see in the distance the flat cone of Mt Hekla, a volcano so fierce it was once believed to be the hell prison of Judas Iscariot. Further down the road was that other volcano—you know, the one that exploded in 2010 sending plumes of ash all over Europe? It took several weeks of patient tutoring from Kári to enable me to say its name which is—I'm still getting it wrong, I'm sure—Eyjafjallajökull. Before then I was calling it Eyefayurklegurkle, which really annoyed him.

So that afternoon in the cabin Kári was telling me he was having a bit of a struggle to assemble all the events of the story in a kind of a linear manner for the radio, and maybe I might want to read the saga in its original form myself—in translated form—so I could see if I could come up with some ideas. So I flopped down on the couch in the cabin and I read his Penguin Classics translation of 'Gísli's Saga', and as I read and as I turned each page I became more and more worried. After 10 pages, I wondered if we'd ever figure out a way to present this Viking story to a radio audience. It certainly wasn't lacking in drama. Hell, no. The question we had to answer was: how do we take this sprawling and complex family story and pour it through the narrow funnel of spoken narrative? And this was an odd question because the saga had begun its life as a spoken narrative.

But the narrative was wickedly complex. Gudrún Nordal, the saga scholar, had a lovely phrase for it. She said the people in Gísli's Saga are doomed in these intricacies. We had to find a way to make those intricacies understandable. The saga of Gísli begins with a conclave of four friends. They go to the local assembly and these four guys make a bit of a show of themselves, and this irritates the onlookers, and one of them predicts ominously those four young men won't be as close in three years as they are now. Now Gísli, who was one of the four, overhears this and he decides that he'll refute this by binding his friends to him and each other through a four-fold pact of blood brotherhoodship—and so they cut their arms to let the blood drip onto the soil and to mulch it up with their hands. That's the ritual.

Now straight away as I'm reading this—that sounds great, but four is not a great number for radio. Four friends, okay? Three is much better. Listeners who might just hang on for a third name tend to switch off after that, and the names were tricky. For a start there's Gísli, then there's his brother Thorkel, then his brother-in-law, Thorgrim who's married to the sister, Thordis, and the fourth man in the circle is Gísli's best friend, Vesteinn. If you had heard those aloud, could you even remember the names of more than one of those characters and how they connect through kinship? Even the most enthusiastic listeners would struggle to sustain that Venn diagram of relationships in their heads, and I knew people would get lost.

Now on the page it's not so bad. The eye can scan the previous page, go backwards and forwards, you can check who's who, and you can still remain immersed in the narrative. But the radio listener can't do that, and if you're listening to it as a podcast, well, you might need to tap the 15-second rewind button to check back on who was the brother again? And who was the brother-in-law? And who was the best friend? But that's not good because the podcast listener has then had to snap out of the medieval world of blood brotherhood and cold iron and icy seawater, and is now standing in the middle of the cat food section of Coles searching for a button on their iPhone.

So what to do? On an audio medium, when you're confronted by a problem of overwhelming narrative complexity, sometimes it's simply best to step back and confess the problem to the listener. So I thought when we introduce the saga I'll just have to say something like, 'Okay so there's four men, Gísli, Thorkel, Thorgrim and Vesteinn. It's complicated, don't get too hung up on the names right now. What matters here is that some of these friends are fated to kill each other. That's a bit better, that's okay, right? We're still listening here, aren't we? We're still with that, okay?'

So still lying on the couch, I pressed on with Gísli's saga, and then the tangled web just got more twisted. It turns out that Thorkel's wife, Asgerð, used to have a thing for Vesteinn, who happens to be the brother of Auð, who's the wife of Gísli—are we keeping up with this? And Aud it seems once had a thing for Thorgrim, Gísli's brother-in-law. Yikes, the web of interrelationships was beginning to look like the Canberra Action Bus map! But it's important to the narrative. It's this crush of family and intermarriage that's going to give the drama that follows all its energy.

The most shocking thing in Gísli's saga sits just below the surface. It's the unspoken implication that Gísli, the chief protagonist and our man of honour, is partly driven by an incestuous attraction to his sister, Thordis, and can't admit it to himself, of course. And this is the moment in the saga—and I knew we could make it work for a radio audience—Gísli decides he must avenge the death of his best friend by killing Thorgrim, his brother-in-law. So in the dead of night, he creeps into the farmhouse with his spear. The room is perfectly dark. Gísli approaches the bed. He slips his cold hand under the covers and places it on his sister's breast. She thinks it's her husband and she says, 'Do you want me to roll over to you, Thorgrim?'

So Gísli has to stand there silently in the dark listening to them couple with each other while impotently clutching his spear. How Freudian is that? Waiting for the couple to finish making love, his sister to make love. Gísli waits for them to fall asleep again and the saga says he raises his spear and plunges it into Thorgrim's chest so hard that his spear lodges in the planks at the foot of the bed. You see now you're listening. Now you want to know what happens next. Again, spoiler alert: things don't end well for Gísli.

Gísli, in his final years, hides out in a remote fjord in the far northwest of Iceland, so Kári and I went all the way out there just to see what it was like, this bleak, rocky fjord—it's like a moonscape. On the day we were there, there was a fierce wind blowing in from the North Atlantic, cold enough to sting the ears, but nothing in the landscape moved—it was that lifeless, just little tufts of weeds. The saga records that Gísli and his wife Auð built a ragged little farm on the water's edge while they were hiding out. One night two killers came looking for Gísli at the farmhouse, but by then he'd escaped into the hills.

So the killers confronted Auð in the farmhouse and offered her 300 pieces of silver to give them his whereabouts. 'After he's killed,' they said, 'we'll arrange a better marriage for you'. 'Maybe you're right,' said Auð. 'Money is better than grieving.' So the killers tipped the silver into her lap. She put the pieces into a small sack and asked one of the men if she could do whatever she wanted with the money. 'Of course,' he said, 'it's yours'. So she got to her feet and swung the bag of silver into his face smashing his nose. 'Now,' she said, 'you can tell everyone the fine story of when your nose was broken by a woman'. That's awesome, isn't it? I mean, that's amazing. It's not hard to imagine another generation of Vikings chortling over that just like you did now.

By the time we finished the radio series of 'Saga Land', I was starting to write my first book, *Ghost Empire. Ghost Empire* is a history of the city of Constantinople, the second Rome: the capital of the later Roman empire which historians called Byzantium. The modern-day version of it is, of course, Istanbul. Sometimes the phrase 'biography of a city' is employed for such books, and it's not a bad analogy. The city is born, it flourishes, weakens, recovers and, in the case of Constantinople, it experienced a terrible, violent death after a long decline with the invasion of the Ottoman Turks in the year 1453.

A great city has a complex, many-sided character, and it can engender a kind of love in people. When you live in a city for a long time, a comfortable intimacy sets in, a bit like a marriage. *Ghost Empire* was peopled with short biographies of great historical figures like Constantine the Great, and the imperial power couple, Justinian and Theodora. It was also a pleasure to meet some compelling but lesser known people like Irene of Athens, Anna Komnene, and the very last of the Roman emperors, Constantine XI, who died at the walls of Constantinople in 1453. And the story of that last emperor, Constantine XI, just haunted me, and I still think about him all the time. Constantine XI possessed deep reserves of courage and fortitude that sustained him in the city's terrible final ordeal. It was his awful fate to inherit the throne just as the empire's final crisis was already engulfing it.

I think biography at some level should be a profound act of sympathy extended across time and space to the subject. So I went with my son to Istanbul to see the sight of the last stand of the last emperor for myself. As we stood atop the ancient Theodosian walls that course through the suburbs of modern-day Istanbul, I tried to imagine the last emperor's sense of horror and futility as he looked down upon the vast army of the Ottoman empire pressing at the gates. And the more I read of the doomed emperor Constantine XI, from the multiple primary sources that document the fall of the city, the greater the affection I felt for him as someone who made the very best of a very bad situation. Writing about him created a strange sense of intimacy with him which of course is entirely illusory, because the poor bugger is dead and he's in no position to reciprocate my affection for him. Yet when I wrote the last sentence of that book I felt a small pang of grief to leave him there, to leave his bones there buried under a wall in Istanbul.

After I finished *Ghost Empire*, Kári and I got to work on the book of 'Saga Land'. We decided to write alternating chapters. One of the narrative tasks I was assigned was to write the life story of the greatest of the saga authors, an Icelander from the thirteenth century named Snorri Sturluson. Now Snorri Sturluson is revered today in Iceland. He wrote three classic works: a family saga, a history saga and most significantly he wrote the *Prose Edda*. This is the source of much of what we know of the Norse gods. All the stuff you're seeing in Marvel comics movies these days—Thor, Odin, Loki, Hela—this all came from the pen of a well-padded Icelandic lawyer writing in a remote farmhouse in medieval Iceland.

Neil Gaiman's bestselling book on Norse mythology owes everything to Snorri Sturluson. Snorri is Iceland's national hero. There's a shrine, a statue, a street and a beer named after him—a good beer too. He was murdered in his cellar by his enemies in the year 1241. One of our missions in Iceland was to find out if something Kári's father had once told him was true: that Kári is a direct descendant of Snorri Sturluson. I thought we better go looking for the historical Snorri instead of the statue, and I found a primary source in 'Sturlunga saga', which happened to be written by Snorri's nephew. The nephew, Sturla, has a slightly flat writing style, but he is decidedly not in awe of his famous uncle, which makes him a reasonably reliable narrator.

Snorri's story appears in dribs and drabs throughout the Sturlunga saga, and I found that when I pulled these bits and pieces together Snorri came sharply into focus—not as a builder, not as a national hero, but as a wrecker. Unlike Constantine, the more I read of Snorri the less I thought of his reputation. Iceland in Snorri's time had moved a long way from its egalitarian habits. Power had become concentrated in the hands of a few powerful families. Snorri, who was the cleverest chieftain of his time, was as responsible as anyone for this awful social distortion. He loved power and wealth and honour too much.

Icelanders treasure their early history when the island was an independent commonwealth in the Middle Ages, but I discovered that Snorri connived to sell out Iceland's independence to Norway so long as he would be appointed the first *jarl* (earl) of Iceland. He undermined the republic so he could be an uncrowned king. An ardent republican, I naturally found this repugnant. Snorri, I discovered, screwed his allies, enemies and family members alike, and was shocked when they came after him for revenge. Even so, just like the last emperor of Constantinople, the moment of Snorri's death is poignant. Hiding in his cellar, Snorri is discovered by his enemies. The seething assassins unsheathe their swords. Snorri is an old man in his sixties, armed with nothing but his chiefly authority to bring to his defence.

The saga records that Snorri's last moment was a defiant one. He utters a command, 'You will not strike'. The men hesitate. Again he commands, 'You will not strike'. One assassin edges forward and then thrusts his sword into Snorri, more sword thrusts follow, and then the cleverest man in Iceland lies dead of his wounds on his cellar floor. Today Snorri's old farm estate at Reykholt in Iceland is a national shrine to the great man. It contains a museum, a church and a library. The statue of Snorri out the front is pleasingly modest but ultimately quite absurd. They've dressed him as a saintly Lutheran even though Lutheranism didn't even exist in the thirteenth century. Snorri loved food and beer and sex and conversation and power way too much to be considered a pious martyr.

Around the corner Kári and I found Snorri's old outdoor thermal bath. Such things are common around Iceland. And there was a small tunnel that connected the bath to his farmhouse. Kári and I sat in that tunnel trying to imagine Snorri's awful, squalid death and I wondered then if his last words had been mistranslated—if instead of 'you will not strike', he really said 'don't strike', which would have been perfectly understandable under the circumstances. I soon had my answer to that question—whether Icelanders could cope with the idea that their national hero cowered in his moment of death—when I entered the museum. As I was looking at a panel in the museum that described these last moments of Snorri, an Icelandic lady sidled up next to me and she whispered, 'You know, I'm very certain Snorri never said, "you will not strike"'. And I said, 'Really? What do you think he said?' 'I think he said "thou shalt not kill" and my priest agrees with me.' I had to take Kári out very quickly before he said something very rude at that point.

Now, when I'm writing, I don't try and place myself above my subject very often. In my mind, I'm really sitting beside them in the car asking them questions about the scenery as it passes by. It's only when I'm finished that I like to take the view from 30,000 feet and draw some conclusions about the life in full, and I try to do the same thing as a broadcaster with my radio program, *Conversations*.

I began with *Conversations* back in 2005, and right at the outset the program had a foundational ethic and aesthetic. To create more space and time for storytelling and reflection, and most importantly that it would regularly feature people who were unknown to the wider community—everyday people who had seen and done remarkable things. We found listeners particularly loved those stories because they felt they could measure their own lives against them more easily than against a Hollywood actor or a powerful politician. But such guests are hard to find and, sometimes when we do find them, they struggle to tell their story coherently, to assemble all the elements of their lives into a shape that would make sense to a listener. And that's hardly surprising because life is messy. It's not like a curated museum of memory where everything is in its place.

Life is more like a teenager's bedroom with dirty clothes all over the floor, rotting school lunches stashed under the bed, and a vague troubling smell lingering over the whole environment. It's messy. That's life. If you reflect on your own life for half a minute, you'll find long stretches where nothing much seems to happen but small achievements build up and some problems are allowed to metastasise. There are moments of love and kindness as well as moments of indifference and mulish stupidity. There are things that have been said and done that make no sense, and would require a decade of therapy to understand. And how reliable is memory anyway?

I have sat alongside a friend while he regaled a dinner party with a funny story about me where this friend was front and centre of the action, except I knew for a fact this friend was not there at all. He had once heard me tell this story, and had somehow transposed himself magically into the scene. When he finished I quietly said to him—I waited for him to finish—and I said, 'You weren't there, you just weren't there'. I can't tell you how shocked he was when he realised he had not indeed been present. He had co-opted one of my memories as his own without ever being aware of it. Lemn Sissay, the British poet who I spoke to recently in Byron Bay, told me that his definition of family is kind of interesting. He said family for him is a group of disputed memories between a group of people over a lifetime. It's a bunch of people arguing over the same photo.

On *Conversations*, we have to take that messiness of life and the subjectivity of memory into account, and make some allowances for it. Most of the time, basic chronology gives us a structure to make the mess of life seem more rational than it really is. One event after another, after another, after another, after another. I think the subjectivity of memory is understood and accepted and taken into account by the listener, partly because the story is carried by the voice. Human fallibility is built into the texture of the human voice, much more so than on the authoritative page. Listeners can hear authentic tenderness, brokenness, regret, evasiveness, disingenuousness and delight. As a presenter, I try to subtly underline the subjectivity of the experience for the listener. This is why so many of my questions are couched in terms of, 'What do you remember?' instead of simply asking, 'What happened?'

The moment I know it's really working with a guest is when a memory suddenly seems to flicker in front of the guest's eyes like a movie, and the guest falls into a kind of a reverie narrating the sequence of events as they unfold before their eyes. When that happens, that's so lovely, it makes such beautiful radio, and while it's happening I try to almost not breathe. I don't move at all, and I try not to breathe at all, absolutely do nothing to break the reverie of that guest. One of my favourite examples of this is when I had Angela Lansbury on the program. Normally, we're a bit allergic to famous actors because they tend to go, 'Oh, what's this show? It's Australia?', and they calibrate their energy accordingly. And I don't think you guys really want to hear how amazing it is to work with Steven Spielberg, do you?

So I was a bit sceptical, funnily enough, but then I looked into her life and career and I realised that no-one had ever given her a good interview. She'd been interviewed by Larry King, and he talked two-thirds the way through the interview. This is Angela Lansbury, yes, from 'Murder, She Wrote', but who was also in 'Gaslight', who was the wicked mother in 'The Manchurian Candidate', who was Elvis's mother in 'Blue Hawaii', who had an amazing career on Broadway as well, who'd seen and done amazing things, and she was so ready to talk. Right at the start, I asked her what she remembered of her childhood in London, and she gave me a complete evocation of what London was like near Regent's Park in the 1920s. She talked about the coal man coming around and calling out, 'Co-al, co-al'. She talked about the sound of horses clip-clopping on the cobblestones. She described the smell, the shape of the streets, and that moment was there, right at the start of the interview, and I was so excited. I was almost shaking, but I just didn't dare move a muscle. And she went in that lovely reverie where she wasn't even seeing me, I think: it was a movie playing in front of her eyes and in her ears as well, which she was narrating to us, the listener. It made such lovely, lovely radio. These moments never fail to move me.

I'm also conscious on the radio that there's some artful deception in the narrative arc of the hour. Such arcs are satisfying, again because they give shape to the chaos. But life doesn't proceed in a narrative arc, and it continues to bump along after the interview is over. It's not finished. So there is some art in the transmission of life into a life story. The story we present to listeners is not the mess itself but more like an audio presentation of the mess. Like the teenager's bedroom on that one day when the real estate agent had to come round and do the house inspection, that's the day. The portrait is not the person. It's just a portrait.

The everyday, non-famous guests that we love so much are treated with great care, particular care by our producers Nicola and Michelle. These guys will conduct a long pre-interview with the guest over the phone for several hours. As they do so, they help the guest shape their stories, they assemble the facts into coherent narrative, and sometimes gently challenge them on the parts of the story that seem a bit contradictory, improbable or too self-serving. During the pre-interview, the guest will sometimes arrive at a new insight that momentarily floors them. For the producer, this pre-interview process can be exhilarating, and harrowing at times, but the process does reassure the guest that they will be treated fairly and sympathetically, and that we'll do all we can to make sure that they're fully understood. When the guests arrive at the studio, they're made to feel as welcome as possible. It's really easy to forget the ABC can be an intimidating place for people who've never spoken on the radio before, who are worried they're not important enough or famous enough to be on the show. And listening to someone for a whole hour is a really powerful thing.

In 2011, I went to meet Ira Glass, the host of the consistently brilliant show *This American Life* in New York City, in their offices, and he asked me how our show worked. I told him and he said, 'Wow, that's an incredibly powerful thing to listen to someone for an hour, to let someone talk for an hour'. He said that he loved his wife very much—lovely person—but he reckoned the amount of time she was prepared to let him talk uninterrupted was about 45–60 seconds: 'So an hour, you give someone an hour. That's amazing, it's really powerful'. Fortunately for us, people are more likely to open up in front of a microphone than they are in front of a camera. Radio is a far more intimate medium than TV. It comes to you not blaring across a room but mysteriously, almost like from somewhere inside your own head.

Radio's also profoundly democratic. It places the great and powerful at the exact same level as a guest for the compelling story whose name is unknown, and we treat them exactly the same way. So you don't get a head start if you're a famous person in this kind of a format. No-one can see how beautiful or famous or rich you are on the radio. That's one of the most beautiful egalitarian forces that exist in the world of public radio, in particular. There's a kind of noble nakedness in all of this. Jay Allison, one of the pioneers of public radio in the United States, once said, and I'm quoting him here, 'Radio gets inside us. Lacking earlids we are defenceless, vulnerable to ambush. Sounds and voices surprise us from within. Our tool as radio producers is oral story, the most primitive and powerful. Invisibility is our friend, prejudice is suspended while the listener is blind, only listening'.

We podcasted *Conversations* right from the start, but I have to admit that for the first years of the show I didn't bother to listen to a single podcast. We treated the podcast as just another damn thing we had to do at the end of the day, that would stop us going home half an hour earlier. It was around 2007 that I finally bought an iPod. Remember those? And downloaded some outstanding public radio shows from the United States like *This American Life* and *Radiolab*, and this changed the way I make the program. I imagine now when I do the show, at the start of every program it's a bit like the moment when you go to the movies, when the trailers have finished and the lights dim and the curtains part a bit more, and then the movie starts. It's like you're going into a kind of a dream world almost.

The ABC began to make promo spots with the tagline *spend an hour in the life of someone else,* because that was the pleasure of it. Listeners could take a brief holiday from their own lives, from the burden of selfhood, from the quotidian business of everyday life, reverse parking, making a sandwich, picking up the kids and they could travel weightlessly through the life story of a guest, and then return refreshed into themselves once more. Like I said, radio can have enormous didactic momentum, but that momentum can be easily derailed by cliché and sentimentality. We keep a watching brief against lumbering try-hard adjectives like 'tragic' and, worse still, 'iconic'. I try to avoid polite euphemisms. When people die, I say they're dead; I don't say they've passed away or, worse still, that they've passed. Passed what?

I avoid guests who are prone to sustained humourless polemic. I don't much care for gurus or sanctimonious people. For my own part, I try to avoid talking to listeners like a priest or a priestess, the old radio presenter model where you impart knowledge down from on high like some godlike figure who knows everything. Ira Glass calls this the mask of omniscience, and it's a terrible lie. Worse still, it makes you afraid to express curiosity, vulnerability, discovery and humour.

When I started at ABC Radio, the standard thinking was that no—I was told this—no interview should go longer than seven minutes because after that people will just tune out. But it turned out there was a great hunger for a well curated, long conversation, particularly in a media environment where so much space is taken up in a boring and destructive culture war where, as one comedian put it, everyone is angry about everything all the time.

As profits continue to shrink there are plenty of media operators who have figured out their best hope of survival is to provoke fear and rage by goading people to run towards their tribes, and I think public radio at its best can take the nation in a different direction. Public radio, as it does engage with the great diversity of modern Australian life, tends to create shared sympathies between people across the nation, between people who might otherwise mistrust or disdain each other. The ABC, with its strong connections to rural and urban people, to young and old Australians, to the First Australians and to those of us who came later, is constantly attempting to construct a kind of commonwealth of shared sympathies. The ABC at its best tries to convene the nation in conversation, and to acknowledge our shared humanity.

And I'd like to finish with this thought. Australians continue to place a great deal of trust in the ABC. This trust rests on a fundamental expectation that ABC journalists will speak truth to power. That in turn rests on an expectation that the ABC's board will act to defend the broadcaster's independence against political interference from ministers who believe it is they who fund the ABC. They do not fund the ABC. It is you who fund the ABC, and we, the employees, are your servants, not theirs.

Public Life, Private Man

Emeritus Professor Judith Brett AM
2019

I'm going to talk about Alfred Deakin. But in order to say, I think, a bit more at a general level about the craft of political biography, I'm also going to talk a bit about Robert Menzies, because in having two case studies I can illustrate a little more clearly what I see as the key challenges of writing political biography. So I'm going to talk about Robert Menzies and Alfred Deakin, both of whom have their papers here. I've spent many, many hours reading them in the Manuscript Room in this building, where the staff have always been courteous and helpful, so I'd like to take this opportunity to thank every one at the National Library.

What I want to do tonight is to use the lives of these two prime ministers to illustrate what I see as the core challenge of political biography, which is to answer the question: 'why politics?' Why did this person become a political actor? What needs did it fulfil? What emotional and psychological resources did they muster for its accomplishment? What were its costs and what were its rewards?

In popular understandings of politicians, particularly amongst cynical Australians, the answers are obvious: ambition, a sense of destiny, immense self-belief, the will to power. For some lesser players, material self-interest. Australians are typically cynical about politicians' motives and the pushing, shoving types who inhabit our Parliament. Deakin, I'm sure, is exceptional.

But if you ask politicians themselves why they go into politics you'll get a very different answer. They will talk about the desire to give back, to contribute, to serve the party, the class, the faith, the community, the people or the nation. Both of these answers are true. There is ambition in a political life but there are also ideals, and especially in the political lives that attract biographers: the lives of the men and women who win high office and have a lasting influence on the polities they lead.

So ambition and ideals, these are the two poles of political motivation. And biography is essentially a narrative art. It tells the story of a life but in ways that make that life intelligible. The biographer works within a time, producing a chronology of events in their historical context. It narrates a plot but we also work with interior time, with our subjects, in our lives. This is described by the English biographer Richard Holmes as patterns of impulse and imagery, repetitions and recollections, constellations of self-myth and self-understanding, links between childhood and adult experience, which obey the (quite different) unhistorical or dream laws of memory and imagination.

Now the patterns that Holmes is describing only reveal themselves when a biographer lifts their attention from the moving edge of time, from the chronicle of events, the sequence of people and of issues which make up the subject's outer life, to an essentially spatial contemplation of the whole, to the life spread out like a landscape with the biographer's life roving back and forth for patterns and disruptions.

For me as a political biographer, the key pattern that I'm looking for is to find the balance between ambition and ideals in that political subject's life, and to chart how they interact and shift over a lifetime. It means that it's actually not until you in some ways get to the end of the life that you can go back and see the patterns. So tonight what I want to do is say a little about the patterns that I found in my work on Alfred Deakin and Robert Menzies, and I'm going to begin with Menzies even though he's later in history. He's psychologically less complicated than Deakin, and he's no doubt a bit more familiar to people here.

Now in many ways Menzies was the quintessential man of ambition. He was born in 1894 in the small and very new Wimmera town of Jeparit, which is up in the northwest of Victoria. Jeparit at that stage was only five years old. His parents had moved there to open a store, and 50 years earlier its surrounds had been part of the hunting grounds of the dispossessed Wotjobaluk peoples. Here's a description that Menzies wrote of his childhood home. He wrote this in 1948 in a piece that was called 'What the Empire Means to Me'.

> To me the British Empire means … a cottage in the wheat lands of the North West of the state of Victoria with the Bible and Henry Drummond and Jerome K. Jerome and Burns on the shelf. It means the cool green waters of the Coln as they glide past the church at Fairford, the long sweep of the Wye Valley above Tintern with a Wordsworth in my pocket. King George and Queen Mary coming to their jubilee in Westminster Hall.

On it goes for two pages of associations about what the Empire means to him. He didn't publish it until 1949, and he had to change it to 'Commonwealth'. The empire had gone but the emotional pattern stays the same.

Now what I'm interested in here is the way Menzies is placing his childhood home securely inside the British Empire. He's associating it with its landscape and literature, and with the monarchy he loved so well. His first trip to England was for the coronation of King George.

Notice his description of what was actually a weatherboard and iron dwelling behind a shop—the general store—as a cottage and the books on the shelf. The Menzies home may have been in the 'outer empire', as he sometimes talked about Australia, but it was in the empire nevertheless, and this gave meaning to his and his family's limited and difficult lives on the edge of settlement as it did to the lives of so many like them. They may have been at the very edge of the circle of light emanating from London, but they were still inside its glow as members of the British race living out its historic destiny.

Now these books on the shelf appear in most descriptions of Menzies' childhood. For him, the closeness and security of his childhood home seem best expressed in the family activity of reading together. Through these books the family created and shored up its sense of belonging, of being part of something greater. Books were the links, the lifelines from the remote, alien place of Menzies' birth to another world, and Menzies quickly learned that if he could master the knowledge they contained, they would provide a way out of Jeparit, and perhaps pave the way to the centre.

Very early on, young Menzies set his sights on high office. A visiting phrenologist foretold it. Phrenology is reading the future and your character by feeling the bumps on your head. It was very popular in the late nineteenth century. Deakin also consulted a phrenologist. But for Menzies, I think, the family took him along. It was a bit of entertainment, I suppose, and the phrenologist said that he would be a public speaker and a barrister. Menzies was a very young boy. He was very pleased with this, and he told his family he wouldn't just be any old barrister—he'd become the Chief Justice of Victoria. The way out of Jeparit for him was through education, and as the family was not well off, and at that time there were no government secondary schools, this meant he had to win scholarships, and his mother made that pretty clear to him early on.

Menzies was hardworking and he was clever. He matriculated, studied law and he was soon a successful barrister. In 1920, while he was a relatively junior member of the Bar, and only 26, he argued the Engineer's Case which reshaped Federal and State relations and brought him sudden fame. After a brief stint in the Victorian Legislative Assembly, he won the Federal seat of Kooyong in 1934, which he then held for the rest of his political life, and Prime Minster Joe Lyons made him Attorney-General. So at 40 years old, the boy from Jeparit was now Australia's chief law officer.

On his own account, Menzies gave up his successful legal career and entered politics in order to serve. Democratic politics, he often wrote, was the noblest and highest of civil vocations. The one mar on his reputation at the Bar had been his air of superiority, which sometimes put a jury offside. In politics, this air of superiority was an even greater liability for this young man in a hurry. He was impatient to test his skills against the demands of high office, he was very conscious of his own considerable gifts, and he was not too tolerant of the inadequacy of others.

When he won preselection for Kooyong, the Victorian Premier, Stanley Argyle, reputedly told one federal minister, thank God we got rid of him, you're welcome to him. Argyle had felt the pressure of Menzies's ambition, and soon Joe Lyons would feel it too. When Lyons died suddenly of a heart attack at Easter in 1939, Menzies, who had resigned from Cabinet, was accused of contributing to the pressure that killed him.

Although Menzies was consciously choosing a life of service to his ideals, his ambition often got the upper hand and led him into actions which contemporaries saw as expressing his own competitive urge to succeed rather than as the principled actions he wanted them to be. Despite some opposition, Menzies did succeed Lyons as prime minister, and five months later he was the prime minister when Australia entered World War II.

Early in 1941, now the Prime Minister of Australia, Menzies went to England where he sat, while he was there, in Winston Churchill's Cabinet. Menzies was very critical of Churchill. He was critical of the great man's dictatorial methods, and of the subservience of his ministers as well as of Churchill's disregard for wider imperial defence as Churchill focused on defeating Germany.

Menzies was angling for a permanent dominion presence in the Cabinet so that the war would be seen as an imperial war, not so much just a national defence of England. He thought he would be the best person to take up this position. At least he wanted a lot more consultation with the dominions on war strategy. If he had been able to persuade Churchill, it would have been the pinnacle of his political ascent: a position of power in London helping to defend the Empire (which was the source of the cultural and political values which had shaped him). But this was not to be. Churchill didn't want a permanent dominion presence in his Cabinet, and he certainly didn't want Menzies staying in London, and after four months abroad Menzies had no choice but to return to Australia.

A short time later Menzies resigned the prime ministership in the face of continuing carping and disunity in his party, and in his government. The disunity, though, needn't have been fatal. Menzies himself initiated his resignation and some thought he folded too easily. But in this moment in his political life, his ambition and his self-confidence deserted him. Soon Labor's John Curtin was prime minister, and Menzies didn't become prime minister again until 1949.

Now Menzies' loss of the prime ministership at this time has been generally attributed to his personality, his air of superiority, his lack of the common touch, and his inability to rub shoulders in the party room. The humiliation of the defeat has been seen as teaching him a necessary lesson in human relations, after which he was a wiser man and a far better politician.

My reading of Menzies' loss of the prime ministership, and the subsequent mellowing of his political personality, is a little different. It places the decisive defeat not in the party room in Canberra but in London at the hands of Churchill. This was the most absolute defeat of Menzies' political life. All others had been temporary setbacks after which his career resumed its upward path.

The pattern of his first 40 years was of easy success. To be sure, he worked hard and he was capable, but he was also ambitious, and to me it seemed that this ambition was not so much to reach the top, but to reach the centre. The metaphor I had in mind wasn't the ascent of a ladder that you get in lives that are essentially about upward class mobility. It was the movement from the outer edge of a circle to the centre of that circle, and at the centre was London, Westminster and the monarchy. In 1941 his movement to the centre was decisively checked by Churchill. He, Menzies, would not be the man to save the Empire. What political future he had would be in Australia.

Out of office and on the back bench, he did contemplate leaving politics altogether and returning to the Bar, but he stayed, and in staying he had to find new answers to the question, 'why politics?' This ushered in the most creative period of his political life as he rethought his reasons for staying in politics, and discovered new purpose and new energy for his political life.

Between 1941 and 1949, I'm suggesting the balance between Menzies' ambition and his ideals shifted decisively. His most substantial achievement in this period was the formation of the Liberal Party. In the wake of the United Australia Party's disastrous election result in 1943, he worked indefatigably to bring the splintering non-Labor organisations together into a new non-Labor party, and he worked hard to rethink and reshape non-Labor ideology to give this new Labor Party a set of ideals to guide its pursuit of political power in the post-war world. To do this he had to be able to speak convincingly to Australians of the ideals that were embodied in Australian life and Australian political actions.

We can see him doing this most clearly in his 1942 radio broadcast to the forgotten people. It was one of a series of radio broadcasts that he made at this time in which he was exploring his core political beliefs, but for a biographer it's the most revealing because it's got the most personal content. It was reading this speech, in fact, that first sparked my interest in Menzies. At an obvious political level he was arguing for individualism against the collectivist values of the Labor government which looked set to dominate Australia's post-war reconstruction. In 1942-43, Curtin's Labor government is immensely popular. Against these collectivist values, Menzies set the home and the family and the thrifty hardworking middle class.

Now what interested me as a biographer was the way the speech drew on his own family and childhood. He cited Robert Burns' poem, *The Cotter's Saturday Night,* to illustrate the virtues of humble family piety, this taking him back to the cottage in the field with Robert Burns on the shelf. At this low point in his political life what you can see is Menzies re-mooring his sense of political purpose in this close childhood home, and his relation with his parents: the lives of his parents which embodied the values of hard work, independence, service and frugality for which he praised the Australian middle class.

He went on to become the most successful twentieth century representative of the values of the Australian middle class, and he was only able to do this, I would suggest—to become such a convincing representative of shared group goals—when he accepted the inevitable limits of being Australian, and the limits that these placed on his political ambition. He could still adore the Empire turned Commonwealth, and he could adore the monarch, but this was now more of a sentimental attachment than a focus for personal ambition.

Now to Alfred Deakin, who became Australia's second prime minister in 1903 when Edmund Barton went to the High Court. He was prime minister three times in the early Commonwealth's first decade. In this decade, key institutions were built, and he was instrumental in this, and in laying the foundations for the protective policies that underpinned Australian politics until the advent of neoliberalism in the 1970s and 1980s. When Menzies retired in 1966, he nominated Deakin as Australia's greatest prime minister, and in many ways Menzies saw himself as Deakin's heir. He named the new Liberal Party that was founded in 1944–45 after Deakin's party of that name.

Most politicians leave very few intimate papers. Their life is lived in the public world. They make speeches, they do deals, they win and lose elections, they suffer public triumphs and public humiliations. They live politics day and night, and it is there that the biographer must look for answers to the question, 'why politics?' Menzies was a man like this. There were some memoirs written late in life, a couple of diaries from his trips to Britain which were very revealing, some occasional personal reflections in speeches, but his private papers are not rich. I looked for the pattern of his life as much in his public words and actions. I mean, obviously you're using both, but that's where there was much more material.

Deakin is very different. After his death his family found, in his study, notebooks filled with his private writings mainly on literary and religious topics but also manuscripts, including two on politics. There was one about the very early period of his political life when he first becomes a Member of Parliament, and one on Federation. There are autobiographical reflections, and there's a prayer diary which he kept from 1884 until his retirement from Parliament in 1913. Such a voluminous record of a rich inner and spiritual life is a rare resource for a political biographer, even if it's a little daunting. Some of it was typed up by his children later, but there are pages and pages of nineteeth century handwriting.

Deakin became a politician, he wrote, by sheer force of circumstance rather than by independent choice, and he repeatedly flirted with the possibility of resigning and leaving politics altogether to do something different, but he never did. Despite this disavowal, his is, again, an intensely political life. But he always disavowed simple political ambition, which was a challenge for a political biographer. As with Menzies, the answer to the question 'why politics?' shifts across his life, though as I said it's harder to answer initially. Menzies went into politics because he was ambitious, and he consciously sought political office. Deakin didn't consciously seek political office. He entered politics almost accidentally when David Syme, the powerful editor of the Melbourne *Age* suggested his name to a committee of electors who were looking for a candidate to contest a by-election. They couldn't find anybody, and Syme said try Deakin.

At the time Deakin was 22. He was born in Melbourne in 1856. He was the only son of gold rush immigrants. The family was of modest means but they only had two children, and because of this they could afford to educate them well so, for a son of the lower middle class, Deakin was extraordinarily well educated. He attended Melbourne Grammar and he later studied law as an evening student at the university. But he wasn't very interested in law. His passions were literature and philosophy, including theology and comparative religion.

He contemplated various futures for himself. Perhaps he could become a preacher or an actor or a dramatist or an essayist, and pursuing the latter, becoming an essayist, he approached David Syme hoping to write literary essays for his papers. Instead Syme sent him to cover Parliament and then, on Syme's suggestion, he was whirled into politics. Whirled into politics is a phrase that Deakin himself uses to describe the beginning of his political life. This phrase captures the headlong rush of events that followed his rather impulsive decision to contest the by-election. He became a candidate on Friday, he addressed his first campaign meeting the following night, and then he was off on the campaign trail—and to his and everyone else's amazement, he won the seat.

This phrase though, 'whirled into politics', is more than a description of the hectic activity of Deakin's first days in politics. Whirling is an image of motion and energy—worldly, natural, cosmic and spiritual. With it, Deakin aligned his entry into public life with larger forces. At the time he entered politics, Deakin had been an active spiritualist for about four years. He was a member of a prestigious seance circle, and he was a successful medium. He wrote a book, *The New Pilgrim's Progress*, that was dictated by the shade of John Bunyan, and he was an office-bearer in the Victorian Association of Progressive Spiritualists.

Later on, when he re-read the book when he was a bit older, he decided it hadn't been dictated by John Bunyan. He said it didn't have Bunyan's style, and it seemed to be preoccupied with all the things he was preoccupied with as a man at the time he wrote it, so he had some insight. But he still held onto some of spiritualism's core beliefs, in particular the divinity of the universe, the immortality of the soul, and the possibility of communication across the grave.

As well as consulting a phrenologist, he went regularly to seances—not ones in which he was a medium but in which he was seeking guidance from the spirit world as to what he should do with his life. There was a series of prophecies made, and Deakin believed that these prophecies were actually fulfilled in the events that unfolded over the next few years. They included that he would marry his fellow spiritualist, Pattie Browne, and that he would soon be back in Parliament. It turned out he did marry Pattie Browne, and he was soon back in Parliament and so this shored up his spiritualist convictions.

Now in these early days as a Member of Parliament, as I said he regularly sought guidance from the spirits through a suburban medium. The shades of John Knox, Thomas Macaulay, John Bunyan, John Stuart Mill all appeared, and all were very keen to help him become a great reformer. Deakin recorded their advice in a diary which is held in the National Library, and it's a pretty astonishing document. Deakin regularly culled his papers, but this survived.

The spirits urged him not to yield to depression, and they advised him on reading and on his health, and on shares. His share investments on the spirits' advice were not good—he lost quite a bit of money—so some prophecies weren't fulfilled. But the diary, as well as the share advice, returns again and again to the question of his life's purpose. The spirits tell him he will be a great reformer, but he's not sure whether that will be in the law, in politics or religion. The spirits weren't entirely clear about where this great reforming work would take place.

Now if we put to one side the bizarreness of his belief in the spirits, we can ask what psychological role were these seances playing for the young Deakin? The answer, I think, is that they reassured him and gave him confidence, and shored up in him a sense of destiny. They fed the conviction that he was special, singled out for great work. But more than the belief that one is special is needed to succeed in politics. One needs skills and aptitudes, and in his early political campaigns Deakin revealed his extraordinary gift for oratory. And this, I think, is one of the reasons he actually stayed in politics: that words, phrases, images, arguments, quotations, examples streamed from his mouth with great rapidity. He didn't have written scripts like today's politicians. He extemporised. He could do this on his feet for an hour at a time, and he would work the crowd. So it was very similar to evangelical preaching of the time. There was a sort of call and response structure where people would cheer and boo, and the orator and the crowd would, in a sense, work up their emotions together.

On the platform or on his feet in parliament with his mind and body working in unison like this, his senses alert, Deakin was fully alive and present in the moment, and it was an exhilarating experience for him. He is at various times plagued with a sense of depression and of lassitude, and I think that this exhilaration of the political platform is crucial for understanding, in a sense, why he got into politics and stayed there initially. Because politics provided him with the drama, excitement and a great deal of attention from important older men, and with his political successes apparently prophesied, it satisfied his yearning for work that served a higher purpose. As his life in politics unfolded, he did have periods of doubt, and he soon learned that public life had its fair share of tedium and repetition.

But during the next decade his political fortunes rose with those of the city of his birth. The colony of Victoria was riding a wave of prosperity, and marvellous Melbourne was in full swing. He was soon in the ministry, and by 1885 he was the leader of the Liberal Party, and Chief Secretary in a coalition government. He visited California to explore irrigation, and he invited the Chaffey brothers to establish the irrigation colony on the Murray that became Mildura.

Now in 1887, he visited London for the first time as a member of the Victorian Delegation to the 1887 Imperial Conference. This trip, he believed, had been prophesied, and while he was there he boldly challenged the British Prime Minister, Lord Salisbury, over Britain's reluctance to annex the New Hebrides. The Victorians were very keen that the New Hebrides be annexed, and he refused a knighthood. It was a thrilling series of triumphs and he returned from it a local celebrity, especially among the young native-born of the Australian Natives' Association.

In 1888, though, as the Australian colonies celebrated the centenary of the arrival of the First Fleet, cracks were starting to appear in their prosperity, especially in Victoria where a speculative land boom was in full swing, and government debt was mounting as it borrowed to build infrastructure to support the growing population. The Gillies-Deakin Government was defeated in 1890, and the following year the boom came to a shuddering end. Soon banks and building societies were closing their doors, bankruptcies and unemployment were soaring, people were leaving Victoria.

Now as the colony's prospects plummeted, so did Deakin's spirits and his conviction that politics was his destiny. He was being urged to return to the leadership to help calm the panic that was turning the financial crisis into a disaster. He told his supporters, though, that he was staying out of office until he could be sure that he could realise his Liberal principles, but his prayers tell a different and more psychologically interesting story. In 1892 he confessed to his God,

> I even dread the influence I seem to possess because uncertain of it being exercised for good, and I still more dread to increase my responsibilities. Blind as I am, how should I lead the blind?

Deakin didn't take the leadership at this time because he didn't have a clue what to do with it and what could be done to restore the colony's finances. He was a facilitator of the spirit of progress, a leader for when times were good. But he was not a man for a crisis, and he stayed on the back bench and returned to law to rebuild his finances. He was seriously thinking of leaving politics at that point, but he doesn't leave, so the big question for the biographer is why doesn't he leave at this time? Things had really gone pear-shaped for him.

The answer was the promise of Federation, and for the rest of the 1890s it was this promise that held him in political life. Australia's six colonies had been talking seriously about federating since the early 1880s, and in 1893 the Corowa Plan made it much more achievable. From 1893 onwards, Deakin basically throws himself into the cause of achieving federation. For the rest of the 1890s he refused all pleas to return to the ministry, and the achievement of Federation became the focus of his energies.

The achievement of Federation and the birth of the Australian nation became for Deakin a redemption project after the humiliation of the financial crisis, and was his second answer to the question, 'why politics?' The sense of destiny which had carried him through the first decade of his political life had found a new focus in the birth of the nation, and he believed that destiny was behind the federation movement—that it was the destiny of the colonies to form into a nation and that he would then be an agent of that destiny. So there was now a much more achievable focus compared with the rather diffuse sense of destiny that he had in the first decade of his political life.

Once Federation was achieved Deakin became attorney-general in the first Commonwealth government, and after Edmund Barton retired to the High

Court, he was the second prime minister. He was 47. Over the next decade the answer to the question 'why politics?' shifts from his belief in his special destiny, and the destiny of the achievement of the nation, towards a sense of duty and service.

When the constitution was finally law and the Commonwealth was inaugurated, Deakin saw it as the duty of those who had argued for federation to make it work. It was a compact he believed between the people who had voted yes and their elected representatives, and this compact he believed was something of a sacred compact and to be served. The constitution provided a framework for the government of the nation but that was all—it was only a framework. Federal institutions had to be built and federal laws had to be passed for areas of federal responsibility. Federal sentiment and a wide federal perspective had to be nurtured. Again and again in his speeches in this period, Deakin conjured up the map of Australia, and he reminded his audience that they were no longer just Victorians or South Australians or Tasmanians: they were now Australians.

This was his great mission in the Federal Parliament now, to make real the promise of the nation carried in the Constitution. But it wasn't easy, and he was often downhearted and not at all sure what to do. The rapid rise of the Labor Party's electoral support had turned Federal Parliament into an unstable three-cornered contest, with a series of minority governments and recurring political crises. Deakin's Liberal Party was the middle party, between Labor on the left and the conservative Free Traders antisocialists on the right.

Its most productive period of government from 1905 to 1907 was in alliance with Labor. At the end of the decade, in 1909, Deakin reluctantly joined with the conservatives to form a united non-Labor Party in what became known as the Fusion. He was abandoning his erstwhile Labor allies. Labor's Billy Hughes furiously attacked Deakin in the Parliament for his inconstancy.

> What a career his has been. In his hands, at various times, have rested the banners of every party in this country. He has proclaimed them all, he has held them all, he has betrayed them all ... There is surely some moral obliquity about a nature such as his. No act that he commits, no party that he betrays, no cause that he abandons affects him at all. He regards himself as the selected and favoured agent of Providence.

Now here we can see Hughes attributing to Deakin the cunning, self-justifying, steering by the chances for power that would mark his, Hughes', future political career, but even so Hughes recognised a recurring pattern. Deakin did see himself as an agent of providence. It was just often he wasn't quite sure what providence had in mind for him, and where it was heading. His prayer diaries (mostly the prayers don't have much political content but they are dated, which is immensely helpful for the biographer because you can line up when the prayer is written with the events that are happening) are of two main types of prayer. One prayer is, 'Thank you God for my many blessings, for my fortunate life', and the other is, 'Oh Lord, show me the way, I don't know what to do, what is it that you want me to do?' In the Commonwealth Parliament he's no longer seeking occult help with seances and divinations as he was in the early 1880s. But he would step back and let events unfold, and he'd wait for providence to show its hand while all around speculated as to what Mr Deakin would do.

Fusion ushered in Deakin's final term as prime minister. An election was due in 1910, and Deakin hoped that the new united non-Labor Party would sweep the polls. He was wrong. Labor won a decisive victory to become the first Commonwealth Government with a clear Parliamentary majority. At a personal level though, Deakin was relieved. Since 1907 he'd been complaining about failures of memory, his insomnia had become chronic, and he had periods of what was then described as 'nervous exhaustion'. Politics was taking an increasing psychological toll on him, and as he trudged on he felt, he wrote to his sister, Catherine, that a continent was strapped to his shoulders.

Deakin stayed in Parliament for another three years leading a shell-shocked opposition, as his once brilliant mind slipped away in what was most likely early-onset Alzheimer's. For a time he watched and recorded the deterioration of his mental capacities, but by the time he died he didn't know who he was, and he was only 63. Pattie was devoted to him in the last years of his life but it's a very sad end that he had.

Now Deakin and Menzies are very different biographical subjects. The absence of conventional ambition made Deakin the more challenging, I found, as a biographer, as did his deeply religious nature. Particularly when you're writing for a largely secular readership, it's quite challenging to convey the role that religion played in the lives of earlier generations. It's not just the spiritualism which was pretty challenging to work out how to write about, because some of the material was really bizarre. What I decided to do was often to just provide the primary material, and to minimise the comments, and look for the psychological role that this was playing. But even with what became more conventional Christianity, and with a politician who is at the end of every day praying—it's quite hard to convey what that meant when you know that many of the people interested in political biography are essentially secular.

There are some striking similarities between the two lives. Both men were gifted and hardworking, and they experienced early success and an effortless rise to political office, though Deakin's early triumphant celebrity were greater and more heady than Menzies'. Both left office voluntarily in midlife after experiencing setbacks and losing confidence. They had achieved little at this time, when they left office, and their early promise was unfulfilled, but both stayed with politics. In both cases this happens, if you like, at midlife, the point when a man realises he has stopped growing up and started to grow old. It's a very confronting moment for men of ambition and destiny. Opportunities remain for achievement and success but the limitless horizons of youth are gone, and with them youth's reckless energies and unquestionable self-belief.

Both Menzies and Deakin hit limits at midlife—Menzies, the limits to his political ambition imposed just by the fact that he was Australian, and Deakin, the limits to the optimism which had buoyed up his political career as his self-belief and faith in progress, as the financial crisis engulfed the colony. They both withdrew for a time from high political office to sit on the back bench, during which they rediscovered their political purpose with more limited and achievable goals. This tamed and focused their ambition, and grounded their commitment to service in something tangible. Menzies founded the Liberal Party and took it to electoral victory. Deakin was crucial in the achievement of Federation and the shaping of the new Commonwealth. Both went on to become great Australian prime ministers.

So what I hope to have shown you tonight is that political biography can do more than chronicle the events of a political life. By asking the question, 'why politics?', it can explore a politician's deep motivations, and the way these change across their lives, and so help to explain their achievements. It can I think also help us understand failure, but that's another story for another time.

The Donald Rumsfeld Theory of Biography

Dr Jacqueline Kent
2022

It's a particular pleasure to be here. Like everything else in life, this lecture has been postponed and rejigged for a couple of years because of COVID. So I'm very happy to be here tonight, speaking to you all.

When you start thinking about biography, you think you should start with great biographers of the past, like Tacitus, or Suetonius. Or Boswell, or even Lytton Strachey. I've decided not to do that tonight.

What I want to do is lower the tone considerably and talk to you about, of all people, Donald Rumsfeld. Well, not talk about Donald Rumsfeld, actually, but start off with him. What people remember about Donald Rumsfeld, who was of course the US Secretary of Defense in the George W. Bush administration, is his comment about the lack of evidence linking the government of Iraq with supplying weapons of mass destruction to terrorist groups.

What he said was, and this is exactly what he said: 'As we know, there are known knowns, there are things we know we know. We also know that there are known unknowns'. You've got to say all this fairly slowly because it's a bit vertiginous otherwise. 'We also know that there are known unknowns, and that is to say we know there are some things we do not know. But there are also unknown unknowns, the ones we don't know we don't know.'

When you think about it, that's actually quite sensible, and it also goes with another quote which I'm quite fond of, by one of Abraham Lincoln's favourite humorists, a guy called Artemus Ward, one of those homespun, backwoods humorists of the nineteenth century in America. He said, 'It ain't what you don't know that hurts you, it's what you do know that ain't so'.

I think all those comments are very worthwhile bearing in mind when you're talking about biography, and I think it's slightly unfair that Donald Rumsfeld was pilloried—or ridiculed, rather—for saying what he did. What I'd like to do tonight is to go through what Donald Rumsfeld said, and evaluate it in terms of writing and researching biography. Because they're the biographies I know best, I'll be mostly talking about my own work. In the last 20-odd years, I've been writing the life stories of notable women. I thought it was most interesting, trying to set the course of their lives against their times, to explain the pressures of various kinds that led them to do what they did, and to challenge others' expectations of them.

So this is where the Rumsfeld effect, if you can call it that, comes into operation, because it means: what do we know? What do we, or don't we, know? What can we, or can't we, know about the lives of our fellow humans?

Known Knowns

First of all the easy one, which is what you know about a subject for biography. What you know is usually a series of facts that you find intriguing, that you think need to be examined further, or think haven't been given their due, or else there's a central mystery in this person's life that you really want to tease out. I have to say, and we'll get to this later, the central mystery is the most intriguing aspect for a biographer, and I'm sure most people who write biography would agree with that. What made them do what they have done? Why did they do it? Why were they there? What did they think they were doing? (You can also be exasperated: what on earth did they think they were doing?)

I think there are lots of reasons why people choose subjects for biography, and one of them of course is because the person is worthy—because they're a famous person, they are worthy of having their life memorialised. To which point, I might tell you a story about a celebrated Australian biographer, who was asked by his editor to write the life story of a well-known Australian politician with whom he was not in sympathy. He did not feel that this was a congenial subject. The editor said, 'Oh look, come on, no-one's done it, you've got to do it'. And he said, 'I have done a lot of work like this, I know how long biography takes, and I am not having that little [expletive] in my head for five years'. One can sympathise because some people start off writing a biography and about halfway through they think, 'I don't really like this person, I really want to stop'. They may be so far into it that going back would be as difficult as continuing.

But for me the reason for getting into a biography is always personal. My first full biography was of Beatrice Davis, the Angus and Robertson book editor from 1937 to 1973. I never knew her well. I started out as a baby editor, and Beatrice was the 'grand dame', and I mean both those words very seriously. We were all terrified of her at the same time as resenting her because we were the next generation along, the writers coming up—and writers like Helen Garner and Kate Grenville wrote books that Beatrice Davis was not at all sympathetically disposed towards.

I decided it would be good to write a book about her for several reasons. One is that, as anyone who's been involved in book publishing knows, it's an absolutely mad industry. It gets written about reverently, but that seems unnecessary when you think of the extreme difference in the personalities involved—those who write books and those who publish them. I thought, 'Why hasn't anyone written a book about publishing saying what fun it is, and what fun these people are, and what reserves of tact, human kindness and sheer keeping-your-temper you need if you're working as an editor?'

I thought, well, Beatrice knew about all that, and I'd been an editor. So I read a lot of her correspondence, which is in the Mitchell Library in Sydney, and, oh, the Angus and Robertson files are a glory to behold. They really are wonderful. They're got everything in them. It's a sort of archive where people filed everything, including theatre tickets and bus tickets—the sort of archive you really want to look at. And because I knew Beatrice's job and I'd been seeing the letters that she wrote, I could tell how clenched her teeth were occasionally, how happy she was about somebody's success, how well she got on with her writers, how sympathetic she was towards them, and how cranky she could be—because she was a pretty multifaceted creature. But I wanted to write about someone doing a job in an industry unlike any other. And because I'd worked with other people's words, I did want to give my profession, as it was then, its due.

It was also interesting to see how editing has changed over the years: nowadays you can go straight from having an idea for a book to print without going anywhere near paper, which is really something to think about. The proofs are on screen, proofreaders read on screen, people do corrections on screen. It's almost completely non-paper now. So another reason for doing the book was to keep a record of an industry that was changing very fast.

My second biography was about Hephzibah Menuhin, the sister of the celebrated violinist Yehudi Menuhin. It's a name that's not known much now by anybody over 40; there are so many celebrity musicians now. But in the 1930s, up to the 1960s or 1970s, Yehudi and his pianist sister Hephzibah were rockstars. Hephzibah was particularly interesting because she, her brother and sister were all child prodigies, the three of them. I happen to come from a family where precocious intelligence is wildly overvalued. I will not go into detail, but

I've got a few fairly dodgy relatives who were forgiven for some of the things they did because they were bright; I often heard, 'Oh, but he's got an IQ of 140' or something like that. So I've always been interested for personal reasons about what happens to people who show precocious talent, whether they crash and burn, whether they catch up emotionally after they have been hothoused when they were young. Hephzibah and Yehudi never went to school. They were intensely trained into being stars, really.

When he was young my father also happened to see Yehudi and Hephzibah, and Yehudi Menuhin was the greatest violinist the world has ever known as far as my father was concerned, and Hephzibah was a very good pianist. It was actually quite interesting that her role was subordinate to his in performances, but she was never—as far as my father was concerned—less important. She was a talent in her own right.

Hephzibah married at 17, and she married a rich grazier, Lindsay Nicholas, who lived in the western district of Victoria. She was ready to play at Carnegie Hall, and she gave that up to marry Lindsay; she'd just being playing the piano since she was three, and she was really sick of it and wanted to discover life. Well, she did but the life she discovered wasn't exactly what she thought it'd be. A sheep farm in Australia was nothing like Europe, only with sheep. During and after World War II, she had two kids. In the mid-1950s, she gave it all up, left her husband and two children, two boys aged nine and eleven, and went off and married somebody else—a man named Richard Hauser, whose daughter, by the way, was the feminist activist Eva Cox.

I wanted to try and work out: why did she do that? What leads a woman to do that? I was very angry with her at the end because she really did hurt many people. Because of her background, because of having been brought up to think of herself as a special person who could do as she liked, she'd had little idea what her walking out did to those other people. I'm not entirely sure she ever came to terms with that, and I found that difficult to emphathise with.

My third biography, of Julia Gillard, was not really in the same category as either of those two. It was in about 2009, I think, when she was Deputy Prime Minister to Kevin Rudd and was getting a lot of publicity. It was suggested to me that she might be a good subject for a biography. I thought, yes. I mean she's the first woman who's got this far, so let's have a look.

I wanted to see what drove her, and what were the steps in her becoming Australia's first woman Deputy Prime Minister, and afterwards, of course, in June 2010 becoming Australia's first woman Prime Minister. Gosh, I remember that night when she deposed Kevin Rudd. It was a Wednesday night in winter, it was freezing cold, and I remember yelling at the television, 'Julia, no! It won't be good'.

And of course the mystery in her life was what led her to usurp her leader, as the deputy—what led her to do that? That was what I wanted to try and elucidate.

Now the thing about Julia Gillard, of course, is that her story isn't finished yet. Since 2013, she's gone on to have an extraordinary, stellar career as a public figure, and the other thing that she's done with enormous dignity is not becoming involved in Australian politics. She's the only former Prime Minister in a long time who hasn't felt it necessary to comment on what her successors are doing, for good or ill. Having the self-discipline and the self-respect to walk away as she has done is pretty good, I think. But her story, of course, isn't finished, so I'd like to revisit my book, but it'll have to wait for a while. So far, she's my only subject who's been alive when I've been writing about her. I mentioned this to her and she said, 'I'm not crossing the road with you!'

She was always guarded, we saw it on television again and again. I know she was, unless you were close to her. I was coming from outside, I wasn't a friend, I wasn't part of the byzantine—God help us—Victorian Labor Party. I didn't have the connections. I didn't have the history. So she was understandably very guarded and that was okay, if a bit frustrating. But she was really good. I met her a few times and I became fond of her, though never close, because she doesn't offer friendship. She offers friendliness without friendship. I suspect a few of them are a bit like that. I think they think you've got to keep a kind of Perspex shield between you and the rest of the world. Not great if you're trying to write biography, but understandable.

Vida Goldstein was much easier: first of all, because she didn't have a family still alive. I think it was Brenda Niall who mentioned having to get on side with the descendants—very important and it's often not possible. Goldstein was the first woman to put her hand up to be elected to the federal parliament anywhere in the Western world, in Victoria in 1903. That book had a strong personal element for me too because, many years ago, when I'd just finished being a student—I was about 19 I think—I had a friend, Dianne Scott, who was the first woman I'd ever met who'd done a history thesis at Sydney University about Australian suffragists. I hadn't known there were any. I hadn't heard of Rose Scott, and I hadn't heard of Vida. I hadn't heard of any of them, but Dianne told me about them and they kind of lodged in the back of my head.

Vida had been written about in a rather worshipful way, so I thought it would be really good to look at that struggle, and look at all the women involved, because she was not the only campaigner for the vote. There were heaps of women who were out there on the hustings, and there were some very brave women doing the work, and they had to put up with a great deal. So I was fascinated to hear about her. I dedicated *Vida* to Dianne because I'm extremely grateful to her.

Known Unknowns

It can be pretty disheartening when you're interviewing people. I'm sure other biographers have had this experience: you find someone who insists that she's the best friend of the person you are writing about, and knows every single thing about them, and you think, 'Oh good'. With Hephzibah, in particular, there were several people who said they were her best friends, who told me what I already knew about her. It was the same with Beatrice Davis. People were presenting well known facts as if they were entirely new.

Now that's interesting in itself, really, because what that says—in Hephzibah's case in particular—is that people were dazzled by her. They were happy to have her as a friend. She was glamorous, so anything she chose to tell them—she had this way of saying, well I'm telling you and only you—was flattering.

One of the big blank spots in the story of Hephzibah was her divorce. The whole thing caused a terrible scandal, as you can imagine, because the parents thought they'd got her happily settled in Australia bringing up healthy children, and that all was fine. But when she announced she was leaving Lindsay and they were getting divorced, the Menuhin parents were furious, they were absolutely ropeable. I knew that, but I had no correspondence from them or anything at all about that time. I could have pasted over the cracks—there are always ways of doing that—but you never feel happy about it, you really don't.

So when I was in London researching the book, I interviewed Zamira, who was Hephzibah's niece and Yehudi's eldest daughter. She was the daughter of Nola, who was Yehudi's first wife, and it hadn't been a happy marriage. I just said something anodyne and sympathetic about how it must have been so hard for her. She just looked at me and said, 'Just a minute', and she went away, and she went into another room and she came back with a pile of paper—I swear it was about 30 centimetres high.

She said, 'Here'. And I said, 'Oh what's that?' She said, 'These are all the letters that Hephzibah wrote to her parents, and that her parents wrote to her, around the time, in 1953 and 1954, of the separation and the divorce'. I thought, oh my God. I said, 'How did you get those?' She said, 'Oh, Moshe, her father, kept carbon copies of every letter he wrote'. Don't you love people like that? Before he died, he handed them over to his eldest grandchild, who happened to be Zamira, who had kept them ever since, hadn't given them to a library, hadn't given them back to the family. She had them in her spare room. I said, 'Um, look, I've got my computer here. I'll sit in the back room, and I'll come every day, and I'll type it all out, and I'll be terribly careful'. She said, 'Oh no, you don't have to do that, just take them away'. So there was I getting on the tube at Paddington with a Waitrose plastic bag in my right hand containing this amazing cache of letters. I spent a fortune on photocopying—of course I did—and then handed all the letters back.

But without them I would not have been able to complete the book. It's the greatest stroke of luck I think I've ever had as a biographer, and it happened completely out of the blue. That's the weird thing about biography on any level, the unexpected things that happen to you and the things you find out. Those were good letters too. I quoted them extensively in the book, and Zamira trusted me for that too. She just said, 'Oh no, this is all right'. She believed, I think, that handing them over was some kind of family duty. It was quite something. Anyway the thing was that those letters were written by two very angry people, and it was really good to have them.

Unknown Knowns

One of the most interesting aspects about writing biography is the bit that Rumsfeld left out, which is the unknown knowns, the things you didn't realise you knew, and the little things you can put together in your own head. It happened a lot with Beatrice Davis because I knew her background and the stories of her authors, and I'd done her job. But the most interesting example, I think, of this was *Beyond Words*, the memoir I wrote about my marriage to Kenneth Cook, author of *Wake in Fright*. I married him several months before he died in 1987. I didn't want to marry him—he wanted to marry me but I wasn't all that keen—but I thought, oh well, I suppose you have to do it once. Better to marry than burn, and so on.

Ken wrote about ten novels and scripts and radio plays and talks and stage plays. He has an enormously large body of work but he's most famous for *Wake in Fright*, published in 1961. The movie made from it some years later, by the way, is an absolute shot list for the book. You could just about take that book and write a film script from it, scene by scene, it's really so visual. But it's very interesting, he was in his early thirties when he wrote his first book—it was his first and biggest success—and he always said that it was a young man's book. He'd learned a lot since he wrote it and said he had done better stuff since then; writers always say things like that.

But it always puzzled me because the subject matter's pretty bleak, as most of you know. But it's the tone of the work that's interesting. It's got a slightly jocular tone; it's not grim and spare at all. He asks all the way through: who are these people and why do they drink so much? For goodness sake, who are they? What are they doing?

Do you know the book it seemed most like? You'll be really surprised—I was: *They're a Weird Mob* by Nino Carlotta (John O'Grady). It's the same story, if you look at it. Person comes along to new society of which he knows nothing, is thrown into a deep end, has to make sense of it all. I mean, of course, *Weird Mob* is played for comedy, and *Wake in Fright* isn't precisely played for comedy, but it's the same story. I'd looked, I'd checked it out, and that book was published about 1957, and *Wake in Fright* was only four years later, and Ken had two or three goes writing it.

I came upon that little gem some time after Ken had died. He would have been very dismissive of such a view: whatever floats your boat, he would have said. But he used the same kind of story in a totally different novel: *The Wine of God's Anger*, which is about a young conscript in Vietnam. A young conscript, wide-eyed good Catholic lad, goes to war, thinking he'll find life. And is shocked and demoralised. It's one of Australia's very few—in fact I think possibly the only—anti-Vietnam war novel; the other accounts have been mostly memoirs.

Unknown Unknowns

The hardest part of writing biography—and we're getting to the serious end of the subject now—is the unknown unknowns. The bits you find out when the book is ten minutes into print, or you never find out at all, or the little connections you just cannot possibly make. It's very frustrating. To which point I would like to read you one of my favourite quotes. It's from the *New Yorker* writer Louis Menand. In 2003, he wrote that when you undertake historical research—and it also applies to biography—'two truths that seem banal come to seem profound'.

> The first is that your knowledge of the past—apart from, occasionally, a limited visual record and the odd unreliable survivor—comes entirely from written documents. You are almost completely cut off, by a wall of print, from the life you have set out to represent. You can't even know most of what has not been written about. What has been written about therefore takes on an importance that may be spurious. A few lines in a memoir, a snatch of recorded conversation, a letter fortuitously preserved, an event noted in a diary all become luminous with significance, even though they are merely the bits that have floated to the surface. The historian, biographer, clings

> to them, while somewhere below the huge, submerged wreck of the past, of the person you're writing about, sinks slowly out of sight.[1]

There's a lot of truth in that. How can you know someone? What do you do when there are gaps in the record, gaps you absolutely need to fill?

What you can't do is make stuff up, and this is what people have done. Which brings me to the story of Edmund Morris, who was given the job of writing the first authorised biography of Ronald Reagan. He found out so little, he said, from Reagan and those who knew him that he abandoned a straight biography and turned the book into a sort of hybrid novel. He invented characters who never existed in scenes in which they interact with real people, and other scenes that were dramatised or made up. He even invented sources and footnotes. I mean, seriously. He called the book *Dutch* and it was published in 1999 after 14 years of work.

You can imagine why he did all that, how desperate he must have felt knowing that he'd got all this money and he didn't have a book. He was being paid to write it from more than just *New York Times* cuts, and so he didn't have it. You have to sympathise with him to some extent. The problem was that when it was finished, it was presented to the public as if it was a proper, researched biography.

I think that's absolutely wrong. Without getting too sanctimonious about this, as a biographer there's a certain contract between writer and reader. The reader's got to believe that you've done your work, and you know what you're writing, and that what you're writing is, as far as you can judge, true. This is something I keep telling younger writers: you're allowed to speculate, provided you flag that that's what you're doing. You can say something happened because of this, maybe, but, it could also be because of that. The balance of probability is that it's this, but we do not know because of X. It's a little frustrating but it's a hell of a lot better than presenting fiction as fact. I know there is a lot of hybrid material that's part fact, part fiction. There's *The Crown*, for heaven's sake. I've got no great quarrel with *The Crown*—the conversations that may or may not have taken place and probably didn't—but it's never been presented as absolute documentary fact, and I think that's okay.

But the *New York Times* had such trouble with *Dutch*. A 1990 review said:

> a reader who surrenders to Morris's self-indulgent blend of scholarship and imagination will be led through a riveting story to a transcendent conclusion with a surprise twist. If there is 'higher truth' justifying the book's technique, it is that Ronald Reagan lived in a world of his own fictions, far more extensive than the fictions of Edmund Morris. Who better suited to plumb a phantom subject than a phantom narrator?

Sorry, I don't buy it. And clearly a lot of other people didn't either. As far as I know, that book did not sell its socks off and neither should it have done.

When I was thinking about this lecture, I remembered certain details about the subjects I've dealt with, and how small details can tell you a lot about the person and give you new insights into them.

In the early 1990s, I helped Lindy Chamberlain write her autobiography, and that was an assignment and a half, I can tell you. I spoke to her about 12 or 13 years after her baby had been taken. She told me two things that I wish had been known at the time. The first one: in August 1980, she and her husband Michael went home without their baby, with their two little boys, and she described lying awake in bed at night in Cooranbong, which is close to the Watagan Mountains, and hearing dingoes howling to each other. Imagine what that would have been like. The other things she told me was that because she and Michael were broke, she had to return the baby formula she had bought for Azaria to the chemist and get a refund.

With Beatrice, the thing I learned about her which was interesting was that in 1937 she married a much older man, Frederick Bridges. It was the time when married women were not allowed to work. So what did she do? She was working as Miss Davis at Angus and Robertson. She went off one lunch hour to the Registry Office, married Frederick, took her wedding ring off, came back to work and didn't tell anybody what she had just done. I think that was very Beatrice—'my private life is my private life, and I'm not telling anybody about it'—and she wanted to keep her job.

With Hephzibah it was her wedding photo. There's this photograph of her and Lindsay: he's putting the ring on her finger, and she's wearing the most ridiculous wedding dress. It's a crinoline, with one of those high nineteenth-century bonnets, and I couldn't work out why. I finally worked it out. Lindsay was a sheep farmer. She was being Little Bo Peep. She was only 17, and that shows you how young and naïve she was. Needless to say she found that life was a little different from that, and she wasn't going to run around with a little shepherd's crook, so that was that.

The other thing I found out about her was—and I had this corroborated not 24 hours ago, actually—when she couldn't get a piano and practice, she used the edge of a shelf or a table as a practice keyboard. A reviewer said, 'Oh, that's ridiculous, nobody's that good'. But because she had studied her repertoire so thoroughly from the age of three, she could hear the piece in her head. She and Yehudi had played together so often that she really knew it.

With Vida it was her washing. It really bugged me, when she was going around Victoria, speaking to town meetings, she was much more often praised for looking pretty and ladylike than for what she said. (That still happens: you only have to think how Julie Bishop's fashion sense got more attention than her words.) Vida travelled everywhere by train, and it was really hot and dusty. How on earth did she manage to look so good in that era? Who did her washing when she was travelling around Victoria with a tin trunk? I found out that, first of all, she was staying with well-to-do people, who often had servants to do the washing. There were railway hotels, but I can't imagine her giving her precious petticoats to someone in a hotel. Also, of course, all the railway lines radiated out from Melbourne, so she could go out and come back fairly readily. She could wait for her person at home—Lizzie McPherson—to do the necessary tidying. But just imagine all that: it was hot, it was dusty, buttons, no zips until after World War II.

It's questions like that that can drive you mad. You have to know.

So all these little things just turn up. You've got to be on the lookout for them, but when you find them they're absolutely valuable. I think things like that are what make people come alive on the page if you can possibly do it.

Just one more thing about Gillard. I told you she gave expected, considered answers to pretty well everything I asked her, or she evaded the issues like a politician. I asked her, 'What was your first car?' She said, 'No-one's ever asked me that before', in an accusing voice. I can't remember what it was now—I think it was a Cortina. The interesting thing about it was that her parents bought it for her to go from Adelaide to Melbourne. That tells you something about her parents: they saved up enough money to get their eldest daughter a car so she could travel to Melbourne. No wonder she was so close to her family, which she always was. That was just another little way of showing how close.

I'd just like to finish by quoting Tom Crewe in the *London Review of Books*:

> We must remember that the past is more unknown than known, that the vast majority of lived experience is penetrable only to the guided imagination. If we pursue the dead, it is because they have left so many clues behind, and because we can't help being curious as to what they looked like before they turned their backs.[2]

1 Louis Menand, 'The Historical Romance', *The New Yorker* (24 March 2003), newyorker.com/magazine/2003/03/24/the-historical-romance.

2 Tom Crewe, 'Found Objects', *London Review of Books* (12 August 2021, 43(16)), lrb.co.uk/the-paper/v43/n16/tom-crewe/short-cuts.

Published by National Library of Australia Publishing
Canberra ACT 2600

ISBN: 9781922507723

The National Library of Australia acknowledges Australia's First Nations Peoples—the First Australians—as the Traditional Owners and Custodians of this land and gives respect to the Elders—past and present—and through them to all Australian Aboriginal and Torres Strait Islander people.

First Nations Peoples are advised this book contains depictions and names of deceased people, and content that may be considered culturally sensitive.

Publisher: Lauren Smith
Managing editor: Amelia Hartney
Designers: Nada Backovic (cover) and Kerry Cooke (internals)
Image coordinator: Madeleine Warburton
Printed in China by Asia Pacific Offset Ltd on FSC®-certified paper

Cover image: J.W. Power, colourised study from *Cubist and Figure Studies Sketchbook 3*, National Library of Australia, nla.obj-139017988

Find out more about NLA Publishing at nla.gov.au/national-library-publishing.
A catalogue record for this book is available from the National Library of Australia.